Crisis and Trauma Counseling

UNIQUE FORMS OF HELPING

First Edition

Eric W. Owens and Richard D. Parsons

West Chester University of Pennsylvania

cognella® | ACADEMIC PUBLISHING

Bassim Hamadeh, CEO and Publisher
Abbey Hastings, Associate Production Editor
Jess Estrella, Senior Graphic Designer
Alexa Lucido, Licensing Coordinator
Don Kesner, Interior Designer
Natalie Piccotti, Senior Marketing Manager
Kassie Graves, Director of Acquisitions and Sales
Jamie Giganti, Senior Managing Editor

Crisis and Trauma Counseling

UNIQUE FORMS OF HELPING

CONTENTS

Preface

He told me he was going to kill himself. I couldn't believe it. I knew he was depressed. I knew he was struggling, and I knew his struggle was getting worse. I knew a lot. What I didn't feel like I knew was what to do to help. But I knew I had to figure it out, and I was so thankful that he trusted me enough to tell me.

We believe that those who choose to become professional counselors accept a serious and critical responsibility. To sit with another person and listen to the stories those clients tell us is no small task. When a client enters in to a counseling relationship, success depends on a host of factors, and there are many textbooks that identify the theories, skills, and techniques necessary for success in this relationship.

We believe that there are two factors that cannot be overlooked in the successful practice of professional counseling. The first is trust. Clients must develop a trusting relationship with the counselor if the process is to be effective. We speak of resistance often in counseling and psychology; resistance being the reticence on the part of clients to fully disclose, to completely engage, to *trust the counselor with the thoughts, feelings, and stories that they cannot share with others*. For counseling to work, trust is essential.

So, we often ask ourselves, how is this trust developed? For us, one crucial element to the development of trust in the therapeutic relationship is for counselors to not only acknowledge, but respect and value, the awesome responsibility they accept when they sit down with clients in the therapeutic milieu. Too often, counselor educators focus excessively on presentation of theory and rote recitation of microskills. These are important, of course. But it is just as important to remember that the person sitting across from you is more than a "patient" who needs a cure. We have included small vignettes at the start of each chapter and case illustrations throughout the book in an effort to remind the reader that the clients with whom we work are *human beings*, who come to us hoping for not only skill and knowledge, but also for compassion and trust.

The second factor we believe is critical to success in the counseling process is the intentional use of empirically supported theories and skills in the treatment of client concerns. It is for this reason we have written this text, *Crisis and Trauma Counseling: Unique Forms of Helping*. As we discuss throughout, crisis intervention and counseling survivors of trauma is no easy task and requires a special set of skills and cognates that are not the focus of many counseling texts or coursework. Working with clients who have suffered great loss or who have witnessed or experienced unspeakable horrors requires an understanding of theories and skills that are often different than those taught in most counseling programs. It is these skills that help clients to speak of those things they may think are unspeakable.

We also acknowledge that a text that addresses crisis counseling is unfortunately needed and will continue to be. As we completed the final phases of this manuscript, 59 people were killed when a gunman opened fire on a concert in Las Vegas. By the time this text goes to print, we are sure there will be countless more stories to be told in various places across the globe. Our world can be a dangerous place, but with every unspeakable horror, there are many who want to help. This text is written to help those who wish to learn how to do it better.

As Mr. Fred Rogers famously said, "The world could have come to seem a scary place to live ... There was something my mother did that I've always remembered. 'Always look for the helpers,' she'd tell me. 'There's always someone who is trying to help.'" Mr. Rogers' mother was right. It is our hope that this text can help those who want to help when the world seems like a very scary place.

Acknowledgments

Any work of this magnitude is the result of the contributions of many, not just the authors. We wish to recognize those who have participated in this endeavor.

First, we must acknowledge the support of our families in this project. Their patience and support during the writing of this book helped to make the process a little less traumatic. We are eternally grateful for their willingness to smile when we frowned, to laugh when we scowled, to be patient when an idea sprung forth at the worst possible moment, and to hold their tongues when we would wake early on vacation to do some last minute editing. Thank you Ginny. Thank you Shannon, Ryan, and Katherine.

Also, we must recognize the tireless efforts of Clara Morgan. Her research assistance was outstanding and her editorial work was remarkable. As a graduate student, it would have been easy for her to defer to her faculty, but instead, she was unafraid to make suggestions, and those recommendations have made this book much better. We look forward to your growth as a counselor and a professional.

Finally, we would be remiss if we did not acknowledge the assistance of Kassie Graves, Director of Acquisitions at Cognella. Her patience, support, and encouragement were invaluable. Additionally, we would like to thank Rejoice Addae at Arkansas State University, Deborah Fenton-Nichols at Colorado Christian University, Wendy Killam at Stephen F. Austin University, and Diana Suffridge at the University of California for their feedback and suggestions in the development of this project.

This book is dedicated to the helpers. Sure, there is pain and suffering in the world, but there is also beauty, joy, and happiness. We wish those good things for you.

SECTION 1

The Nature of Crisis and Crisis Work

CHAPTER 1

Crisis Intervention: Conceptualizing Crisis Intervention for Helpers and Clients

Seeing the blood everywhere? Seeing those kids shaking, crying, or so scared they couldn't even move? It absolutely changed me.

It was a typical Saturday night on a college campus. Students were milling around the main quad, some heading to see friends, others getting ready to leave for a night on the town. Things were happening across the bustling, sprawling campus, from movies in the main auditorium to a dance in the student union.

As the dance continued, the night turned anything but typical. Several people inside the union were arguing; the reason now seems unimportant. The verbal dispute turned physical, with one student pushing another. The push was met with a punch, and it did not take long for a large fight to break out. There was no security at the event; this campus was so small and friendly that security would never have been a consideration before tonight.

As the combatants moved outside of the union building, the fight continued. Punches were thrown; people were kicked. Passersby stopped to watch the melee as it continued unabated.

People began moving faster after a gunshot shattered the tranquility of this autumn night, followed by over a dozen more. Two shooters ran from the scene, leaving five students shot and bleeding on the usually pristine campus walk. Most of those who had stopped to watch the fight had run, but a few helped carry or drag the injured students into buildings and, hopefully, to safety. Sirens sounded, security officers raced across the campus, and a lone counselor who happened to be around for a different event raced across campus to help. There were five students with gunshot wounds, but so many more had witnessed the violence and were deeply affected by it.

"Seeing the blood everywhere? Seeing those kids shaking, crying, or so scared that they couldn't even move?" the crisis interventionist said when asked what the experience was like. "It absolutely changed me."

Crises will, almost always, change those who are impacted by them. Whether it is a campus shooting, a plane crash, natural disaster, or act of terrorism, a crisis is something that challenges our typical means of coping and forces us to view the world differently. Some crises are newsworthy and become the source of widespread discussion and dissection, while others are far less obvious. Regardless of the number of news stories or people impacted, a crisis will have lasting effects on those who experience it. The goal of the crisis worker is to help mitigate the negative effects of crisis, while challenging and encouraging clients to grow and become stronger as a result.

The current chapter will examine the basic nature of crisis, including how crisis is defined, types of crises, why crises cause distress, the cycle of crisis, and the importance of multicultural competence when working as a crisis interventionist. After reading this chapter you should be able to:

1. Define what a crisis is and what makes it different from other events;
2. Differentiate between the various forms of crises;
3. Explain why crises have such a significant impact on those who experience them, specifically related to Maslow's (1954) Hierarchy of Needs;
4. Describe the typical cycles that occur during and after a crisis; and
5. Discuss the impact that culture plays on individuals who experience crises and the interventionists who work to help the survivors.

Defining a Crisis

The term "crisis" is difficult to define for a number of reasons. First, crises can take on a variety of forms, from national tragedies to a flat tire in a thunderstorm. Another nuance to the notion of crisis is that its definition is personal. For example, one person might not experience much dissonance after a national tragedy, while another may be traumatized by experiencing a flat tire during a thunderstorm. The perception that something is a crisis is a subjective one, which is influenced by personal factors, material considerations, coping strategies, and a host of other dynamics that will be discussed at length later in this book.

While the concept of crisis is subjective and socially constructed, there are a number of definitions found throughout the literature. Caplan (1961) defines crisis simply as "an upset in the steady state of the individual" (p.18). This definition includes additional elements, such as encountering obstacles to meeting goals, especially when one's traditional choices and behaviors no longer work to resolve the crisis. Carkhuff and Berenson (1977) argue "crisis is a crisis because the individual knows no response to deal with the situation" (p.165).

Belkin (1984) includes an element to the definition of crisis that adds a sense of immobilization and the inability to consciously control one's life. Brammer (1985) views crisis as a disruption in the meeting of life goals, but goes on to explain that it is the affective reaction to the disruption (e.g., fear, shock, distress, etc.) that constitutes a crisis, not the event itself. Kanel (2007) identifies three specific elements of crisis that include: (1) a precipitating event; (2) a perception of the event that causes subjective distress; and (3) the failure of the person's usual coping methods. The failure to cope causes the individual to function at a lower level than he or she did prior to the precipitating event (Kanel, 2007). James and Gilliland (2012) include in their discussion of crisis that it presents an opportunity for growth as well as danger.

For the purposes of this book, we offer the following summary of these definitions that will serve to operationalize the term crisis hereafter. *Crisis is the subjective experience of an event or events that: (a) causes significant difficulty or distress for the person who has experienced it; (b) cannot be resolved through the individual's current means of coping; (c) can cause significant dysfunction if left unaddressed (e.g., affective, cognitive, and behavioral); and (d) can provide an opportunity for growth if addressed appropriately.* In order to better understand how the term crisis will be used throughout the book, it is important to examine each of these elements individually.

Crisis is the Subjective Experience of an Event or Events

As described previously, the term *crisis* is socially constructed and subject to individual interpretation. Each of us experiences life differently, and each of us constructs meaning based on our own unique experiences. How we construct meaning is influenced by a host of factors, including our family of origin, others in our lives who influence our beliefs, past experiences, and resolution (or lack of resolution) of previous difficulties, to name a few. To illustrate the notion of subjective experience, consider the following statement: *The sky is really blue today.* This is a simple statement, comprised of only six words. However, one person's subjective experience of a *really blue* sky is likely different from someone else's. There are dozens of common shades of blue. To which shade is this statement referring? Also consider the use of the term *really* to describe the color blue. How does that change your perception of the sky that is being described?

Another important element is that while a crisis is often considered a single event, crises can be comprised of a series of events that, if considered individually, may not constitute a crisis. While one single event may not cause a crisis, the compilation of those events may cause a state of disequilibrium from which the individual cannot recover quickly or without assistance. For example, for some, experiencing a flood in their home might constitute a crisis while others may not experience it as such. However, if the day after the flood occurs, water causes the home's electrical system to short circuit causing a fire, the threshold for a crisis may draw closer. Add to the experience the possibility that the homeowner missed a recent insurance payment due to a job loss, and what began as a challenge that could be overcome can escalate to a full blown crisis. Exercise 1.1 highlights the subjective and personalized nature of this thing called "crisis."

Causes Significant Difficulty or Distress for the Person Who has Experienced the Event(s)

Events can occur every day that challenge us. Maybe you walk outside on a beautiful summer day to complete some much needed yard maintenance. After getting your lawn mower, you attempt to start it, only to find that it simply will not run. You make every effort to start the mower, but to no avail. For your neighbor, this may be distressing, causing frustration and disappointment. Perhaps rather than becoming upset, you simply return the mower and sit on your porch and enjoy a cold drink. The point is that for a crisis to occur, the individual impacted by the event or events must experience a significant level of distress.

EXERCISE 1.1

SUBJECTIVE EXPERIENCES AND SOCIAL CONSTRUCTION

Directions: In small groups (two to four), consider the following potential life events. For each event, determine for yourself how distressed you would be if this happened to you, using a Subjective Units of Distress (SUDs) scale from 0–10 (0 = no distress whatsoever; 10 = extreme, unbearable distress). Share your responses with your fellow group members. Discuss within your group why you chose a given SUDs level for each example.

- Driving a vehicle that was involved in a two-car accident where individuals in the other vehicle were injured but you were not.
- Experiencing the death of a parent.
- Being mugged by an individual with a handgun during the middle of the day on a heavily traveled sidewalk.
- Watching on television while a terrorist attack occurs in another country.
- Experiencing the death of a close family pet.
- Having your house burglarized while you were out at dinner.
- Watching a person you know commit suicide by jumping out of a window.
- A hurricane (or tornado if you are no-where near a coast) destroys your home and the homes of your neighbors.
- While at home, a bomb explodes in the center of your town/city.

Cannot be Resolved Through the Individual's Current Means of Coping

While the first element of this definition requires an individual to experience distress, that suffering need not be lasting or out of the individual's control. Each of us possesses our own methods of coping with life's stressors (which will be discussed later in this chapter), and while some stressors are greater than others, some coping strategies are more powerful than others, as well. In order for an event to reach the level of a crisis, the person who experiences it must be overwhelmed to the degree that her or his traditional means of coping are overcome and do not adequately address the stress that resulted from the crisis event.

Can Cause Significant Dysfunction if Left Unaddressed

Once the previous criteria for a crisis have been met (i.e., an individual experiences significant distress and is unable to cope), it stands to reason that if the disequilibrium is left unattended, negative results may occur. Individuals in crisis who do not seek resolution are often left with physical, affective, cognitive, spiritual, and behavioral concerns that can become debilitating if unabated (See Chapter Two for a more detailed discussion). Many people who survive crises but do not fully resolve the experience are faced with severe anxiety, intrusive thoughts, and ineffective and unhealthy behaviors, such as addiction, self-injury, and violence toward others.

Can Provide an Opportunity for Growth if Addressed Appropriately

It is too often assumed that crisis will inevitably lead to negative consequences, and that is possible if the experience is not addressed appropriately. However, those who identify that they are experiencing a crisis and begin to resolve it through assistance from others can begin the process of growth and self-realization (Aguilera & Messick, 1982; Brammer, 1985). Moreover, emerging research has suggested that the potential for growth is quite significant, and the term *Post-Traumatic Growth* describes the "experience of positive change that occurs as a result of the struggle with highly challenging life crises" (Tedeschi & Calhoun, 2004, p.1). Post-Traumatic Growth can manifest in a variety of ways, including increased self-esteem, improved personal relationships, increased self-efficacy, and greater degrees of personal strength.

Crisis Domains

After establishing that an event meets the definition of a crisis, the next step of conceptualizing the crisis condition is determining which of the crisis domains applies to the specific situation. A crisis typically occurs within one of four domains: (1) *developmental* crises, (2) situational crises, (3) environmental crises, and (4) existential crises (James & Gilliland, 2012). Each of these crisis domains will be explored in greater depth.

Developmental crises are events that occur within the normal process of human development and are typically expected and somewhat predictable (Kanel, 2007). The developmental aspect that constitutes the crisis is the individual response to the developmental change. Examples of developmental crises may include such life events as: graduation from high school or college, career changes, marriage, the birth of a child, retirement, or other events that commonly occur across the lifespan.

Situational crises ensue when an uncommon and extraordinary event occurs that is unpredictable and uncontrollable (James & Gilliland, 2012). These events are random, sudden, unexpected, and tend to be emergent (Slaikeu, 1990). Situational crises may also have impact beyond the individual extending to the community at large and may include catastrophic events. Examples of situational crises include death, divorce, illness, terrorist attacks, job loss, sexual assault, or other crimes.

Environmental crises may be classified as situational crises or may be considered in a separate domain. These crises occur when a natural or human-caused disaster impacts a group of people through no fault of their own (James & Gilliland, 2012). Environmental crises may impact every member of a community if the disaster occurs on a large enough scale. Examples of natural environmental crises include: floods, hurricanes, tornadoes, earthquakes, tsunamis, blizzards, forest fires, famine, and drought. Other forms of environmental crisis may be caused by man and include widespread biological disasters, such as oil spills or nuclear accidents, as well as small-scale events, such as a single family house fire. Environmental crises may be political in nature, such as wars and genocide, or result from severe economic crisis, such as major economic recessions or depressions.

Finally, existential crises occur when one's internal conflict becomes too great to be managed through typical coping skills. Existential crises generally result from issues related to the purpose of life, freedom, independence, or commitment to others or oneself. Existential crises may occur when one is faced with the possibility of never achieving a life goal, such as marrying or having children. Such crises may also occur later in life when individuals reflect on their accomplishments and believe they have failed to meet their potential or contribute enough to the greater society.

Significance of Crises

Assuming someone has experienced an event that meets the criteria for a crisis, it is important to understand why that event can have such a significant impact on the person's functioning. One method of conceptualizing the significance of crisis on the individual is through the lens of Maslow's (1954) now famous Hierarchy of Needs. He argued

---

EXERCISE 1.2

BRAINSTORMING VARIOUS TYPES OF CRISES

Directions: Brainstorm as many examples of each as you can for each of the crisis domains (developmental, situational, environmental, and existential). After doing so, compare your responses with 1–2 other people, and create a master list of the many crises that can occur in each of the domains.

Developmental	Situational	Environmental	Existential

that individuals have a variety of needs, ranging from the most fundamental for sustaining life through those that are more interpersonal and intrapersonal. Those fundamental, life-sustaining needs are represented at the bottom of the hierarchy, while those that are inter- and intrapersonal are at the top. Maslow (1954) argued that the most basic needs are physiological (e.g., food, water, oxygen); followed by needs for safety (e.g., shelter, physical health, financial safety); then love, belonging, and esteem; and finally the need for self-actualization.

A crisis can exist in any of these levels of hierarchy. For example, an existential crisis may be found at higher levels of the continuum. The retired banker who finds herself in crisis, because she has reached retirement and feels like she never met her goals of contributing humanistically to society, may find herself struggling with esteem-based needs. The middle-aged male who never married or fathered children may find himself in an existential crisis related to the need for love.

When we consider most crises, however, we tend to think first of those that impact Maslow's (1954) most basic needs, the physiological and safety necessities that are most core to our survival. These crises tend to be situational or environmental and can impact our most basic human necessities. In the example of Hurricane Katrina, a widespread natural environmental crisis, physiological and safety needs were challenged throughout the crisis. The need for safety was jeopardized by rising floodwaters, loss of homes, lack of shelters, and widespread crime, coupled with a lack of public safety personnel to ensure the safety of the citizens of New Orleans. Physiological needs were endangered by a lack of food, lack of potable water, and the absence of accessibility to medication and medical care.

A crisis escalates in severity as the lowest needs on Maslow's (1954) hierarchy are jeopardized. While crises that impact the needs for love, esteem, and self-actualization can certainly have adverse effects on the individual, they tend not to lead to the severity of effect as those crises that expose more fundamental needs, such as physical and financial security, and the basic physiological needs that are paramount to survival.

The Crisis Cycle

In order to fully understand the impact of crisis on the individual, it is first important to understand the process by which people process and cope with disturbing and difficult events. Drawing on the work of James and Gilliland (2012), Janosik (1986), and Kanel (2007), what follows is a method of understanding how clients experience and process traumatic events, conceptualizing the client's experience in a crisis, and how the experience of crisis can become cyclical and recursive if not addressed appropriately. Figure 1.1 represents the crisis cycle, various stages and counseling concerns that occur at each stage, and where the cycle may be disrupted.

Figure 1.1 The Crisis Cycle

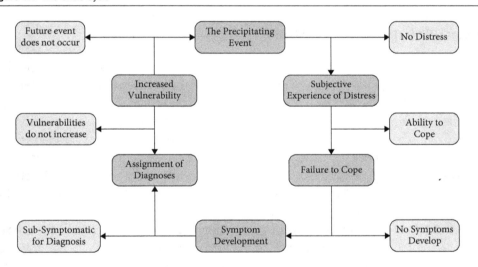

The Precipitating Event

As described previously in the definition of crisis, in order for a crisis to occur, it must begin with a precipitating event. These events can be developmental, situational, environmental, or existential. The occurrence of a precipitating event can be expected; for example, graduation from high school is a typical developmental event that may lead to the experience of crisis. However, when considering the precipitating event, we often assume the event to be unexpected and drastic, including situational and environmental events, such as violent crimes, natural disasters, man-made disasters, and so forth.

It is important to note that the precipitating event may be a compound event, that is, a series of multiple events that, alone, may not constitute a crisis. However when considered aggregately, the compounding of the events becomes distressing to the person experiencing the crisis. The event, in and of itself, does not constitute a crisis. The event must cause the client to experience distress in order to meet the definition of crisis. A negative event that does not cause distress is simply a stressor, much like those that occur every day in each person's life.

Bronfenbrenner (1979, 2005) discussed how events might negatively impact the individual's expected developmental trajectory. Specifically, Bronfenbrenner (1979, 2005) suggested that negative events in a person's life could disrupt the conception of normal human development. This theory posited that continued interaction with par- ticular negative environmental factors could create the risk of abnormal development. Bronfenbrenner referred to these negative factors as *risk factors*. Lynch and Levers (2007) define risk factors as "those that have the potential to interrupt the individual's normal developmental pathway or trajectory" (p. 590).

Subjective Experience of Distress

In order to meet the definition of a crisis, the precipitating event must cause the client to experience distress. It is important to note that each individual experiences the precipi- tating event differently, and as a result, the experience of distress is subjective. Factors such as the client's mental health prior to the occurrence of the precipitating event, the severity of the event, and previous experience with similar events can all have an impact on the client's subjective experience. Slaikeu (1990) suggests that a client's cognitive processes and the meaning the client assigns to the event can greatly impact the client's subjective experience. Slaikeu (1990) refers to the meaning the client assigns to the precipitating event as the *cognitive key.*

The notion of the cognitive key is that the meaning the client assigns to the precip- itating event can be the key to unlocking the individual's experience with the crisis. For example, car crashes occur every day and are often considered minor accidents that are easily resolvable, both practically and emotionally. The meaning most people will assign to a car accident will include a focus on cognitive processes such as who was at fault, how the accident could have been avoided, or the steps that need to be taken to repair a damaged vehicle. However, if the individual involved in a minor car crash was previously a survivor of a major accident that included fatalities, the meaning assigned to the precipitating event might be very different. That meaning might include the belief that the client was lucky not to have died, that others involved in the accident may die as a result, or that riding in a car is inherently unsafe and will never happen again. These beliefs might certainly cause distress, and the assignment of meaning serves as the cognitive key to understanding the distress and addressing it therapeutically.

Discussion of subjective distress and assignment of meaning raises the issue of the difference between *stress* and *crisis*. While crises most certainly involve high levels of stress, the two terms are not synonymous. Stress is a ubiquitous element of life. Stress occurs every day and can be caused by a wide range of events and factors that can be represented by developmental, situational, environmental, and even existential events. However, what differentiates stress from crisis is the subjective experience of the individual experiencing the event. People manage stress through their typical methods of coping, effective behaviors that have been successful for mitigating stressful events in the past. However, when the event is too large in scale, extremely stressful, or triggers the individual in some unexpected manner, the client may fail to cope effectively, and a crisis may ensue.

Failure to Cope

The third element of the crisis cycle is the individual's failure to cope. When considering coping skills, a host of thoughts typically come to mind. Some people exercise, others listen to or play music, while others will call on support from family or friends. Just as Bronfenbrenner (1979, 2005) discussed risk factors as those events that might negatively impact a person's developmental processes, he also suggested that *protective factors* can mitigate those risks. Protective factors are "those that can serve to buffer the individual from the influence of risk factors, such as the presence of a caring or nurturing adult" (Lynch & Levers, 2007, p. 590). Protective factors create a defense between the individual and the risks the person identifies in the environment. In the absence of protective factors, these risks may cause an interruption or change in the individual's developmental progress.

There are a multitude of factors that may serve a protective role against the risk of a crisis event. A few of these protective factors include:

- **Material resources:** Resources, such as wealth, transportation, clothing, shelter, and other material goods can provide a means of better coping with a precipitating event. For example, a man who is the victim of a violent mugging may better cope with the experience if he is able to afford treatment at a local hospital for his injuries, returns to a safe home in a wealthy neighborhood, and is able to afford to install a state-of-the-art security system. If the money that was stolen in the assault was a small fraction of his disposable income, he may better recover than if losing the money left him destitute.

- **Social resources:** Individuals with strong *support systems* (i.e., family, friends, spiritual connection, colleagues, academic peers, etc.) have more social resources at their disposal in times of stress. These social supports provide resources to assist the individual in coping with the precipitating event.

- **Personal resources:** There are a host of internal resources that individuals possess that can provide protection in the face of a difficult situation. For example, people with certain *personality traits* may recover more quickly from adversity, while individuals with other personality traits may struggle. Traits such as perseverance, maturity, and optimism may have protection against the risks of crisis, while traits such as negativity, dependence, and pessimism may lead to failure to cope with the disequilibrium that follows a difficult experience. Individuals who are physically healthier or possess high levels of intelligence or education also tend to cope with challenges more effectively (Kanel, 2007). Additionally, higher degrees of *ego strength* tend to lead to better coping strategies. Ego strength, or the ability to understand how the world works and meet one's needs, is a strong predictor of positive coping (Kanel, 2007).

When considering protective factors and coping skills, we most often think of those behaviors that constitute *effective coping skills*. Effective coping skills are those that help to mitigate the subjective distress the client experiences after the precipitating event and can prevent the event from developing in to a crisis. Effective coping skills are those that alleviate the client's distress, while leading to positive, healthy outcomes that do not create new complications for the client. Caplan (1964) identified seven characteristics of effective coping skills. These are included in Table 1.1.

Table 1.1 Seven Characteristics of Effective Coping (Caplan, 1964)

1. Actively exploring reality and being willing to seek out information
2. Frustration tolerance and a willingness to express both positive and negative feelings freely
3. Actively seeking out help from others
4. Breaking problems into manageable parts and working through them individually
5. An awareness of fatigue and exhaustion, an ability to pace coping efforts, and an ability to maintain control in as many areas of functioning as possible
6. Mastering feelings where possible, being flexible, and possessing a willingness to change
7. Having trust in oneself and others and maintaining a positive outlook on outcomes

However, sometimes the distress a person experiences is greater than the effective coping skills available to the individual, or perhaps, the person lacked effective coping skills prior to the occurrence of the precipitating event. In these cases, people will still attempt to mitigate the distress they experience after the precipitating event but will lack effective means of doing so. In the absence of effective means of coping with the disequilibrium caused by the event, they will turn to *ineffective coping skills*. Ineffective coping skills are those that do not mitigate the distress experienced after the event, and may lead to increased tension or the development of new problematic situations in the client's life. Ineffective coping skills may include alcohol or other drug abuse, risky sexual behaviors, or violence toward others.

Symptom Development

Assuming all of the stages in the crisis cycle have occurred (i.e., a precipitating event, subjective distress, and ineffective coping), the individual who is in crisis may begin displaying symptoms that result from failing to cope with the disequilibrium caused by the precipitating event (see Chapter Two). Survivors of crisis events initially conduct a form of initial cognitive review that includes the following: disbelief that the event occurred, shock, denial, and disorientation (Levers & Buck, 2012). Following a crisis, survivors will often report feelings of numbness, sometimes followed by anger. Those in crisis may blame others for the precipitating event, leading to the desire to seek retribution, or may blame themselves, causing feelings of guilt or self-loathing.

The U.S. Department of Health and Human Services (2004) identified five categories of symptoms that crisis survivors may experience, including physical, cognitive, affective, behavioral, and spiritual. These are discussed in greater detail in Chapter Two.

Assignment of Diagnoses

As symptomology develops, the individual will likely meet criteria for diagnosis as defined in the *Diagnostic and Statistical Manual of Mental Disorders, Fifth Edition* (DSM-5). Considerable attention will be paid in Chapter Five to the various diagnoses that may be identified through the symptoms that manifest following failure to cope with a critical event. The diagnoses that will be discussed in Chapter Five include:

EXERCISE 1.3

EFFECTIVE AND INEFFECTIVE COPING SKILLS

Directions: Consider the various means individuals cope with crises, both effectively and ineffectively. Below, brainstorm as many examples of effective coping skills as you can. After doing so, brainstorm as many examples of ineffective coping methods as you can.

Effective Coping Examples

Ineffective Coping Examples

- Trauma-Related Disorders (including Acute Stress and Post-Traumatic Stress Disorders)
- Anxiety Disorders
- Depressive Disorders
- Substance Abuse Disorders (typically developing from ineffective coping strategies)
- Adjustment Disorders
- Reactive Attachment Disorder
- Social Engagement Disorder
- Personality Disorders
- Somatic Experience of Trauma

Increased Vulnerability

If the individual is deeply affected by the precipitating event, is unable to cope with the stress of the experience, and develops symptoms that meet the criteria for a mental health diagnosis, there is the possibility that the person may become *crisis prone* (Kanel, 2007). If the individual is unable to cope with the event on his or her own and does not receive adequate or appropriate crisis interventions, the person may be more apt to experience crises in the future.

A crisis can be a physically and emotionally exhausting experience. Following such an occurrence, the individual may be left without adequate psychological resources to successfully cope with future precipitating events, and thus, the crisis cycle becomes self-perpetuating. As the individual struggles to cope with the crisis and the symptoms of the mental health diagnosis continue unabated or worsen, the individual is less equipped to cope with future stressful events. Following an unresolved crisis, the individual's ego strength is damaged, and most of the person's resources are devoted to coping with the symptoms of the initial crisis, such as heightened anxiety, sadness, intrusive thoughts and dreams, and so forth.

With a damaged ego and exhausted personal resources, the individual lacks the coping skills necessary to prevent what would have once been a manageable life stressor from becoming a full blown crisis. For example, an individual may survive a house fire but lose a loved one to the flames. If this experience is left unresolved, it would not be surprising for the individual to struggle with such experiences as heightened anxiety, major depression, or the fear of death for oneself or others. While he or she is struggling with these concerns, forecasters begin tracking a hurricane. They do not believe it will impact the town where this person lives, yet it may still evoke a crisis response, as the unresolved previous crisis has increased vulnerability to future crises. Case Illustration 1.1 provides an example of how the same event can lead to very different outcomes.

Multicultural Considerations in Crisis Counseling

There is little doubt that we live in an increasingly diverse society and that cultural considerations have become critical to effective helping (Sue & Sue, 2007). As our culture becomes more pluralistic, helpers must be attuned to the varied needs of those to whom we provide helping services. The American Counseling Association (ACA) speaks to the importance of culturally competent helping as an ethical mandate (2014) and the Council for the Accreditation of Counseling and Related Educational Programs (CACREP) places significant emphasis on multicultural competency in its accreditation standards (2016).

Still, counselors are apt to make biased assumptions when working with clients. For example, citizens of the United States have been fortunate to escape the large-scale situational and environmental disasters that occur throughout the world, such as war, plague, genocide, and other social upheaval. This provides a sort of insulation that makes it difficult to fully understand the experiences of those who have lived through these traumatic experiences. Additionally, Silove (2000) argues that Western therapists assume that Post-Traumatic Stress Disorder (PTSD) and other crisis-based mental health diagnoses follow linear and predictable patterns. Rather than making culturally based assumptions regarding diagnosis, symptomology, and treatment, those

CASE ILLUSTRATION 1.1

THE TALE OF TWO COLLEGE DROPOUTS

Dale was a successful high school student and athlete. He lettered in three sports and maintained an almost perfect grade point average (GPA). While his high school didn't have formal votes, everyone knew Dale was "most likely to succeed." He had succeeded at everything he had ever done. While he attended a school district that wasn't necessarily known as high achieving, *he* was high achieving. He had almost perfect scores on his Scholastic Aptitude Tests (SATs), had already earned a dozen college credits through successful completion of Advanced Placement (AP) classes, and signed a letter of intent to play football at a well-known, expensive, and prestigious Division I university.

During his first summer of football practices, Dale was seriously injured, tearing several ligaments in his knee. Team doctors told him his playing career was likely over. His coaches were supportive and invited Dale to continue to participate with the team and assured him his scholarship would still be honored despite not being able to play. When the semester began, Dale attended classes, performed well academically, and made new friends. But as the semester went on, he began to withdraw. He stopped going to class, stopped completing work, and no longer spent time with the football team. When he went home for Thanksgiving break, he felt he had to tell his parents about his academic situation. They decided to withdraw him from the university and told him they would discuss whether or not he might return in the Spring term. Dale fell in to a deep depression while at home, barely leaving his room.

In contrast, Monica went to the same high school as Dale and was an average student, earning mostly B grades and scoring above the national average on the SATs, but nowhere near the top scores. She had friends in school, had a small group of very close friends, and was involved in some activities but often preferred to stay out of the spotlight. Monica attended a local state university and worked two jobs in order to afford tuition while living at home. Monica had the support of her parents throughout the semester, neither of whom had attended college themselves. Monica struggled to make ends meet while also balancing her academic course load. She contributed some of her earnings to the household budget, especially after her father's hours at work were cut back.

By Thanksgiving break, Monica realized that she wasn't performing well academically and was exhausted from months of "burning the candle at both ends." She approached her parents about withdrawing from the university for a semester while she continued to work to save money and contribute more to the family budget. While saddened, her parents were supportive of the decision. As soon as she completed the withdrawal, Monica felt great relief, as if the weight of the world had been lifted from her shoulders. She re-engaged with friends that she had missed while she was balancing academics and was happier during the holiday break than she had been in months.

who take a multicultural approach to crisis work argue that trauma and crisis are socially constructed within the context of the culture in which they occur and in which the individual exists (Silove, 2000). This approach aligns with the subjective distress model described previously in this chapter.

Pedersen (1987) outlines 10 culturally biased assumptions typically made by crisis intervention agencies in their training of new staff:

1. Individuals share a common understanding of what constitutes "normal" behavior.

2. The individual, rather than the community, should be the focus of crisis intervention.

3. Academic disciplines (e.g., counseling, social work, medicine, nursing, anthropology, etc.) define the concepts of problems, stress, crisis, and so forth, rather than the individual or the cultural system.

4. Western culture is dependent on abstractions to describe the various elements of crisis and counseling. This dependence assumes that the counselor and client will understand one another's language implicitly and will have no misunderstandings related to linguistics.

5. Independence is valued, and dependence is assumed to be a weakness.

6. Formal counseling processes are more important and more effective than natural support systems.

7. Linear thinking is universal. For example, assumptions related to cause and effect and dualistic thinking (e.g., good vs. bad, right vs. wrong) can create cultural misunderstandings.

8. Counselors must work with individuals to help them conform to society and systemic norms (rather than systems changing to adapt to the needs of their constituents).

9. The client's history is irrelevant in the context of a current crisis.

10. Counselors and crisis workers are aware of their biases and cultural assumptions.

With the context of multicultural competence in mind, it is important for crisis workers to be aware of their own culture-based assumptions and biases when working with clients in times of crisis. This can be especially difficult given that the current research has not focused a great deal on the relationships between culture, crisis, and intervention (James & Gilliland, 2012). While crisis work is a unique form of helping, it is still helping, nonetheless and, in that regard, is no different than other forms of counseling. Knowledge, attitudes, and skills related to multicultural counseling are critical to be an effective crisis interventionist, just as they are necessary to any counseling process. However, in the depths of catastrophe, the helper may have difficulty accessing the knowledge and skills necessary to have a positive impact on those in crisis. Case Illustration 1.2 describes how culture can impact those experiencing a crisis.

Summary

- Crisis is the subjective experience of an event or events that: (a) causes significant difficulty or distress for the person who has experienced the event(s); (b) cannot be resolved through the individual's current means of coping; (c) can cause significant dysfunction if left unaddressed

CASE ILLUSTRATION 1.2

THE CHALLENGE OF MULTICULTURAL CRISIS INTERVENTION

Michael was a German exchange student living in the United States for a year while on an exchange program. He was succeeding academically and had made a number of friends, played on the school's soccer team, and by all accounts, had acclimated well to life in the States. However, Michael was hiding a severe depression that worsened as the year went on. When Michael returned to the United States after the winter break, he seemed especially despondent and unhappy.

Michael's mood continued to worsen through the winter months. When asked about it, he would typically reply without much emotion, "I'm just homesick. I'm fine." People took Michael at his word that he was "fine," but he wasn't. Michael's host family contacted his parents in Germany several times, expressing concern for him and suggesting that he may want to return home. Michael's parents assured his host family that Michael would be OK and that he would sometimes struggle with brief periods of sadness but would always work his way out of them.

One morning, Michael didn't join the family for breakfast. His host parents went to his room to check on him to find that Michael had taken his own life. Of course, everyone in the house was distraught; Michael had been part of their family, and they had grown very close to him. Their initial reactions ranged from shock to sadness as they began to grieve. Michael had left a note on the dresser, but it was written in German, and no one in the house could understand it.

Michael's parents were informed of his death and immediately flew to the United States to arrange for his transportation back to Germany. His host family expected to encounter the same range of emotions from Michael's family as they had experienced, but instead, they were met with two stoic figures. Michael's parents curtly thanked his host family for all they had done for Michael and asked to read the suicide note. After reading it, Michael's parents showed little emotion and asked how they could begin making arrangements for Michael's transportation back to Germany.

(e.g., affective, cognitive, and behavioral); and (d) can provide an opportunity for growth if addressed appropriately.

- Crises occur in four domains: developmental, situational, environmental, and existential.

- Developmental crises are events that occur within the normal process of human development and are typically expected and somewhat predictable.

- Situational crises ensue when an uncommon and extraordinary event occurs that is unpredictable and uncontrollable.

- Environmental crises occur when a natural or human-caused disaster impacts a group of people through no fault of their own. They may be natural, man-made, or may be political or economic in nature.

- Crises negatively affect some element or elements on Maslow's hierarchy of needs. Those crises that impact needs that are physiological or safety-related tend to have greater impact on the individual than those that affect belonging, esteem, or self-actualization.

- Crises typically follow a cycle, although that cycle can be disrupted at any stage. The crisis cycle consists of: The Precipitating Event, Subjective Experience of Distress, Failure to Cope, Symptom Development, Assignment of Diagnoses, and Increased Vulnerability.

- The *cognitive key* is a term sometimes used to describe the meaning an individual assigns to a crisis event. The cognitive key represents the issue(s) that needs to be resolved in order for the individual to move past the crisis.

- While crises represent risk factors that can disrupt an individual's normal development and functioning, protective factors help an individual cope with difficult life circumstances.

- Material, social, and personal resources can serve as protective factors against the development of a crisis for an individual following a precipitating event. Personal resources may include things such as personality traits and the individual's ego strength.

- Individuals use coping skills as a means of dealing with the distress caused by a crisis. Effective coping skills will help the individual move past the distress; ineffective coping skills are employed when effective coping skills no longer work or are absent. Ineffective coping skills will often make the crisis worse.

- Individuals who fail to fully process a crisis event may be subject to increased vulnerability to future events, which can, in turn, lead to future crises and can leave an individual as a crisis-prone person.

- Just as in any other form of helping, effective crisis work requires that the helper develop the knowledge, skills, and attitudes necessary to work with individuals from diverse cultures and with different worldviews.

Important Terms

Cognitive key

Crisis

Crisis-prone person

Developmental crisis

Economic environmental crisis

Effective coping skills

Ego strength

Environmental crisis

Existential crisis

Failure to cope

Ineffective coping skills

Maslow's hierarchy of needs

Man-made environmental crisis

Material resources

Natural environmental crisis

Personal resources

Personality traits

Political environmental crisis

Post-Traumatic Growth

Protective factors

Risk factors

Situational crisis

Social resources/support systems

Stress

Subjective experience of distress

Additional Resources

In Print

Jackson-Cherry, L.R., & Erford, B.T. (2010). *Crisis intervention and prevention*. New York, NY: Pearson Education, Inc.

McAdams, C.R., & Keener, H. J. (2008). Preparation, action, recovery: A conceptual framework for counselor preparation and response in client crises. *Journal of Counseling & Development, 86,* 388–398.

Ripley, A. (2009). *The unthinkable: Who survives when disaster strikes-and why.* New York, NY: Three Rivers Press.

On the Web

Boatlift: An Untold Tale of 9/11 Resilience: https://www.youtube.com/watch?v=MDOrzF7B2Kg

Crisis and Trauma Resource Institute (CTRI): http://www.ctrinstitute.com/

International Association for Suicide Prevention (IASP): https://www.iasp.info/

Love and Strength: Subjective response to the tragedy at Sandy Hook: https://vimeo.com/119009935

References

Aguilera, D. C., & Messick, J. M. (1982). *Crisis intervention: Theory and methodology* (4th ed.). St. Louis, MO: C.V. Mosby.

American Counseling Association (2014). 2014 ACA Code of Ethics. Alexandria, VA: Author.

American Psychiatric Association (2013). *Diagnostic and statistical manual of mental disorders* (5th ed.). Arlington, VA: Author.

Belkin, G. S. (1984). *Introduction to counseling* (2nd ed.). Dubuque, IA: William C. Brown.

Brammer, L. M. (1985). *The helping relationship: Process and skills* (3rd ed.). Upper Saddle River, NJ: Prentice Hall.

Bronfenbrenner, U. (1979). *The ecology of human development: Experiments by nature and design*. Cambridge, MA: Harvard University Press.

Bronfenbrenner, U. (2005). *Making human beings human*. Thousand Oaks, CA: Sage.

Caplan, G. (1961). *An approach to community mental health*. New York, NY: Grune & Stratton.

Caplan, G. (1964). *Principles of preventative psychiatry*. New York, NY: Basic Books.

Carkhuff, R. R., & Berenson, B. G. (1977). Beyond counseling and therapy (2nd ed.). New York, NY: Holt, Rinehart & Winston.

Council for the Accreditation of Counseling and Related Educational Programs. (2015). 2016 standards. Alexandria, VA: Author.

James, R.K., & Gilliland, B. E. (2012). *Crisis intervention strategies* (7th ed.). Belmont, CA: Thomson Brooks/Cole.

Janosik, E. H. (1984). *Crisis counseling: A contemporary approach*. Monterey, CA: Wadsworth.

Kanel, K. (2007). *A guide to crisis intervention*. Belmont, CA: Thomson Brooks/Cole.

Levers, L. L., & Buck, R. P. (2012). Contextual issues of community-based violence, violence-specific crisis and disaster, and institutional response. In L. L. Levers (Ed.), *Trauma counseling: Theories and interventions* (pp. 317–348). New York, NY: Springer.

Lynch, M. F., & Levers, L. L. (2007). Ecological-transactional and motivational perspectives in counseling. In J. Gregoire and C. M. Jungers (Eds.), *The counselor's companion: What every beginning counselor needs to know*. (pp. 586–605). Mahwah, NJ: Lawrence Erlbaum Associates.

Maslow, A. (1954). *Motivation and personality*. New York, NY: Harper.

Pedersen, P. (1987). Ten frequent assumptions of cultural bias in counseling. *Journal of Multicultural Counseling and Development, 15*, 16–24. doi: 10.1002/j.2161-1912.1987.tb00374.x

Silove, D. (2000). A conceptual framework for mass trauma: Implications for adaption, intervention, and debriefing. In B. Raphael & J. P. Wilson (Eds.), *Psychological debriefing: Theory, practice, and evidence* (pp. 337–350). New York, NY: Cambridge University Press.

Slaikeu, K. A. (1990). *Crisis intervention: A handbook for practice and research* (2nd Ed.). Needham Heights, MA: Allyn & Bacon.

Sue, D. W., & Sue, D. (2007). *Counseling the culturally diverse: Theory and practice* (5th ed.). Hoboken, NJ: Wiley.

Tedeschi, R. G., & Calhoun, L. G. (2004). Posttraumatic growth: Conceptual foundations and empirical evidence. *Psychological Inquiry, 15*, 1–18. doi: 10.1207/s15327965pli1501_01

U.S. Department of Health and Human Services (2004). Mental health response to mass violence and terrorism: A training manual. DHHS Pub No. SMA 3959. Rockville, MD: Center for Mental Health Services, Substance Abuse and Mental Health Services Administration.

CHAPTER 2

Crisis and Trauma: Experiences with Wide Ranging Impact

Each time the airlock opened I thought—they are going to tell me he was okay ... that they made a mistake ... that he was ALIVE.

As advertised, it was a night "to remember." However, it was and continues to be remembered for all the wrong reasons.

It was the night of the high school senior prom and the school psychologist, whose reflection is quoted above, was in his car, following a teacher friend as they left the downtown hotel where they served as chaperones. As the light turned green, they both moved through the intersection when, out of nowhere, came a drunk driver who not only ended the psychologist's friend's life, but dramatically changed this psychologist's life forever.

The reference to the airlock was his memory of standing in the emergency room (ER) and the fact that an airlock entry separated those receiving care from those waiting. The sound and the memory centered on the moment of being told that his friend, a young man of 24, who just two months prior became a newlywed, had died. For what seemed like an eternity, he stood there, detached, disassociated from time and place only to be drawn back to the moment by the sound of the opening ER airlock door.

With each passage through the door, he anticipated—no, *fantasized*—that the doctors would rush out to tell him that, miraculously, all was well, that they had made a mistake. But this was not to be.

He was experiencing the event almost as two different people. He "knew," even as he stood there, that such thinking was irrational and fantastical, yet he was unable to stop. He "knew" that he was in the grips of major psycho-emotional crisis, but that knowledge alone did not immediately ground him in the horror of the moment. His reaction illustrated an acute disruption in his psychological balance or homeostasis. His normal coping mechanisms were inoperable. The distress and functional impairment he experienced were all the hallmarks of a crisis.

The current chapter will review the expansive impact and areas of disruption encountered by those experiencing stress induced by crisis or trauma. While most are aware of the psycho-emotional effects of crisis and trauma, the research cited will highlight not only the impact of crisis on one's affect, but also the potential impairment to cognition and judgment, as well as the immediate and long-lasting physiological changes that may result. After reading this chapter you should be able to:

1. Describe the physiological and neurological systems disrupted by the experience of crisis and trauma;

2. Explain the mechanisms accounting for the impairment to memory and judgment that results from the experience of crisis and trauma;

3. Describe the psycho-emotional response, both immediate and prolonged, typically presented by those experiencing personal crisis and trauma;

4. Explain the potential impact of crisis and trauma on one's values and worldview.

Effects: Both Immediate and Enduring

The impact of crisis and trauma, while highly individualized, can be both immediate and enduring while affecting multiple domains, including one's physiology, affect, cognition, and behavior. If we consider the opening case and the response of the psychologist to the news of his friend's death, we can see the breadth of the impact that crisis can impose on an individual.

As he attempted to process the news and the reality of his loss, his adaptive mechanisms appeared to simply overload. The immediate response, and one quite typical of those encountering a crisis, was disbelief. As the news took center stage, it felt as if time had slowed down. He found himself dissociating as if he stood outside of himself, watching the events unfold. He felt frozen in the moment, pushed to approach the situation in order to understand and resolve, yet at the same time having an equally strong desire to escape.

While the impact of crisis or trauma is broad, the specific experience and response is highly individualistic. Reactions to a crisis or traumatic event vary considerably from person to person. It is not unusual for such reactions to be delayed for a few hours, days, or even weeks. Further, the impact can last a few days, several weeks, months, or even longer depending on the severity of the event, one's personal experience with crisis or trauma, and one's developed style of responding. As might be expected with an increased frequency and duration of traumatic events, the impact of the traumatic event and symptoms are likely to increase. Exercise 2.1 invites you to gather anecdotal data supporting the variance of individual responses to crisis or trauma.

EXERCISE 2.1

A VARIATION OF RESPONSES

Directions: As noted in the text, numerous variables can contribute to an individual's immediate and long-term reaction to crisis or trauma. In this exercise, you are invited to interview your classmates or colleagues for their own experiences of personal crisis or trauma. The goal is NOT to have the interviewee reveal deep personal information about the situation, but rather, to identify the impact the experience had on their thinking, feeling, and acting, at the moment and/or shortly thereafter.

Incident	Did it affect my thinking?	How did I feel at the moment?	Did I behave in ways that were atypical of how I would normally act?	Did the impacts change over time (Get worse? Better?)

Crisis and Trauma: Impacting One's Body

The physiological systems that are activated at times of stress, while potentially serving to protect an individual, can also produce significant damage to one's body (Selye, 1956). This is especially true when an individual is in crisis, and the nature of the stress overwhelms a person's adaptive mechanisms. fight/flight

Crisis-related stress can result in numerous physical symptoms (see Table 2.1). Common symptoms include headache, loss of appetite, stomach and digestive upset, joint pains, and fatigue (see Exercise 2.2). Beyond the short-term disruption of these systems, crisis- and trauma-related stress can result in longer-term disruption and illness to one's cardiovascular, immunological, gastrointestinal, and neuromuscular systems.

EXERCISE 2.2

PERSONAL EXPERIENCE WITH CRISIS-INDUCED STRESS

Directions: Most crises are part of the normal range of life experiences. Experiences ranging from the loss of a pet, the momentary panic of a parent who has lost sight of a child, or the shock of being in a car accident, can all be perceived as an intolerable difficulty that exceeds one's current resources and coping mechanisms and thus by definition are crises. Identify a personal experience with crisis and, using the list of possible responses listed below, check off those that you experienced. You may find it of value to compare/contrast your response to your personal crisis to that of a colleague or classmate.

Physical	Mental	Emotional	Behavioral
Nausea	Slower thinking	Anxiety	Crying
Upset stomach	Fearful thoughts	Guilt	Hyperactivity/agitation
Tremor	Memory problems	Grief	Withdrawal for interaction
Sweating	Detached as if not in the moment	Sadness	Increase in drug or alcohol use
Diarrhea	Flashback—images of the event	Overall numb	Snapping at others
Headache	Feeling insecure	Irritability/anger	Inability to get motivated and do anything
(other)	(other)	(other)	(other)

Table 2.1 Physical Response to Crisis and Trauma

- Gastrointestinal problems–constipation/diarrhea
- Decreased appetite
- Decreased libido
- Startle response
- Fatigue
- Insomnia
- Sleep disturbance
- Hyperarousal—easily startled
- Somatic complaints—sudden sweating and heart palpitations
- Impaired immune response—more susceptible to colds and illness
- Headaches—miscellaneous pain

Cardiovascular Illness

There is extensive support linking crisis-related stress and acute trauma to impairment of cardiovascular functioning (Holman et al., 2008). Brydon, Magid, and Steptoe (2006) reported an increased risk of coronary events for those who have experienced a traumatic event. Likewise, individuals with crisis-related stress have been found to present with high blood pressure (Uchino, Holt-Lunstad, Bloor, & Campo, 2005) and atherosclerotic plaque (McEwen, 2005).

Immune Functioning

Research on the relationship between stress and immune functioning suggests that acute stress may immediately enhance the immune system, whereas chronic stress is linked with immunosuppression (McEwen, 2005). Thus, while stress may initially activate one's immune reaction, continued exposure can lead to a dramatic suppression of immune functioning and increase vulnerability to disease. This finding would certainly explain the experience many of us have when we find ourselves more likely to catch a cold when we experience ongoing academic or employment stress.

Gastrointestinal Conditions

The loss of appetite and experience of nausea, which often accompanies the experience of crisis-induced stress, has been explained as a result of increased visceral sensitivity (Murray, et al., 2004) and exaggerated arousal and dysrhythmic gastric activity (Muth,

Koch, Stern, & Thayer, 1999). These gastrointestinal changes can account for not only the experience of nausea, but also general gastric pain and discomfort reported by those in crisis.

Musculoskeletal and Pain Disorders

Dorn, Yzermans, Spreeuwenberg, Schilder, and van der Zee (2008) found that in a sample of accident survivors, musculoskeletal problems were elevated relative to community controls. Further, Haviland et al. (2010) noted that trauma increases the risk of one of the most common musculoskeletal conditions, fibromyalgia, which can be experienced as an overall body ache and specific points of extreme touch sensitivity.

The Neurological Basis for Physical Disruption

While a review of the specific neuro-physiological mechanisms affected by trauma is beyond the scope of this text, one concept that has been offered as an explanation of connection between crisis- or trauma-induced stress and health problems is worth review.

Allostatic load (Friedman & McEwen, 2004) refers to the effect of stress on the regulation of hypothalamic-pituitary-adrenal axis and the autonomic nervous system. It can be thought of as the wear and tear placed on the body as a result of toxic stress. It has been used to explain how the frequent activation of a body's response to stress can damage or wear down the systems it was intended to protect (Taylor, 2006), thus resulting in the physical symptomatology often associated with crisis and trauma experience.

Interfering with Cognitive Function

As will be described below, research has demonstrated that the experience of crisis and trauma can impair one's ability to think rationally and plan decisively (see Table 2.2). However, advanced neuropsychological study now provides insight into the more long-term, structural effects of crisis and trauma on the brain and the resulting negative impact on memory, arousal, and fear response.

Table 2.2 Impact on Cognitive Functioning

- Impaired concentration
- Impaired decision-making ability
- Memory impairment
- Disbelief
- Confusion
- Distortion
- Decreased self-esteem
- Decreased self-efficacy
- Self-blame
- Intrusive thoughts/memories
- Worry
- Nightmares

Impaired Problem Solving and Decision Planning

When in the grip of a crisis, the ability to cognitively focus, process data, and engage in rational problem solving and decision making is often impaired. Consider a typical scene from a movie in which a character finds himself stuck on a train track in a car that has stalled. With the awareness of the impending disaster, the camera focuses intensely on the character, who is clearly in crisis and responds by continually grinding the ignition with no effect, pumping the accelerator to the point of further flooding the engine, and finally accepting his apparent fate, stares hopelessly into space.

While the depiction certainly adds to the drama and excitement of the scene, the character's responses appear less than functional or adaptable to the circumstance. If you were to take a more objective view of the event, unlike our movie character, you would realize there was time to abandon the car and find safety. But the ability to process those data can easily be impaired in moments of crisis.

Our higher-order cognitive skills, those supporting purposeful, goal-directed activity, are the result of the executive functioning of our prefrontal cortex. These executive functions, which are mediated in the frontal lobes and prefrontal cortex, are critical to higher-level reasoning (Carlson, 2010). They help us direct and maintain our attention, remain focused in the face of distractions, plan future behavior under conditions of uncertainty, anticipate outcomes, and use feedback—all cognitive activities that are essential to complex decision-making. Further, these are all cognitive activities that can break down during periods of crisis (Lezak, 2004).

It appears that the prefrontal cortex of our brain, the area that supports our highest cognitive abilities, is sensitive to the detrimental effects of crisis- or trauma-induced stress. When we find ourselves in crisis, our lower brain centers, specifically the amygdala and hypothalamus, activate higher levels of noradrenaline and dopamine release. These hormones not only impair prefrontal cortex regulation but also elevate fear response and strengthen fear conditioning. Under these conditions, regulation shifts from executive functioning to more of a bottom up control, and the brain response pattern switches from slow, thoughtful, prefrontal cortex regulation to a reflective, rapid emotional response characteristic of amygdala control (Arnsten, 2009).

Impairment Beyond Information Processing

While impairment to information processing is even more pronounced with those who have been trauma exposed (Brewin, Kleiner, Vasterling, & Field, 2007; Karl et al., 2006), the impact of trauma on cognitive functioning goes beyond such processing impairment. Those who have experienced trauma often exhibit intrusive thoughts, hyperarousal, flashbacks, nightmares, and sleep disturbances, changes in memory and concentration, and increased startle response with reduced inhibition of impulses and fear (Buckley, Blanchard, & O'Neill, 2000; Brewin et al., 2007).

These symptoms are hypothesized to represent the behavioral manifestation of stress-induced changes in brain structure and function specifically to those areas felt to play an important role in stress responding. Karl et al. (2006) meta-analyzed data from 50 studies examining structural brain abnormalities of those with trauma exposure. These authors reported that those who had experienced trauma and were exhibiting Post-Traumatic Stress Disorder (PTSD) had significantly smaller amygdala and anterior cingulate cortices, areas that are responsible for coordinating responses to fear. Further, these data reveal that those with PTSD exhibited smaller frontal lobe functioning that may account for reported difficulty with planning and judgment, as well as failure to modulate emotional responsiveness through inhibition of amygdala function. In addition to difficulty monitoring arousal and fear responses, those who have been trauma exposed were found to show alterations in memory function following traumatic stress (Elzinga & Bremner, 2002).

Impacting Values and Worldview

Traumatic experiences can affect and alter cognitions, including our perception of connection to self, others, the world, and the divine. From the outset, trauma challenges the core life assumptions that help individuals navigate daily life (Janoff-Bulman, 1992).

Not only can one's fundamental assumptions about safety in the world be undermined, but so can one's trust in self, others, and even in God. Trauma truly can result in a shattering of one's worldview (Roberts, 2000). In this outcome of a new worldview, there is no meaning, control, connection, safe place, or dependable individual (Ochberg, 1993).

While one's worldview can be shattered, others may respond to crisis and trauma with a clarified sense of values, worldview, or purpose. Exercise 2.3 invites you to look at one such individual.

EXERCISE 2.3

INCREASED COMMITMENT AND VALUES-DRIVEN BEHAVIOR

Directions: While trauma can often shake the fundamental values and worldview of an individual, there are individuals who have responded to crisis and trauma with a clarified sense of values, worldview, and purpose. You are invited to research the experience of an individual whose life work/commitment is the result of his or her response to a personal crisis or trauma. Examples can range from political and social activists, such as Malala Yousafzai or Nelson Mandela, to celebrities, such as Oprah Winfrey or Tony Robbins. As you review the individual's life and response to personal crisis or trauma, try to identify the factors that facilitated their positive response.

The Psycho-Emotional Impact of Crisis and Trauma

Being in crisis elicits emotions such as fear, frustration, and anger, which are responses to a perceived threat and reflect the mobilization of our protective "flight or fight" response. While an initial response may reflect our survival mode of flight or flight, these responses will often be followed or accompanied by one or many of the emotional reactions found in Table 2.3.

Table 2.3 Emotional Response to Crisis and Trauma

- Shock
- Anger
- Despair
- Emotional numbing
- Dissociation
- Terror/Fear
- Guilt
- Depression or sadness
- Grief
- Irritability
- Hypersensitivity
- Helplessness/Hopelessness

One's emotional reaction to crisis and trauma can range from mild arousal or feelings of sadness to those signifying trauma-related mental disorders. While the emotional reactions are highly individualized, it is not unusual to have those impacted by crisis- or trauma-induced stress to report experiences of emotional dysregulation, a general sense of numbing, or even dissociation, depersonalization, and derealization.

Emotional Dysregulation

Emotional regulation refers to the ability to have control over not only how and when, but also the intensity and positive/negative valence with which emotions are felt, experienced, and expressed. Those encountering crisis- or trauma-induced stress often report having difficulty regulating emotions, particularly anger, anxiety, sadness, and shame (van der Kolk, Roth, Pelcovitz, & Mandel, 1993).

There appear to be two different forms of emotional dysregulation with distinct patterns of cortical and subcortical activation and symptoms (Steuwe, Lanius, & Frewen, 2012). Undermodulated emotion (e.g., anxiety, hyperarousal, dysphoria) is related to the classic pattern of heightened amygdala activation and reduced prefrontal inhibitory activation. Overmodulated emotion (e.g., dissociation, emotional numbing), by contrast, is related to extensive midline prefrontal inhibition of limbic activity (Lanius et al., 2010).

Problems with emotional regulation play a role in the development, maintenance, and treatment of many psychiatric conditions. Maladaptive coping with challenging emotions is common in depression, bipolar disorder, borderline personality disorder, substance-use disorders, eating disorders, and somatoform disorders, among others (Berking, 2012).

For most adults, such emotional dysregulation is typically short lived and tied to the moment. However, children who, due to increased cortisol reactivity and decreased emotion regulation, may exhibit unpredictable, explosive emotions (Lopez-Duran et al., 2009); without assistance, this experience can be more enduring (D'Andrea, 2012).

Dissociation, Depersonalization, and Derealization

While dissociation, depersonalization, and derealization are typically encountered in conditions of serve crisis or trauma-induced stress, they also can be employed by those encountering less traumatizing and more temporary conditions of stress. When confronted with an overwhelming experience from which actual escape is not possible, such as that encountered at times of crisis, one may find escape from distress by way of dissociation, depersonalization, and derealization. These states provide an altering of consciousness to accommodate overwhelming experience, thus allowing the person to continue functioning.

Perhaps you have found yourself driving a road that you have often traveled and, at some point, realize that you were not really clear or paying attention to how you got to a certain spot. The fact that dissociation helps distance one from an experience makes it a process often used by those experiencing a moment of crisis or a history of trauma. Consider Case Illustration 2.1.

JAN–DRIVING SOLO

Jan is a 16-year-old high school student who just recently passed her driver's test. Having gotten her license, she spent the entire weekend cajoling her parents into allowing her to drive to school on Monday, rather than take the bus. As might be expected, Jan's parents required her to use the weekend to provide evidence of her competence and attention to safety details. After receiving the thousand and one parental reminders, Jan was given the keys to her mother's car with the final instruction, "Be careful."

As she turned into the entrance of her school's parking lot, feeling proud of her first solo effort, she excitedly took the occasion to beep and wave at her best friend, Keisha. The look on Keisha's face was priceless. "Boy was she surprised." Surprised!

The sound of the broken glass pulled her attention back to the front window and the car that was just backing out of the parking spot, the car that she just rear-ended.

Sitting in the car, staring straight ahead, she was only faintly aware of the voices and people now surrounding her car. The people expressing concern and asking if she was okay appeared to exist in another time and space, and for Jan, it appeared for several moments as if nothing was happening, as if time stood still.

Certainly Jan's first fender bender was experienced in a way that simply overwhelmed her adaptive systems. As such, temporary relief was achieved by simply detaching from the time, the place, and the experience. While just momentary "escapes" can be functional, in its extreme, such dissociation can disrupt normal integration of consciousness, memory, and identity (APA, 2013).

Depersonalization is generally experienced as a detachment from self and the immediate experience as if one were a detached observer of oneself, rather than the experiencing self. It is not usual for those experiencing such depersonalization to report feeling as if in a dream-like state. This was certainly true for the psychologist whose ER experience opened the chapter.

He noted that he felt *"As if he was two people—he 'knew', even as he stood there, that such thinking was irrational, fantastical, yet he was unable to stop."* It was as if he was observing himself and all the events around him from a perspective far above the ER, watching as if from a distance. At the same time, he was experiencing the entire event as not real—even though the evidence was all too clear that it was. This process of seeing or experiencing the event as "not real" is derealization and is an attempt to soften the pain.

As with all of these coping mechanisms, chronic depersonalization and derealization are signs of significant dysfunction and evidence of a dissociative disorder (APA, 2010).

Of Major Concern

While most individuals experiencing a crisis- or trauma-induced stress may experience the emotional responses listed above, most will find the effects short lived, assuming the presence of coping skills and support. However, the power of crisis and trauma is such that it can result in mood disorders, substance abuse, and in more severe, longer-lasting forms of dysfunction, which can include but is not limited to: Major Depressive Disorder, Generalized Anxiety Disorder, Panic Disorder, Substance Abuse Disorders, Post Traumatic Stress Disorder, and Acute Stress Disorder (Kessler et al., 1997).

Behavioral Responses to Crisis and Trauma

An individual's reaction in the midst of a crisis or trauma is highly idiosyncratic and is affected by the individual's history with crisis and trauma, the availability of support systems, and one's own modes of coping and general life skills. The behavioral responses can range widely from mildly disruptive to those defined as pathological. Table 2.4 lists a number of behaviors often exhibited by those encountering crisis or trauma-induced stress. What these behaviors appear to have in common is that they reflect attempts to manage the intensity of the experience and to gain some control over the distressing experience.

Table 2.4 Behavioral Response to Crisis and Trauma

- Alienation
- Social withdrawal/Isolation
- Increased relationship conflict
- Vocational impairment
- Refusal to go to school
- School impairment
- Avoiding reminders
- Display excessive temper
- Exhibit regressive behaviors
- Anxious, fearful, and avoidant
- Show irritability, sadness, and anxiety
- Socially withdrawn

Avoidance

A common response to stressful life events, such as rape, is engagement in avoidance coping strategies or effortful attempts to avoid or reduce negative affect (Littleton, Horsley, John, & Nelson, 2007). Some people reduce tension or stress through avoidant behavior. They will go to great lengths to avoid people, places, things, or situations that remind them of the experience and elicit a re-experiencing of the unpleasant emotions and memories tied to the event.

While such behaviors may be of service in the short run, this avoidance reinforces the belief in danger in the absence of reality-testing; these behaviors typically result in additional problems. Consider Case Illustration 2.2, where the expanding employment of avoidance moved from mildly disrupting to severely impairing the client's life.

Social/Interpersonal

After experiencing a traumatic event, it is common to see a disruption in relationships with others. In part, this may be due to the withdrawn behavior that frequently accompanies sadness and depression. Survivors may readily rely on family members, friends, or other social supports, or they may avoid support. It is not unusual for survivors of trauma to feel ashamed of their response to crisis, or believe that no one could understand. They may even feel betrayed by those whom they assume should have "saved" them from the experience. Each of these perspectives lends to a desire to withdraw and/or avoid social interaction.

Self-Medicating

Self-medication, in these instances, is an effort to mediate painful memories and feelings associated with adverse events and situations. It has been hypothesized that survivors of trauma often turn to substance use to sedate or numb the effects of traumatization (Cappell & Greeley, 1987; Stewart & Israeli, 2001). For many responding to the stress induced by crisis or trauma, substance use is viewed as having been an essential part of their psychological and emotional coping.

CASE ILLUSTRATION 2.2

A LONG DRIVE TO THE GROCERY STORE

The accident, which totaled the car and resulted in Raul breaking his wrist, occurred as he exited the local grocery store. While there were no other serious effects of the accident, at least not immediately, within three weeks after the occurrence, Raul began to make significant adjustments to his behavior.

Even though he lived less than a quarter mile from the local grocery store, going to the store caused him to experience much distress and anxiety. As such, he began to drive in the opposite direction to shop at a different store. He saw this as a minor inconvenience.

As time passed, he began to notice the anxiety and distress returning, and he associated to the fact that this new store was of the same chain and, thus, had the same signage and layout as that of the original store. In hopes of avoiding these experiences, Raul began to drive to the next community, where he found a store from another chain, one that had a unique layout and even different store brands.

The shift in location changed his travel time from 10 minutes to the original store to 20 minutes to the first option to, finally, 70 minutes to his final store of choice.

Re-Enactment

Many traumatized people expose themselves, seemingly compulsively, to situations reminiscent of the original trauma. These behavioral re-enactments are rarely consciously understood to be related to earlier life experiences (van der Kolk, 1989). Attempts to explain re-enactments are very complicated, as re-enactments occur for a variety of reasons. While there is no single reason for engagement in these reenactments, one position is that re-enactments are attempts at gaining a sense of mastery over the dangerous situation (van der Kolk,1989).

Re-enactments can include behaviors, such as hypersexuality; driving recklessly; positioning oneself in dangerous situations, as with walking alone in unsafe areas; or involvement in repetitive destructive relationships (e.g., repeatedly getting into romantic relationships with people who are abusive or violent).

High-Risk and Self-Injurious Behaviors

In addition to such high-risk behaviors as those listed as re-enactments, survivors may engage in self-harm or self-injurious behaviors. It has been proposed that such self-harm is an attempt to cope with the emotional and physical distress that seems overwhelming (Santa Mina & Gallop, 1998). See Case Illustration 2.3.

Among the self-harm behaviors reported in the literature are cutting, burning skin by heat (e.g., cigarettes) or caustic liquids, punching hard enough to self-bruise, head banging, hair pulling, self-poisoning, inserting foreign objects into bodily orifices, excessive nail biting, excessive scratching, bone breaking, gnawing at flesh, interfering with wound healing, tying off body parts to stop breathing or blood flow, swallowing sharp objects, and suicide.

Summary

- The impact of crisis and trauma can be both immediate and enduring, affecting multiple domains, including one's physiology, affect, cognition, and behavior.

- Crisis-related stress can result in symptoms that include headache, loss of appetite, stomach and digestive upset, joint pains, and fatigue.

- Crisis-related stress and acute trauma can impair cardiovascular functioning.

- Continued exposure can lead to a dramatic suppression of immune functioning, thus increasing the vulnerability of disease.

- Crisis-induced stress has been explained as a reflection of increased visceral sensitivity and exaggerated arousal and dysrhythmic gastric activity.

- Those who have experienced crisis or trauma-induced stress experience increased risk of one of the most common musculoskeletal conditions, fibromyalgia, which can be experienced as an overall body ache and specific points of extreme touch sensitivity.

CASE ILLUSTRATION 2.3

RELIEF THROUGH SELF-INJURY

Anyone who knew Tisha would be hard pressed to describe her as anything but a sweet girl. She was an honor student, an all-star high school tennis player and senior class president. She truly had it all going for her—or at least that was what everyone else believed.

As for Tisha, she hated herself. She hated that everyone thought she was perfect, that she was a "goody-too-shoes," that she couldn't do anything wrong. She especially hated the comments made through social media, comments that were hurtful, rejecting, and truly humiliating.

The social bullying began in 6th grade and only escalated throughout high school. On the outside, she showed no ill effect. The adults in her life never knew of the abuse or the grave impact it was having on Tisha. Concluding it was somehow her fault resulted in her concluding it would always be like this, that she would be isolated and alone and truly unlovable. She hated herself. She hated her life. She hated the way she was treated, and the only relief she could find was by cutting herself. As she explained it, "Cutting seemed to release the pain, not just blood. It made me feel great as if everything was going to be okay … at least for now."

- Allostatic load, which refers to effect of stress on the regulation of hypothalamic-pituitary-adrenal axis and the autonomic nervous system, has been used to explain how the frequent activation of a body's response to stress can damage or wear down the systems it was intended to protect.

- Crisis and trauma can impair one's precortical executive function. This impairment can lead to a reduction in the ability to think rationally and plan decisively.

- Traumatic experiences can affect and alter cognitions, including our perception of connection to self, others, the world, and the divine. From the outset, trauma challenges the core life assumptions that help individuals navigate daily life.

- Those impacted by crisis- or trauma-induced stress often report experiences of emotional dysregulation, a general sense of numbing or even dissociation, depersonalization, and derealization.

- It is not unusual, after experiencing a trauma, to see a disruption in relationships. This may be due, in part, to the withdrawn behavior that frequently accompanies sadness and depression.

- It has been hypothesized that survivors of trauma often turn to substance use to sedate or numb the effects of traumatization.

- Many traumatized people expose themselves, seemingly compulsively, to situations reminiscent of the original trauma as an attempt to gain a sense of mastery over the dangerous situation.

- It has been proposed that self-harm, often employed by those who have experienced crisis or trauma-induced stress, is an attempt to cope with the emotional and physical distress that seems overwhelming.

Important Terms

Adaptive mechanisms

Allostatic load

Avoidance

Cardiovascular illness

Depersonalization

Derealization

Disbelief

Disconnection

Disorientation

Dissociation

Emotional regulation

Executive functions

Fatigue

Gastrointestinal conditions

Headache

Hyperarousal

Immune functioning

Loss of appetite

Musculoskeletal and pain disorders

Overmodulated emotion

Prefrontal cortex

Problem solving and decision-making

Re-enactments

Self-injurious behaviors

Self-medication

Undermodulated emotion

Additional Resources

In Print

Marshall R. D., & Garakani A. (2002). Psychobiology of the acute stress response and its relationship to the psychobiology of post-traumatic stress disorder. *Psychiatric Clinics of North America., 25*, 385–395.

McFarlane A. C.,Yehuda R, & Clark C.R. (2002). Biologic models of traumatic memories and post-traumatic stress disorder. The role of neural networks. *Psychiatric Clinics of North America., 25*, 253–270.

Shalev A. Y. (2000). Biological responses to disasters. *Psychiatric Quarterly, 71*, 277–288.

On the Web

Friend, T. (2003). Jumpers: The fatal grandeur of the Golden Gate Bridge. *The New Yorker*, October 13, 2003. Available online at: www.newyorker.com/archive/2003/10/13/031013fa_fact

PTSD Symptoms and Signs (Post Traumatic Stress Disorder) https://www.youtube.com/watch?v=FPTFhaj7BhM

References

Arnsten, A. F. T. (2009). Stress signaling pathways that impair prefrontal cortex structure and function. *Nature Reviews. Neuroscience, 10*(6), 410–422.

American Psychiatric Association (2013). *Diagnostic and Statistical Manual of Mental Disorders* (Fifth ed.). Arlington, VA: American Psychiatric Publishing.

Berking M. (2012). Emotion regulation and mental health recent findings, current challenges, and future directions. *Current Opinion Psychiatry; 25,* 128–134.

Brewin, C. R., Kleiner, J. S., Vasterling, J. J., & Field, A. P. (2007). Memory for emotionally neutral information in posttraumatic stress disorder: A meta-analytic investigation. *Journal of Abnormal Psychology, 116,* 448–463.

Brydon, L., Magid, K., & Steptoe, A. (2006). Platelets, coronary heart disease, and stress. *Brain, Behavior, and Immunity, 20,* 113–119.

Buckley, T. C., Blanchard, E. B., & Neill, W. T. (2000). Information processing and PTSD: A review of the empirical literature. *Clinical Psychology Review, 20,* 1041–1065.

Cappell H, Greeley J. (1987). Alcohol and tension reduction: An update on research and theory. In Blane H. T., Leonard K. E., Eds., *Psychological Theories of Drinking and Alcoholism* (pp. 15–54). New York, NY: Guilford.

Carlson, N. R. (2010). *Physiology of behavior* (10th ed.). Boston, MA: Pearson, Allyn, and Bacon.

D'Andrea W., Ford J. D., Stolbach B., Spinazzola J., van der Kolk B. A. (2012). Understanding interpersonal trauma in children: Why we need a developmentally appropriate trauma diagnosis. *American Journal of Orthopsychiatry, 82,* 187–200.

Dorn, T., Yzermans, J. C., Spreeuwenberg, P. M. M., Schilder, A., & van der Zee, J. (2008). A cohort study of the long-term impact of a fire disaster on the physical and mental health of adolescents. *Journal of Traumatic Stress, 21,* 239–242.

Elzinga, B.M., & Bremner, J.D. (2002). Are the neural substrates of memory the final common pathway in posttraumatic stress disorder (PTSD)? *Journal of Affective Disorders, 70,* 1–17.

Friedman, M. J., & McEwen, B. S. (2004). Posttraumatic stress disorder, allostatic load, and medical illness. In P. P. Schnurr & B. L. Green (Eds.), *Trauma and health: Physical health consequences of exposure to extreme stress* (pp. 157–188). Washington, D.C.: American Psychological Association.

Haviland, M. G., Morton, K. R., Oda, K., & Fraser, G. E. (2010). Traumatic experiences, major life stressors, and self-reporting a physician-given fibromyalgia diagnosis. *Psychiatry Research, 177,* 335–341.

Holman, E. A., Silver, R. C., Poulin, M., Andersen, J., Gil-Rivas,V., & McIntosh, D. N. (2008). Terrorism, acute stress, and cardiovascular health: A 3-year national study following the September 11th attacks. *Archives of General Psychiatry, 65,* 73–80.

Janoff-Bulman, R. (1992). Happystance. A review of subjective well-being: An interdisciplinary perspective. *Contemporary Psychology, 37,* 162–163

Karl, A., Schaefer, M., Malta, L. S., D., D., Rohleder, N., & Werner, A. (2006). A meta-analysis of structural brain abnormalities in PTSD. *Neuroscience & Biobehavioral Reviews, 30,* 1004–1031.

Kessler, R. C., Anthony, J. C., Blazer, D. G., Bromet, E., Eaton, W. W., Kendler, K., & Zhao, S. (1997). The US national comorbidity survey: Overview and future directions. *Epidemiologia e Psichiatria Sociale, 6,* 4–16.

Lanius R. A., Vermetten E., Loewenstein R. J., Brand, B., Schmahl, C., Bremner, D., & Spiegel, D. (2010). Emotion modulation in PTSD: Clinical and neurobiological evidence for a dissociative subtype. *American Journal of Psychiatry, 167*, 640–647.

Lezak, M. D. (2004). *Neuropsychological assessment* (4th ed.). New York, NY: Oxford University Press.

Littleton H., Horsley S., John S., & Nelson D. (2007). Trauma coping strategies and psychological distress: A meta-analysis. *Journal of Traumatic Stress, 20*, 977–988.

Lopez-Duran N. L., Olson S. L., Hajal N. J., Felt B. T., & Vazquez D. M., (2009). Hypothalamic pituitary adrenal axis functioning in reactive and proactive aggression in children. *Journal of Abnormal Child Psychology, 37*, 169–182

McEwen, B. S. (2005). Stressed or stressed out: What is the difference? *Journal of Psychiatry & Neuroscience, 30*, 315–318.

Murray, C., Flynn, J., Ratcliffe, L., Jacyna, M., Kamm, M., & Emmanuel, A. (2004). Acute physical and psychological stress and its influence on autonomic outflow to the gut in irritable bowel syndrome. *Gut, 53*(4), A29.

Muth, E., Koch, K., Stern, R., & Thayer, J. (1999). Effect of autonomic nervous system manipulations on gastric myoelectrical activity and emotional responses in healthy human subjects. *Psychosomatic Medicine, 61*, 297–303.

Ochberg, F. M. (Ed.). (1993*). Posttraumatic Therapy*. New York, NY: Plenum Press.

Roberts, A. R. (Ed.). (2000*). Crisis intervention handbook* (2nd ed.). New York, NY: Oxford University Press

Santa Mina E. E., & Gallop R. M. (1998). Childhood sexual and physical abuse and adult self-harm and suicidal behaviour: A literature review. *Canadian Journal of Psychiatry, 43*, 793–800.

Selye, H. (1956). *The stress of life*. New York, NY: McGraw-Hill.

Steuwe C., Lanius R. A., Frewen P.A. (2012). Evidence for a dissociative subtype of PTSD by latent profile and confirmatory factor analyses in a civilian sample. *Depress Anxiety, 29*, 689–700.

Stewart, S.H., & Israeli, A.L. (2001) Substance abuse and co-occurring psychiatric disorders in victims of intimate violence. In C. Wekerle & A Hall (Eds.) *The violence and addiction equation: Theoretical and clinical issues in substance abuse and relationship violence* (pp. 98–122). New York, NY: Hogrefe & Huber.

Taylor, S. E. (2006). *Health psychology*. New York, NY: McGraw-Hill Education.

Uchino, B. N., Holt-Lunstad, J., Bloor, L. E., & Campo, R. A. (2005). Aging and cardiovascular reactivity to stress: Longitudinal evidence for changes in stress reactivity. *Psychology and Aging, 20*(1), 134–143.

van der Kolk, B. A. (1989). The Compulsion to Repeat the Trauma: Re-enactment, Victimization and Masochism. *Psychiatric Clinics of North America, 12*(2), 389–411.

CHAPTER 3

Crisis Intervention:
A Unique Helping Process

The cell phone went off, and they told me there was a client holding a piece of broken glass against her throat, threatening to commit suicide. I didn't know what to do; I feel like everything I ever learned went right out the window.

Many counselors are called upon to intervene in crisis situations throughout their careers; yet, few have had specific training in how crisis intervention differs from other types of helping. Intervening with a client who is threatening suicide is a difficult and frightening experience and requires skill, training, and practice in assessing the nature and likelihood of the threat. Understanding the differences in crisis helping, as well as understanding various models of prevention, intervention, and postvention can help a counselor feel more prepared in the moments when the cell phone rings.

This chapter will examine the differences between crisis intervention and other forms of helping, and will also explain how various theories of counseling are integrated into crisis intervention theory. This chapter will also examine models of crisis prevention, intervention, and postvention, in addition to discussing the concept of transcrisis. After reading this chapter, you should be able to:

1. Differentiate between crisis intervention and other forms of helping;
2. Understand how primary, secondary, and tertiary prevention strategies can be important in averting crisis situations;
3. Identify various models of crisis intervention and postvention models to use with individuals;
4. Describe three approaches to crisis intervention on the systemic level; and
5. Discuss the importance of transcrisis and how transcrisis states impact individual functioning and growth.

Distinguishing Crisis Intervention from Other Forms of Helping

Intervening in a crisis is no easy task. Successfully helping individuals and communities through difficult events can be a challenge, even for the most experienced helpers. Effective crisis interventionists must be able to balance a number of important skills and areas of knowledge. First, they must embody a number of unique characteristics. Second, they should employ the fundamental skills of helping while demonstrating the ability to discern the specific skills necessary at the time of the crisis and how these may be different than those typically employed in a counseling dynamic. Finally, crisis interventionists must understand the theoretical underpinnings of crisis work.

Characteristics of Crisis Counselors

When one enters the world of crisis intervention, it can be advantageous if the helper has, or can develop, some personal characteristics that are often found in those who help in crises. James and Gilliland (2012) identify a number of important characteristics of the effective crisis worker. While this list is not exhaustive, it does highlight a number of characteristics that can help the crisis interventionist be more effective:

- Life experience—A host of life experiences tend to allow the crisis worker to be more empathetic with the client in crisis, in addition to developing a sense of maturity that is important in this work.

- Poise—Crises often cause disequilibrium. While this experience is subjective by definition, often, a crisis can impact people who experience it. Being able to remain calm under pressure is important.

- Creativity and Flexibility—In the midst of an emergency or a disaster, knowledge learned in textbooks or skills learned through experience often must be adapted or abandoned altogether. The ability to be creative and adaptable can be extremely helpful during a crisis.

- Intellectual Quickness—Time is critical during a crisis. The helper should be able to think quickly and adapt to the constantly changing context of a crisis. This intellectual quickness is also related to the ability to be creative and flexible.

- Energy, Resilience, and Optimism—Working with people during a crisis event, such as a disaster, requires the ability to find untapped personal energy and optimism in the face of difficulty.

- Multicultural Competence—As described in Chapter One (and, again, in Chapter 11), it is necessary for crisis workers to understand how culture influences reactions to crises and how the helper can be culturally competent in providing interventions.

- Balance of Optimism and Realism—In order to be effective, the crisis interventionist must believe in the ability of the client to grow and overcome the effects of the crisis. At the same time, a crisis is a real event, full of danger and difficulty. The helper cannot take a Pollyanna approach to the challenges inherent in the crisis but must be realistic about outcomes and dangers.

- Courage—Working in a crisis situation can often be frightening. Environmental crises, such as floods and fires, or situational crises, such as crime or terror, can tap in to the helper's greatest fears. Showing courage in the face of fear can often serve as a modeling technique for clients.

- Identifying Client Strengths—In order to help clients overcome the negative impacts of a crisis discussed in Chapter Two, it is important that the helper be adept at identifying the strengths a client possesses and encourage the client tap into those strengths during the helping process.

Exercise 3.1 is designed to help you assess your own characteristics, including those that you may need to develop further as you enter the field of crisis intervention.

Beyond the "Typical" Application of Counseling Skills

For those with a background in the fundamentals of helping, crisis work can be difficult in that it often challenges the basic tenets taught to new helpers. Consider the question, "How does that make you feel?" While asking a question that elicits an emotional response is often one of the most fundamental techniques in the helping process, it is

---

IDENTIFYING YOUR CHARACTERISTICS

Directions: Below is a list of characteristics often found in crisis workers. For each of the characteristics, identify (a) if you believe you possess that characteristic, (b) if others have given you feedback that you possess that characteristic, and (c) what you might do to help develop that skill more fully (if necessary). If possible, brainstorm with one or two others (classmates, colleagues, etc.)

Characteristic	Do you believe you posses it?	Do others believe you possess it?	How can you develop it more fully?
Life Experience			
Poise			
Creativity/Flexibility			
Intellectual Quickness			
Energy, Resilience, & Optimism			
Multicultural Competence			
Balance of Optimism & Realism			
Courage			
Identifying Client Strengths			

often the last question one asks during or immediately following a crisis. Consider the case of a person who has lost everything after torrential rainfall has caused massive flooding, and her home has been washed away with all of her belongings. How do you think that person feels in the immediate aftermath of learning that everything is gone? How will that person respond if, as the rain continues to fall, you ask her, "How does this flood make you feel?"

However, it is important for the helper to use many basic skills while working with an individual in crisis. For example, rapport is often helpful when asking people to share their most intimate thoughts with you. However, in crisis work, rapport is difficult to develop, as crisis intervention is often limited and context prevents multiple meetings with clientele (Kanel, 2007). Attending behaviors, such as active listening, are critical, as are effective questioning skills. Clarifying skills, such as paraphrasing and verifying, are important, as is summarizing. Developing and exhibiting empathy are necessary skills in crisis intervention, as well (James & Gilliland, 2012).

However, some skills differ when working with individuals in crisis. For example, interpretation is a helping skill not often used during crisis situations. Interpretation often requires the development of a complex therapeutic relationship that, by definition, does not typically occur in the short-term nature of crisis work (Kanel, 2007). Also, counseling students and novice professionals are encouraged to be non-directive; the helper is asked to take a backseat to the client during the helping process. While this is often optimal, during crisis work, the helper may need to be far more directive than in other forms of helping (James & Gilliland, 2012). For example, an individual in the midst of a panic attack may need to be directly guided through a mindfulness exercise in order to help calm down and focus on the situation at hand.

Other important differences between crisis intervention and traditional counseling can be found in Table 3.1

Table 3.1 Differences Between Crisis Work and Long-Term Counseling

	Crisis Work	Long-Term Therapy
Focus	Resolve immediate concerns and develop short-term coping skills	Resolve life goals through the development of measurable objectives
Goal	Reduce immediate stress and incapacitation. Return client to environment better able to cope	Provide long-term strategies for resolution of life stressors or systemic challenges
Client Intent	Return to normal	Change behaviors, cognitions, affect
Strategies	Psychoeducation and symptom management	Individual or group therapy
Nature and Time	Short-term, directive	Long-term, non-directive
Interventionist	Often multiple helpers who interact with the client at different times/places	One helper who works individually with the client or in small group work
Approaches	Employs multiple forms of intervention based on context and circumstance (e.g., legal assistance, shelter, food, water, social services)	Development of a therapeutic alliance based on empirically supported treatment approaches grounded in counseling theory

Counseling Theory and Crisis Work

While crisis intervention is different from traditional counseling or long-term therapy, there are elements of traditional counseling theories that are instrumental when helping individuals in crisis. For example, while crisis work and psychoanalysis are divergent approaches to helping, there are important elements of psychoanalysis found in crisis counseling (Brenner, 1974; Fine, 1973). The notion of disequilibrium that is a hallmark of psychoanalytic theory is also a critical element of the definition of crisis found in Chapter One. Also, the concept of ego strength is important in assessing a client's ability to cope with crisis, and the notion of psychic energy found in psychoanalysis can be associated with the inability to cope with crisis.

Just as we discussed the concept of existential crises in Chapter One, existential theory is also associated with crisis work. While the traditional existential approach is considered a long-term therapy, the notion that crisis can develop from internal conflict is important. Humanistic theory can help inform crisis work as it relates to locus of control (Raskin & Rogers, 1995). When the client is able to internalize the locus of control, rather than depend on external factors, crises may subside. Additionally, concepts such as optimism, hope, empathy, and safety are all hallmarks of the humanistic approaches employed by Rogers (1951) and others.

Crisis intervention also employs elements of family therapy. For example, human beings exist within systems that consist of interdependent parts, which influence and interact with one another; this systems approach can help to explain how and why people behave the way they do during a crisis (Cormier & Hackney, 1987). Systems theory (Haley, 1973) focuses less on the individual in crisis and more on the interdependence of the individual on others and the relationships between the individual and those in their environment. Additionally, Minuchin's (1974) concepts of independence and nurturance found in structural family therapy can help to explain why some individuals have difficulty overcoming crisis events when they lack these elements.

As discussed in Chapter One, an individual's cognitive perception and meaning of an event are critical elements in understanding how a crisis develops. The subjective perception of a crisis is, in and of itself, a cognitive process, and the notion of a cognitive key is a basic concept of cognitive-behavioral theory. The work of Ellis (1962) and Beck (1979), related to cognitive therapies, offers important building blocks to the development of crisis intervention models and techniques.

Crisis Prevention Programs

Before engaging in a discussion of the various forms and models of crisis work, it is important to understand some terminology regarding the process and the stages a crisis typically takes. Crises typically occur in somewhat predictable phases. Prior to a crisis occurring, intervention strategies are aimed at preventing a potential crisis from occurring. Helpers may intervene with an individual after an event has occurred but before the event causes the subjective distress required for a crisis to develop. While there are a host of prevention programs designed to prevent crises from occurring at all, describing all of them extends beyond the scope of this text. There are as many prevention programs as there are types of crises. However, it is important to understand the different levels at which crisis prevention programs occur and how they work. We will also provide some examples of prevention specific to particular forms of crisis.

Roberts (1991) identifies three levels of crisis prevention: primary, secondary, and tertiary. At the primary prevention level, the goal of the intervention is to be intentional and

---

CASE ILLUSTRATION 3.1

THE DEVELOPMENT OF A CRISIS PREVENTION PROGRAM

John Dewey High School is a public school located on the West Coast of the United States that educates approximately 1,500 students in grades 9 to 12. Dewey High is located in a suburban neighborhood and most students come from lower middle-class homes and from working class families. Dewey High is relatively successful for an American high school; student achievement is above average for the state, and 85% of its students go on to attend 4-year colleges. Many students receive offers from prestigious colleges, and earning scholarships is important to students and parents alike, as families often cannot afford the cost of private colleges without assistance.

Due to the high achievement and financial strain, students at Dewey High feel a great deal of pressure to achieve and succeed, both academically and through extracurricular activities. Students often find themselves in competition with one another to demonstrate who has the best grades, highest Scholastic Aptitude Test (SAT) scores, and most extracurriculars. A year ago, a Dewey High junior took his life through suicide after scoring below his expectation on the December administration of the SAT. The student hung himself in the locker room of the boy's basketball team and was found by two of his teammates after he had missed practice.

The suicide shook the entire Dewey High community. Teachers, administrators, families, and students all came together to discuss the event and why it had happened. Students began sharing their stories of stress, anxiety, and depression that resulted from the expectations they felt to succeed. The school counselors organized an assembly for students and families where students shared stories of their own suicidal ideations and those of friends. While a difficult experience for everyone involved, what resulted was an open and frank discussion about stress, anxiety, depression, and how to cope with these stressors in an effort to keep students safe.

proactive in attempting to prevent a crisis situation from occurring. Primary prevention occurs prior to a crisis event, and is intended to educate or prepare individuals in order to avoid the negative experience. Some examples of primary prevention include sexual assault training in colleges and universities, safer sex programs for adolescents to prevent the spread of sexually transmitted infections and pregnancy, and prevention programs aimed at helping laypeople identify and intervene with those contemplating suicide.

Secondary prevention interventions are aimed at engaging with individuals who may be at risk for developing crisis-related symptoms after a precipitating event so as to mitigate the impact of the event and prevent negative outcomes. Examples of secondary prevention might include parenting programs for people who have been referred to local agencies after accusations of child abuse or neglect or emergency mental heath services provided to individuals who have experienced situational or environmental crises, such as natural disasters or house fires.

Tertiary prevention is a method of intervention that occurs after individuals find themselves in crisis but is intended to mitigate the effects and return people to a state of relative equilibrium as quickly as possible. Examples of tertiary prevention may include suicide prevention hotlines developed to assists individuals who are at risk of taking their own lives or active shooter training aimed at helping people remain safe in the event of an incident of gun violence. Another example is the American Red Cross model of Psychological First Aid (PFA) that will be described later in this chapter. PFA is a specific set of intervention strategies intended to mitigate the impact of crisis on the individual and help the person return to a state of equilibrium as quickly as possible.

Case Illustration 3.1 describes how a high school developed a suicide prevention program for students, incorporating various stakeholders at different points in a potential crisis.

There are a host of prevention programs that are directed at specific crisis situations. Suicide prevention is one of the most commonly found prevention strategies, and there are a multitude of approaches for working with individuals to prevent suicide. One model of suicide prevention is called QPR, which is an acronym that stands for Question, Persuade, and Refer (QPR Institute, n.d.). The idea behind this evidenced-based training program is to educate and prepare anyone to intervene with a suicidal person. The program helps to educate laypeople on the signs of suicidal ideation, as well as provide intervention strategies for helping people and referring them to mental health resources. QPR training can be delivered through qualified workshop leaders or through self-study.

Another example of a prevention strategy used on college campuses is the development of Behavioral Intervention Teams (BIT) or Threat Assessment Teams (TAT). These are committees of various constituents that meet in locations such as college campuses, schools, or sometimes, workplaces. BITs and TATs are comprised of faculty, counselors, student service professionals (e.g., housing officers, student activities staff, etc.), Deans of Students, and others. These teams collect data on concerning student behavior to identify students who may be at risk to themselves or others. These teams then make recommendations on how to best intervene with students to ensure the safety of the individual student, as well as the campus community.

Case Illustration 3.2 provides an example of how a BIT might work in practice on a college campus.

The school counseling staff at Dewey High began working on a suicide prevention program that targeted as many stakeholders as possible within the school system. Classroom guidance lessons were developed with students at every grade level to educate about stress, depression, warning signs of suicide, and resources available both within the school and in the community. Parent programs were held in the evenings to not only educate parents on the warning signs of suicide and how to intervene, but also included strategies for talking with students about stress and how to help reduce their stress to succeed and exceed expectations.

In-service trainings were held for faculty, administrators, coaches, and staff to help educate them on the warning signs of self-harm and suicide, as well as basic intervention and referral skills. The school counselors advocated with administrators and school board members to secure additional resources (e.g., funding, staffing, outside resources, etc.) to provide these additional services to students, families, staff, and others. The school counselors worked with administrators to secure grant funding to bring in outside speakers to help educate stakeholders throughout the system on these issues.

The school counselors also collected data on their efforts. They surveyed students and families about their experiences, their perceptions, and their behaviors. The counselors found that their efforts had been successful. Student stress was decreasing, families were talking about these issues more, and teachers, coaches, and administrators felt empowered to ask the right questions and refer when necessary. The program was so successful that it was implemented throughout the district, and the counselors began consulting with other districts on how to replicate the results.

THE USE OF A BIT

Delaney was a 20-year-old sophomore at a large, public university in the Midwest United States. Delaney had spent her first two years living on campus and had been very successful in almost every way since joining the campus community. She had earned Dean's List honors every semester and maintained a 3.85 GPA, was the Vice President of one of the largest sororities on campus, was a member of the Student Government Board, and assisted one of the most prestigious professors with work in her biology lab. In short, Delaney was the student others looked up to and envied.

That's why it was surprising that Delaney's name was brought up at the campus BIT meeting at the beginning of November. The Director of Greek Life brought Delaney's name to the meeting after she had been approached by the president of Delaney's sorority. The President was concerned that Delaney's behavior had changed in recent weeks. She had become withdrawn and sad. She was no longer participating in activities with her sisters, and members thought she had broken up with her long-time, high school boyfriend. One of the members had approached the chapter president with concerns after seeing Delaney drinking hard liquor alone at the sorority house.

After mentioning Delaney to the BIT, the Director of Public Safety commented that Delaney had been cited by one of her officers after being found passed out in a residence hall lobby on Saturday night. The responding officer determined Delaney had been drinking underage and had sent her back to her residence hall room after citing her for underage drinking and public intoxication. The Director of Residence Life mentioned that Delaney had come to the attention of the Resident Assistant (RA) on her floor, after the RA had found Delaney in the floor lounge, alone and crying. After a short discussion, Delaney told the RA she was just sad after her breakup with her boyfriend.

Models of Individual Crisis Intervention and Postvention

As discussed earlier in this chapter, intervention strategies differ depending on how long the crisis has been occurring and the level of subjective distress the individual is experiencing. Working with individuals in crisis can occur at the intervention phase, which occurs as the crisis is taking place, or at the postvention phase, which occurs following the critical event but while the individual is still in crisis. At these phases, the client is likely experiencing disequilibrium, and these models are designed to prevent the development of negative symptomology, as well as to help the client return to a sense of emotional and psychological safety.

SAFE-R

One intervention strategy is the SAFE-R model developed by Everly and Mitchell (2000). SAFE-R is an acronym that describes five stages of crisis intervention with individual clients. At the first stage, **Stabilization of the Situation**, the helper attempts to mitigate emotional escalation, remove the individual from stressors, and meet basic needs. At the second stage, **Acknowledgment of the Crisis**, interventions are aimed at encouraging catharsis and reducing emotional arousal. The helper also attempts to establish rapport with the client and develop a sense of safety. At the third stage, **Facilitation of Understanding**, the interventionist works with client to conceptualize their reactions as a normal response to an abnormal situation, as well as explain possible symptoms in the context of survival and coping. The fourth stage, **Encouragement of Adaptive Coping**, involves teaching the client basic crisis management skills in an effort to improve short-term coping strategies. Finally, the **Referral** or **Restoration of Independent Functioning** stage includes assessment of the client's functioning as adequate or requiring referral to longer-term care.

Acute Traumatic Stress Management (ATSM)

Lerner and Shelton (2001) developed a 10-step model for ATSM. The 10 stages identified by Lerner and Shelton (2001) include:

- **Assess for Danger/Safety for Self and Others**—Are there important factors that may put the individual at risk, or is there a risk to others?
- **Consider the Mechanism of Injury**—How did the crisis event impact the individual physically and subjectively?
- **Evaluate the Level of Responsiveness**—Is the individual alert? Are there substance use/abuse issues to be considered?
- **Address Medical Needs**—For those trained to assess medical condition or referral, if not trained.
- **Observe and Identify**—Who has been exposed to the crisis situation, and who is displaying evidence of subjective distress or maladaptive functioning?
- **Connect with the Individual**—Begin the process of building rapport. Be sure to state your title and position and attempt to remove the individual from the stressor(s).
- **Ground the Individual**—Discuss the facts, and allow the client to tell his or her story. Discuss psychological and behavioral responses.
- **Provide Support**—Display empathy and active listening. Demonstrate an understanding of the client's affective responses that are the subtext of the content of the story.
- **Normalize the Response**—Normalize, validate, and educate. Remind the individual that the response is a normal response to an abnormal situation.
- **Prepare for the Future**—Review the event, bring the person to the present, describe possible future events, and provide referrals, as necessary.

Assessment, Crisis Intervention, and Trauma Treatment (ACT)

Roberts (2002) developed the integrative ACT model that offers a seven-step framework for providing acute crisis intervention. The model attempts to offer crisis intervention and trauma treatment through a holistic approach that includes bioecological assumptions, cultural considerations, and traditional crisis intervention strategies. The seven steps of the ACT model include:

1. Intake and Assessment: The helper conducts a thorough biosocial assessment and evaluates for lethality/suicidality and other imminent dangers. This stage should not involve an interrogation of the client but rather an attempt to understand the client's situation, allowing the person to feel heard and understood

2. Rapidly Establish Rapport: Through genuineness, respect, and acceptance, the helper works to establish rapport with the client as quickly as possible.

3. Identify Major Problems or Crisis Participants: At this step, the interventionist attempts to identify the major problems that have initiated the crisis (i.e., the precipitating event), which also allows the clinician to prioritize the client's concerns and learn more about effective and ineffective coping strategies.

4. Deal with Feelings and Emotions: This step of the model consists of two elements. One, the helper allows the client to vent, to express feelings, and to feel that his or her feelings have been heard and understood. This is best done through active listening skills, such as paraphrasing, reflection, and probing questions. The second element includes challenging the client to consider alternative cognitions regarding the crisis, loosening the client's maladaptive thinking, and allowing for cognitive reframing.

5. Generate and Explore Alternatives: This is often the most difficult step of the crisis intervention. By definition, clients are in crisis because they are continuing to rely on maladaptive coping skills, despite the fact that those skills are failing and causing distress. Clients often do not see alternatives, otherwise they would have employed them and avoided the crisis altogether. However, once the client is able to address and cope with the difficult emotions associated with the crisis, the helper can begin to work with the client to explore more effective skills and methods of coping with the precipitating event(s).

6. Implement an Action Plan: Implementation of an action plan is both a cognitive and a behavioral process. On the behavioral level, the client is challenged to take action to try new coping skills. For example, clients may be encouraged to join support groups or seek out longer-term treatment options. However, at this step, the client is also challenged to reflect on cognitive responses to the crisis event, as well. How did the client initially respond? Why did the crisis happen? What were the client's expectations prior to the crisis? After the crisis? How can the client think about the crisis event differently?

7. Follow-up: The helper plans a follow-up contact with the client in order to assess physical, cognitive, and behavioral functioning, as well as to assess for new stressors and coping strategies. The helper also makes referrals when necessary.

James and Gilliland's (2012) Six-Step Model

James and Gilliland (2012) developed a six-step model for intervening with individuals in crisis. This model incorporates assessment at all steps and includes three steps that are listening activities and three steps that are acting strategies.

Listening Activities

Step 1: Defining the Problem: At this step, the helper works with the client to define and understand the problem through the use of core listening skills such as empathy, genuineness, and acceptance.

Step 2: Ensuring Client Safety: The second step involves making sure the client is physically and psychologically safe. While employed as the second step it is a process that should occur at all stages of intervention

Step 3: Providing Support: Here, the helper communicates a sense of caring and valuing of the client.

Acting Strategies

Step 4: Examining Alternatives: At this step, the helper works with the client to examine and assess different options for coping with the crisis. This process includes *situational supports* (people who care about the client), *coping mechanisms* (actions, behaviors, or environmental resources that may help the client process through the crisis), and *positive and constructive thinking patterns* (cognitive reframing of the crisis situation).

Step 5: Making Plans: This step includes developing positive, achievable strategies for moving beyond the crisis. The plan should identify people, groups, or referral resources that may be helpful, as well as provide specific coping mechanisms. At this stage, the client should be empowered with control and autonomy as much as possible. People in crisis often feel out of control and powerless. Establishing a sense of agency is important in recovering from the crisis.

Step 6: Obtaining Commitment: The client should demonstrate an understanding and commitment to the plan developed in Step Five. Here too, issues of control and autonomy are important. If the plan is developed collaboratively, commitment should be easier to obtain. It is also important to follow up with the client to ensure the plan is working, and the client is functioning better as a result.

PFA

The American Red Cross developed the PFA protocol as a means of helping those who are impacted by disasters and other crisis events, as well as the volunteers and other workers who are often deployed during a crisis (American Red Cross, 2016a). The PFA protocol has been revised and improved over time, and the process of Enhanced PFA includes 12 strategies that are designed to help individuals cope with crises, as well as the vicarious experience of helping others who have been impacted by a disaster or other crisis event. These 12 strategies are designed to help laypeople intervene with those in crisis and prevent individuals from experiencing excessive distress during or after a critical event. The steps of PFA include:

- Make a connection: The helper makes an introduction and focuses on the individual in need.
- Help people be safe: It is critical to ensure the individual is physically and psychologically safe.
- Be kind, calm, and compassionate: The helper expresses patience and respect and maintains a composed demeanor.
- Meet people's basic needs: Ensuring people's most critical needs are met (e.g., shelter, food, water, etc.) is important to ensuring a sense of safety (see Chapter One and the discussion of Maslow's (1954) Hierarchy of Needs). Connecting people with family and friends is also important in this step.
- Listen: Employing active listening skills helps the individual feel connected, grounded, and heard.
- Give realistic reassurance: Reminding people that their reactions are normal given the circumstances is helpful. Letting people know that their stress reactions will likely go away with time can be reassuring, as well. It is also important not to minimize the client's reaction.
- Encourage good coping: The helper works with the client to identify adaptive, healthy coping skills.
- Help people connect: Connecting people with communication options (e.g., phones, texts, email, etc.) can help mitigate stress reactions. Communicating with loved ones is critical during a crisis. The Red Cross has developed the Safe and Well website (www.redcross.org/safeandwell) as a means for individuals in crisis to communicate with others and let people know they are safe.
- Give accurate and timely information: Not only is it important to communicate with those in crisis to provide a sense of control, but it is also helpful to put an end to rumors and misinformation.
- Make a referral to a Disaster Mental Health worker: When the individual providing PFA is not trained in a mental health field, making a referral to those who are is sometimes necessary.
- End the conversation: When ending the conversation, it is important to ask if there are any unmet needs that can be addressed, and provide contact information for referrals and resources.

- Take care of yourself: A key element to PFA is to model the behaviors used to help others. Vicarious stress is dangerous (See Chapter 13), and those working with people in crisis need to be aware of the possible vicarious effects and seek help when necessary.

Exercise 3.2 provides the opportunity to implement one of these models in a real-world crisis situation.

Approaches to Systemic Crisis Intervention and Postvention

While much of the literature in the area of crisis intervention focuses on models of individual or small group intervention, several organizations have developed approaches aimed at intervention on the systemic level. Specifically, the American Red Cross, the National Organization for Victim Assistance (NOVA), and the Federal Emergency Management Agency (FEMA) have all developed strategies for intervening in large scale crises at the systemic level.

American Red Cross

Inspired by the Swiss Red Cross (or Red Crescent, as it is often known internationally), the American Red Cross was founded by Clara Barton in 1881 as a means of providing assistance to individuals in need (American Red Cross, 2016b). As the Red Cross has evolved over many decades, the organization has provided a host of services to a wide array of constituencies. One of the evolving services provided by the American Red Cross

EXERCISE 3.2

USING A CRISIS INTERVENTION MODEL

Directions: Consider the following case study. Then, develop intervention strategies using one of the models described in the chapter. Make sure your intervention aims to help the individuals in the case cope with the crisis, prevent the crisis from worsening, and help clients back to a state of equilibrium. As you think through the case, consider the various individuals involved and the different approaches you may need to take with each.

Case Study: The Lowell Family:

The Lowells are a family of five who live in a lower-class neighborhood in a large city in the Midwestern United States. The members of the Lowell family who are living together are: Mr. Michael Lowell and Mrs. Deborah Lowell, who have been married for 16 years; their 12-year-old son, Robert; their 9-year-old daughter, Rebecca; and Michael's sister, Elaine Lowell. Elaine moved in to the house last month after separating from her abusive husband.

One evening, an electrical malfunction caused a short circuit in the Lowell's kitchen, causing a fire that spread up the wall and then through part of the first floor of the home. The family was woken early by the sound of fire alarms chirping, and Elaine was able to quickly usher the children out of the house, while Michael and Deborah worked to extinguish the flames. They were unsuccessful, and the flames continued to spread through the house. Deborah pleaded with Michael to get out of the house, but he refused, continuing to work to try to put out the fire. Michael was burned badly by the fire, and Deborah was helping him to the door when firefighters arrived.

Michael was rushed to the hospital by an ambulance, and the family followed. Deborah and Elaine had just been informed by emergency personnel that their home was a complete loss as you (the crisis worker) arrive to assist the family through the crisis. Through her tears, Deborah explains to you that Michael will recover from his injuries, but the family has nowhere to go and no one to whom they can turn for help. She is concerned for her children, but also for her husband's recovery.

She's also not sure how they will pay for the costs associated with his medical care, which may span a period of months before he fully recovers and can return to work.

includes Disaster Mental Health Services. The mission of Disaster Mental Health is "to respond to the psycho-social needs of people affected by disaster, including Red Cross disaster workers, across the continuum of disaster preparedness, response and recovery" (American Red Cross, 2012, p. 1–2).

Based on the assumption that individuals are resilient, Red Cross Disaster Mental Health volunteers are trained to provide an array of services to individuals during crises, from PFA to psychological triage and short-term crisis intervention (American Red Cross, 2012). During a disaster response, mental health volunteers may be deployed for as little as a few minutes to as long as several weeks. Trained volunteers are deployed to emergency and disaster situations in order to assist individuals in coping with the stressors associated with environmental and situational crises.

NOVA Crisis Response Teams

The NOVA was originally founded to assist victims of violent crime but has since evolved to provide an array of services, including crisis intervention services at a systemic level through the National Crisis Response Project (James & Gilliland, 2012). NOVA trains individuals to respond to crisis situations as part of a Crisis Response Team (CRT), through at least 24 hours of skill-based training that been tested in field situations (NOVA, 2016). Over the past 26 years, NOVA has trained over 10,000 people in crisis intervention techniques.

NOVA CRTs are deployed at a state or local level. For example, CRTs may be deployed at the request of a state attorney general in the event of a large scale natural disaster, or by a local school board after a school shooting. CRTs are deployed by NOVA at the request of authorized individuals at the state or local level, but NOVA-trained crisis interventionists may also be deployed from the position of their regular employment or as part of their volunteer experiences.. For example, local police officers or volunteer firefighters may not only be public safety officers in their communities, but may also be NOVA trained crisis interventionists.

FEMA

FEMA was founded in 1979 in response to concerns that the federal government was ill-equipped to respond to crises and disasters due to inter-agency conflicts, bureaucracy, and inefficiency (James & Gilliland, 2012). As FEMA's responsibilities have evolved, the provision of crisis intervention services has developed. FEMA provides services related to disaster and crisis preparation and prevention, as well as training and mitigation following a disaster.

While the majority of these services are logistical and involve provision of basic services, such as shelter, food, water, and other necessities, FEMA also works with local governmental agencies and individual volunteers to provide training in both preparedness and response strategies. For example, FEMA trains Community Emergency Response Teams (CERTs) to support first responders during environmental and situational crises, as well as provide training to local mental health professionals on crisis intervention techniques following large-scale disasters and violence. FEMA also partners with the National Institute of Mental Health (NIMH) to send response teams to areas impacted by large-scale disasters, providing consultation and expertise to local responders. The end of this chapter includes references to websites where individuals can complete online FEMA trainings in disaster response.

Transcrisis

After the event that precipitated the crisis has subsided, individuals may appear to return to a normal state of functioning. People exposed to traumatic or difficult events may believe that the crisis has subsided and that they have returned to normal. However, the notion of transcrisis suggests that individuals may not be functioning as well as it appears. Transcrisis occurs after the precipitating event has concluded, but the individual has not yet resolved the emotional and cognitive difficulty presented by the crisis (James & Gilliland, 2012).

Individuals who are experiencing Post-Traumatic Stress Disorder (PTSD; see Chapter 5) are in a transcrisis state. However, an individual does not have to exhibit symptoms of PTSD to be considered in transcrisis. In fact, a client does not have to meet the diagnostic criteria for a psychological disorder to be in transcrisis. Transcrisis states can take a range of forms, from responding with disproportionate anger or rage, to the experience of extreme sadness after a small emotional disturbance. The point of transcrisis is that it represents unresolved material from the precipitating event, and if left unchecked, can cause significant impairment in cognitive, affective, and behavioral functioning.

Frequently, when individuals are in a transcrisis state, they will experience transcrisis points. Transcrisis points are moments during transcrisis when the client is able to successfully navigate developmental tasks or other elements of the problem (James & Gilliland, 2012). Transcrisis points are benchmarks that represent successful navigation of the crisis and lead to the client's emotional growth. The number of transcrisis points an individual must navigate is not predictable, but as an interventionist, it is critical that the helper be aware that crises may loom for weeks, months, or even years after the precipitating event has passed. However, it is equally important to note that many individuals effectively process the crisis event, and transcrisis does not occur at all or may be very brief.

Summary

- When one enters the world of crisis intervention, it can be advantageous if the helper has, or can develop, some personal characteristics that are often found in those who work with crises.

- It is important for the interventionist to use many basic helping skills while working with an individual in crisis. However, some skills and techniques in crisis work are different. More importantly, the nature, goals, focus, and approaches to crisis work differ significantly from long-term therapeutic interventions.

- There are elements of traditional counseling theories that are instrumental when helping individuals in crisis. Crisis intervention can incorporate elements of psychoanalysis, existential therapies, family counseling theory, and cognitive interventions.

- Crisis prevention is aimed at preventing a potential crisis from occurring, or intervening with an individual after an event has occurred but before the event causes the subjective distress required for a crisis to develop. Crisis prevention occurs on the primary, secondary, and tertiary level.

- Working with individuals in crisis can occur as an intervention, which is typically implemented as the crisis is taking place, or postvention, which is typically implemented following the critical event but while the individual is still in crisis.

- Crisis intervention and postvention strategies aimed at assisting the individual include: SAFE-R, ATSM, Assessment, Crisis Intervention and Trauma Treatment, James and Gilliland's six-step model, and PFA.

- Systemic approaches to crisis intervention have been developed by the American Red Cross (specifically, Disaster Mental Health Services), the NOVA through the use of CRTs, and FEMA.

- The notion of transcrisis suggests that individuals may not be functioning as well as it appears. Transcrisis occurs after the precipitating event has concluded, but the individual affected by the event has not yet resolved the emotional and cognitive difficulty presented by the crisis event.

Important Terms

Acute Traumatic Stress Management (ATSM)

Assessment, Crisis Intervention, and Trauma Treatment (ACT)

Behavior Intervention Teams (BIT)/Threat Assessment Teams (TAT)

Coping skills/coping mechanisms

Crisis Response Team (CRT)

Federal Emergency Management Agency (FEMA)

National Organization for Victim Assistance (NOVA)

Positive and constructive thinking patterns

Postvention

Primary prevention

Psychological First Aid (PFA)

QPR

SAFE-R

Secondary prevention

Situational supports

Tertiary prevention

Transcrisis

Transcrisis point

Additional Resources

In Print

Everly, G.S., & Mitchell, J. (2000). *Critical incident stress management* (2nd ed.). Ellicott, City, MD: ICISF.

James, R.K., & Gilliland, B.E. (2012). *Crisis Intervention Strategies* (7th ed.). Belmont, CA: Brooks/ Cole (Cengage).

Lerner, M.D., & Shelton, R.D. (2001). *Acute traumatic stress management: Addressing emergent psychological needs during traumatic events*. Commack, NY: The American Academy of Experts in Traumatic Stress.

Roberts, A. R. (2002). Assessment, crisis intervention, and trauma treatment: The integrative ACT intervention model. *Brief Treatment and Crisis Intervention, 2,* 1–21.

On the Web

American Red Cross Disaster Services Training: http://www.redcross.org/take-a-class/disaster-training

American Red Cross Safe and Well Website: www.redcross.org/safeandwell

FEMA National Incident Management System and Training Opportunities: https://www.fema.gov/national-incident-management-system

National Association for Victim Assistance: www.trynova.org

National Behavior Intervention Team Association (NaBITA): www.nabita.org

QPR Institute: www.qprinstitute.com

References

American Red Cross (2012). *Disaster mental health handbook*. Retrieved from: www.cdms.uci. edu/pdf/disaster-mental-health-handbook-oct-2012.pdf

American Red Cross (2016a). *12 steps for Psychological First Aid*. Retrieved from: http://www. redcross.org/m/saf/12-steps-for-psychological-first-aid#arcmobile

American Red Cross (2016b). *History.* Retrieved from: http://www.redcross.org/about-us/ who-we-are/history

Beck, A. T. (1979). *Cognitive therapy and the emotional disorders*. New York, NY: Penguin.

Brenner, C. (1974). *An elementary textbook of psychoanalysis.* Garen City, NY: Anchor Books.

Cormier, L. S., & Hackney, H. (1987). *The professional counselor: A process guide to helping.* Upper Saddle River, NJ: Prentice Hall.

Ellis, A. E. (1962). *Reason and emotion in psychotherapy.* New York, NY: Lyle Stuart.

Everly, G.S., & Mitchell, J. (2000). *Critical incident stress management* (2nd ed.). Ellicott, City, MD: ICISF.

Fine, R. (1973). Psychoanalysis. In R. J. Corsini (Ed.), *Current psychotherapies* (pp. 1–33). Itasca, IL: F.E. Peacock.

Haley (1973). *Uncommon therapy.* New York, NY: Norton.

James, R.K., & Gilliland, B. E. (2012). *Crisis intervention strategies* (7th ed.). Belmont, CA: Thomson Brooks/Cole.

Kanel, K. (2007). *A guide to crisis intervention*. Belmont, CA: Thomson Brooks/Cole.

Lerner, M.D., & Shelton, R.D. (2001). *Acute traumatic stress management: Addressing emergent psychological needs during traumatic events*. Commack, NY: The American Academy of Experts in Traumatic Stress.

Maslow, A. (1954). *Motivation and personality.* New York, NY: Harper.

Minuchin, S. (1974). *Families and family therapy.* Cambridge, MA: Harvard University Press.

National Organization for Victim Assistance (2016). *Help crisis victims.* Retrieved from: http://www. trynova.org/help-crisis-victims/overview/

QPR Institute. (n.d.). *About QPR.* Retrieved from: https://www.qprinstitute.com/about-qpr

Raskin, N. J., & Rogers, C. R. (1995). Person-centered therapy. In R. J. Corsini & D. Wedding (Eds.), *Current psychotherapies* (5th ed.). Itasca, IL: F.E. Peacock.

Roberts, A. R. (1991). *Contemporary perspectives on crisis intervention and prevention.* Upper Saddle River, NJ: Prentice Hall.

Roberts, A. R. (2002). Assessment, crisis intervention, and trauma treatment: The integrative ACT intervention model. *Brief Treatment and Crisis Intervention, 2*, 1–21.

Rogers, C. (1951). *Client-centered therapy: Its current practice, implications and theory*. London, UK: Constable.

SECTION 2

From Assessment
to Intervention

CHAPTER 4

Assessment: Models, Strategies, and Tools

I love this part of my job, helping my 11th graders with their post–high school plans. They are usually so excited, so eager. That's what I expected when I met with Alexis. I was not prepared to deal with the cuts and cigarette burn marks I saw on her legs. I felt so incompetent not knowing if I should say something or just continue as planned.

C ontinue as planned? Clearly this high school counselor was not only ill prepared but also responded in a way that served her own need to avoid a potentially difficult situation, rather than responding in the interest of the student. Sadly, the experience illustrated is far from rare or unusual. Counselors, working in all venues and serving a variety of populations, need to be competent in assessing and intervening with clients who may be at risk of harm to self or others.

This chapter introduces the reader to methods and instruments sessment and intervention with those in crisis. After reading this chapter able to:

1. Describe factors denoting increased severity of a crisis;

2. Explain the methods and instruments employed to perform a self-harm suicidal risk assessment;

3. Identify static and dynamic factors correlated with increased risk of violence to others;

4. Describe intervention strategies and approaches that are employed when working with clients at risk for self-harm, suicide, and homicide.

Assessing the Severity of the Crisis

During initial contact with a client in crisis, a counselor needs to evaluate the severity of the crisis and the client's level of affective, behavioral, and cognitive functioning. Effective crisis intervention demands a quick and accurate assessment (James & Gilliland, 2012; Myer, 2001).

While there are many questions to be asked and domains to be assessed, the initial focus of a counselor's assessment should be on the nature and severity of the crisis. The counselor should conduct a thorough lethality/imminent danger assessment. This initial assessment will help identify how urgently a response is required and the type of service response that would best meet the client's needs.

One measure that has been found to be a useful tool to guide the assessment process during crisis intervention is the Triage Assessment Form (TAF) (Myer et al., 1992). The focus of the TAF is on assessing the client's ability to control reactions, the intensity of the reactions, and the stability of the reactions. The TAF helps a counselor identify the severity and overall magnitude of a client's affective, cognitive, and behavioral reactions and, thus, provides the information needed to begin to formulate initial treatment plans. For example, a client who exhibits stable mood with normal variation of affect appropriate to daily functioning is less impacted by a crisis than one who is decompensating. Similarly, the crisis is less severe for the client who exhibits normal problem solving skills and behaviors that are appropriate to the event versus one where there is gross inability to concentrate and erratic, unpredictable, and potentially harmful behaviors.

Two specific areas that need to be assessed are the degree to which the client presents as a risk to self or others.

Specific Client Assessment: Self-Harm

The presentation of self-injury, such as self-inflicted cutting, hitting, burning, and excoriation of wounds, had once been associated with serious mental disorders (Simeon & Hollander, 2001); however, it is now evident among high-functioning populations (Whitlock, Eckenrode, & Silverman, 2006). This increase in non-lethal self-harm within the general population points to the need for counselors to develop and employ formal and informal assessment methods as a basis for their intervention planning.

Assessment Measures

A number of measures, both self-report and clinician rated, are currently available for the assessment of self-harm beha vior (see Table 4.1).

While a structured assessment has value, the use of such a formal measure can be off-putting to the client in the helping relationship (Walsh, 2007). With or without the use of such an assessment measure, counselors need to establish a non-judgmental, supportive alliance in which they can begin to gather data on the history and nature of the client's self-injury behaviors.

Targets for Assessment

History of Self-Injury

When assessing the history of self-harm, the counselor needs to gather data reflecting the following: age of onset, types (e.g., cutting, burning, hitting, excoriation), duration of the problem, frequency of the behavior, number of wounds per episode, and level of physical damage. In general, the challenge in alleviating self-injury increases with the length of time the problem has existed, the longer the course of self-injury, and the greater the number of methods employed (Nock et al., 2006; Walsh, 2007). Another factor to be considered in assessing self-injurious behaviors is the duration and intervals of episodes. Longer episodes suggest greater levels of distress and are, thereby, more concerning (Walsh, 2007).

Nature of the Self-Injurious Behaviors

A second general area for assessment is related to the nature of the most recent episode of self-injury (e.g., within a few hours vs. the last couple of months). Data highlighting possible triggers can be used to not only help in anticipating or predicting future self-injury, but also allow for the development of alternative responses to the trigger. Similarly, it is important to identify the primary function of self-injury. Understanding possible "pay-offs" for these actions will allow counselors and clients to develop alternative ways of achieving those outcomes in the absence of self-harm. For example, if the goal of self-injury is to gain emotional regulation, then treatment will not only target the identification of triggers, but also the development of alternative responses to those triggers (Walsh, 2007).

Table 4.1 Assessing Non-Lethal Self-Harm

Sample of Instruments

Instrument	Description	Reference
Deliberate Self-Harm Inventory (DSHI)	The DSHI (2001) is a 17-item yes/no self-report questionnaire that explores the direct destruction of body tissue. Respondents are also asked about the frequency, severity, and duration of such events. There are items relating to suicide attempts.	Gratz, K.L. (2001). Measurement of deliberate self-harm: Preliminary data on the Deliberate Self-Harm Inventory. *Journal of Psychopathology and Behavioral Assessment*, 23, 253–263.
The Suicide Attempt Self-Injury Interview (SASII)	SASII is used to collect details regarding the time, circumstances, motivations and treatment of each Intentional Self Injury (ISI) that a subject can recollect. Data is collected for either a "lifetime" history (as far back as a subject can recall up to the present) or an "interval" history (covering the intervening time between scheduled assessments or some other arbitrary time span determined by the interviewer).	Linehan, M. M., Comtois, K. A., Brown, M. Z., Heard, H. L., & Wagner, A. (2006). Suicide Attempt Self-Injury Interview (SASII): Development, reliability, and validity of a scale to assess suicide attempts and intentional self-injury. *Psychological Assessment*, 18, 303–312.
The Self-Injurious Thoughts and Behavior Interview (SITBI)	The SITBI is a structured interview that assesses the presence, frequency, and characteristics of a wide range of self-injurious thoughts and behaviors, including suicidal ideation, suicide plans, suicide gestures, suicide attempts, and non-suicidal self-injury (NSSI).	Nock, M. K., Holmberg, E. B., Photos, V. I., & Michel, B. D. (2007). Self-Injurious Thoughts and Behaviors Interview: Development, reliability, and validity of a new measure. *Psychological Assessment*, 19, 309–317.
Self-Injury Questionnaire (SIQ).	The SIQ (1997) is a 54-item, self-report questionnaire with various response options including Likert-style and multiple-choice selections. Examples of items include opening wounds, scratching scabs or lumps, cutting or hurting self, pulling out hair, scratching self, bruising self intentionally, cutting self, and burning self. There are no queries about suicide attempts.	Vanderllinden, J. & Vandereycken, W. (1997). *Trauma, dissociation, and impulse dyscontrol in eating disorders*. Philadelphia, PA: Brunner/Mazel
Adolescent Risk Inventory	The Adolescent Risk Inventory (2007) is a 2-page, 33-item, self-report inventory, with mostly yes/no response options, that explores high-risk behaviors and attitudes. While a majority of items relate to high-risk sexual behaviors, six items explore self-harm behavior including self-cutting and suicide attempts.	Lescano, C. M., Hadley, W.S., Beausoleil, N. I., Brown, L. K., D'eramo, D., & Zimskind, A. (2007). A Brief Screening Measure of Adolescent Risk Behavior. *Child Psychiatry and Human Development*, 37, 325–336

In reviewing the most recent episodes of self-harm, it is also important to identify the extent of tissue damage and location of the bodily harm. Most individuals who self-harm injure the extremities or abdomen (Simeon & Hollander, 2001), thus indication of harm to face, eyes, and genitals may signal major traumatic response or even psychotic decompensation (Walsh, 2007). When presented with this form of injury, the counselor will need

---

EXERCISE 4.1

RESPONDING AT THE MOMENT: MY UNDERSTANDING AND DECISIONS

Directions: Having completed the section on self-harm, reread the brief vignette with which we opened the chapter. Discuss the following with a colleague or classmate.

1. What indications, if any, exist that may suggest a reduced level of severity?

2. What indications or data exist or might be shared by the client that would heighten the level of severity?

3. Assuming that you noticed the scarring, what questions would you like to pose to the client?

4. How would you initiate discussion around the observation of self-harm?

5. How do you feel about the possibility of engaging the client in a discussion around the possibility of her self-harming behaviors?

---

to consider additional diagnostic assessment, as well as the need for further steps to insure safety, including possible hospitalization.

Intervening with Self-Harming Clients

While no single method has been identified as significantly superior in treating self-harm cases, Cognitive Behavioral Therapy (Slee, 2008) or a combination of behavioral therapies and medication, appear effective in symptom reduction (Lukomski, 2004). Alternatively, research has identified a number of interventions that appear ineffective when working with clients who self-injure, including physical restraint, hypnosis, "no cutting" contracts, faith healing, group psychotherapy, relaxation therapy, electroconvulsive therapy, family therapy, and educational therapy (Lukomski, 2004).

The counselor will want to help the client identify the issues or feelings that are at the root of the behavior and assist in challenging the dysfunctional thinking that results in the self-harm activity. However, in the short-term, it may be helpful for the client to employ alternative, less harmful behaviors. For example, anger can be directed to the destruction of a milk carton, punching a pillow, or stomping aluminum cans. When feeling sad, clients might listen to music, engage with a friend, or play with a pet. Though these are not "cures" for self-harm, they may provide the delay needed for the original self-harming urge to fade. Exercise 4.1 invites you to employ the material presented within this section to reassess the case with which we opened this chapter.

Specific Client Assessment and Intervention: Suicide Risk

It has been reported that 35% of counselors have had a client commit suicide (Rogers, 2001). Counselors clearly need the knowledge and skills necessary to assess and intervene with clients who are potentially at risk of suicide.

As is true for other presenting concerns, a comprehensive assessment of a client presenting with potential suicidality is fundamental to effective intervention. Suicide assessment usually refers to a more comprehensive evaluation done by a clinician to confirm suspected suicide risk, estimate the immediate danger to the client, and decide on a course of treatment. Although assessments can involve structured questionnaires, they also can comprise a more open-ended conversation with a client and might include discussion with friends and family members to gain insight into the client's thoughts and behavior, risk factors (e.g., access to lethal means or a history of suicide attempts), protective factors (e.g., immediate family support), and medical and mental health histories.

An effective assessment will entail: a) gathering information related to risk factors, protective factors, and warning signs of suicide; b) identifying the client's ideation, planning, behaviors, desire, and intent; and c) the clinical formulation of risk based on the data collected and the formulation of an intervention plan (Shea, 2009).

Protective Factors, Risk Factors, and Warning Signs

Protective Factors

A number of factors, such as a client's ability to cope with stress, or the presence of social supports, appear to serve as protective factors, reducing the possibility of imminent suicide (Fowler, 2012; Rogers, 2011) (see Table 4.2). However, even when present, these are not a guarantee of absolute protection and may fail to counteract an acute risk (Muzina, 2007).

Table 4.2 Potential Protective Factors

- Effective clinical care for mental, physical, and substance use disorders
- Easy access to a variety of clinical interventions and support for help seeking
- Restricted access to highly lethal means of suicide
- Strong connections to family and community support
- Support through ongoing medical and mental health care relationships
- Skills in problem solving, conflict resolution, and nonviolent handling of disputes
- Cultural and religious beliefs that discourage suicide and support self-preservation

Risk Factors

Just as research has found a correlation between the existence of certain internal and external factors that may serve a protective function, there are conditions that appear to be related to increased risk of suicide. When engaging in suicide assessment, it is important to identify the existence of those factors that have been found to be associated with suicidality. Two of the primary risk factors are mental health problems and/or substance use disorders. The National Institute of Mental Health (2010) reported that over 90% of people who commit suicide have depression and/or substance abuse disorders, often in combination with other mental health disorders.

While mental health and substance abuse are the leading risk factors for suicide (Pompili et al., 2010), there are other biopsychosocial, environmental, and sociocultural risk factors, as well (Haney et al., 2012; Lambert, 2002, Cavanagh et al., 2003) (see Table 4.3).

Table 4.3 Risk Factors

Biopsychosocial Risk Factors	Environmental Risk Factors	Sociocultural Risk Factors
• Mental disorders, particularly mood disorders, schizophrenia, anxiety disorders, and certain personality disorders • Alcohol and other substance use disorders • Hopelessness • Impulsive and/or aggressive tendencies • History of trauma or abuse • Major physical illnesses • Previous suicide attempt • Family history of suicide	• Job or financial loss • Relational or social loss • Easy access to lethal means • Local clusters of suicide that have a contagious influence	• Lack of social support and sense of isolation • Stigma associated with help-seeking behavior • Barriers to accessing health care, especially mental health and substance abuse treatment • Certain cultural and religious beliefs (for instance, the belief that suicide is a noble resolution of a personal dilemma) • Exposure to, and influence of, others who have died by suicide, including through the media

Table 4.4 Warning Signs

General	With the Elderly	With Pre-teens and Adolescents
Talking or writing about suicide, death, or dying	Stockpiling medications	Volatile mood swings or sudden changes in their personality
Giving direct verbal cues, such as "I wish I were dead" and "I'm going to end it all" (suicidal threats)	Buying a gun	Indications that they are in unhealthy, destructive, or abusive relationships such as unexplained bruises, a swollen face or other injuries, particularly those they refuse to explain
Giving less direct verbal cues, such as "What's the point of living?," "Soon you won't have to worry about me," and "Who cares if I'm dead, anyway?"	Giving away money or cherished personal possessions	
	Taking a sudden interest, or losing their interest, in religion	
	Failing to care for themselves in terms of the routine activities of daily living	A sudden deterioration in their personal appearance
Looking for ways to kill himself or herself: seeking access to pills, weapons, or other means	Withdrawing from relationships	Self-mutilation
	Experiencing a failure to thrive, even after appropriate medical treatment	A fixation with death or violence
Increasing alcohol or other drug abuse	Scheduling a medical appointment for vague symptoms.	Eating disorders, especially combined with dramatic shifts in weight (other than those associated with a diet under medical supervision)
Global insomnia		
Isolating himself or herself from friends and family		Gender identity issues
Exhibiting a sudden and unexplained improvement in mood after being depressed or withdrawn		Depression
Neglecting his or her appearance and hygiene		

Warning Signs

Because clients are not always forthcoming with their intent to self-harm or commit suicide, it is important for counselors to be sensitive to potential warning signs (see Table 4.4) and use them as invitations to engage in a more in-depth and comprehensive assessment.

The complexity of assessing and intervening with a client presenting at risk for self-harm is illustrated in the brief case of Mr. Snyder (see Case Illustration 4.1). As noted in the case, the client has strong family support and has been engaged in his church and community. These preventive factors need to be contrasted to the existence of family history, his own current health and work-related problems, and his admittance of depression. While perhaps being viewed as mild-to-moderate risk, the fact that he allowed for the engagement of his wife and sons, and a commitment to return to therapy, bode well for this case.

Risk Assessment

When engaging with a client at risk for suicide, the initial focus should be on the assessment of risk and the provision of client safety. A counselor must first assess the level of risk being presented and respond accordingly. A number of studies (e.g., Brown et al., 2004; Hawton et al., 2013; Rudd et al., 2006) have identified factors that differentiate levels of suicidal risk. Table 4.5 presents a risk assessment matrix that differentiates between low, medium, and high risk for suicide. As level of risk increases, especially in light of low protective factors, more immediate structured and protective interventions (including hospitalization) need to be employed. For clients who present with lower risk and higher protective factors, outpatient counseling, along with engagement of home or community supervision and support may be sufficient.

CASE ILLUSTRATION 4.1

MR. SNYDER

Mr. Snyder (a 58-year-old male) was referred to counseling by his primary care physician as a result of what his doctor felt was evidence of depression. While waiting for his appointment, he was asked to complete some paperwork, including a depression-screening measure.

The intake revealed that Mr. Snyder had a family history of depression and suicide, as both his father and grandfather has shot themselves around the age of 50. Mr. Snyder had recently been diagnosed with emphysema, and as a result, had to take disability leave from his work as an ironworker. This is the first time in 40 years that he has not been employed. Since leaving his job three months prior to the visit, Mr. Snyder has increased his alcohol consumption, reporting drinking about three bourbons a night.

DR. NEAL: Mr. Snyder, I noticed on your survey that you noted that you are feeling down "nearly every day."

MR. SNYDER: Hell yeah! Wouldn't you if you were falling apart?

DR. NEAL: And, here you checked that you have had thoughts that you would be better off dead. Can you tell me more about those thoughts?

MR. SNYDER: Look Doc, shit happens. I can't breathe. I am no longer productive—not even a man—my fate if I am anything like my dad and granddad is that I'm well overdue anyway, so what's the big deal?

DR. NEAL: Have you thought about taking your own life?

MR. SNYDER: Ah … yes, aren't you listening? My life is for the shits.

DR. NEAL: Have you thought about how you may go about that?

MR. SNYDER: Not really—but I clean my gun a lot and you know accidents can happen.

DR. NEAL: Are you currently or have you within the last day or so thought about hurting yourself or taking your own life?

Table 4.5 Suicide Risk Matrix

		Lower Risk	Moderate Risk	High Risk
PLAN	Details	Vague	Some specifics	Well thought out
	Preparedness	Means not available	Has means close by	Has means in hand
	How Soon	No specific time, no immediate plan	Not sure but soon, within hours or days	Has imminent date/time in mind.
	Lethality of Method	Means unavailable, unrealistic or vague reference to pills/slash wrists	Method allows for some likelihood of rescue, such as drugs/alcohol	Method allows for little or no chance of intervention, such as gun/jumping/hanging
	Chance of Intervention	Others present most of the time	Others available if called	No one nearby; isolated
RISK FACTORS	Previous Attempts	None or low lethality	None or low lethality	Multiple with high lethality
	Emotional Stability	Sad, irritable but relatively stable	Mood swings—rare disclosure of feelings	Emotional numbness or emotional turmoil (agitated, anxious, emotional lability)
	Emotional Pain/Distress	Mildly upset, in pain	Moderately intense distress	Feels distress is unbearable
	Depression	Mild	Mild	Severe
	Substance Abuse	None or infrequent use	None or infrequent use	Continual abuse or frequent binges
	Sexual Issues-Identity or Abuse	Questioning identity, no abuse	Questioning identity, no abuse	Confusion, rejection/alienation, abuse
	Family Problems, Losses	Recent, minor believes family and others care	Moderate conflict with concern of limited or fragile support	Intense conflict and/or ongoing and significant, alienation (socially isolated)
	Previous Suicide of Family or Friend	Threat or unsuccessful attempt	Threat or unsuccessful attempt	Recent, directly involved
	School or Legal Problems	Recent, minor	Recent, minor	Ongoing and significant
	Significant Others	Several who are available	Several who are available	Only one or none available
BEHAVIORAL INDICATORS	Giving Possessions Away	Unclear "generosity"	Some treasured items	Treasured or needed items
	Withdrawal or Isolation	Occasional	Frequent	Continual and severe
	Lack of energy or concentration	Mild, occasional	Moderate, frequent	Continual and severe
	Sad, Tearful, Hopeless	Mild, occasional	Moderate, frequent	Marked, significant
	Angry, Hostile	Mild, occasional	Moderate, frequent	Marked, significant
	Change in Eating, Sleeping or Self-Care	None or minor	Noticeable	Marked, significant
	Increased Risky Behaviors	None or minor	Noticeable	Marked, significant
	Dwelling on Death with Music, Writing, Drawing	Vague ideation	Occasional preoccupation	Significant preoccupation

Intervention with Suicidality

When providing a comprehensive approach to intervention, a counselor will need to: a) provide for immediate client safety, b) identify and target underlying risk factors, and c) address and develop coping skills.

Providing for Client Safety

As noted above, when engaged with a client who is in the midst of a suicidal crisis, the immediate focus for counselor intervention is risk assessment and the development of a safety plan. Short-term treatment will aim at protecting the client from impulsive actions and reduce factors contributing to the current crisis experience. The goal is to provide immediate stabilization and safety for the client.

With client safety as the primary goal, the counselor should engage necessary family or community resources in the development and implementation of a safety plan. An initial safety plan might include scheduling frequent sessions and follow-up contacts or providing the client with strategies to be self-soothing and calming at points of stress. With higher or imminent risk, a safety plan may include a process of voluntary or involuntary hospitalization (see Chapter 15 for more information on hospitalization).

Target Underlying Risk Factors

After the client has stabilized and the crisis has diminished, the counselor will begin to address specific underlying risks factors and assist the client in developing both a problem-solving schema and the skills to implement that schema. During this process, it is important for the counselor to develop a strong working alliance with the client. In its *Practice Guidelines for the Assessment and Treatment of Patients with Suicidal Behaviors*, the American Psychiatric Association (2003) acknowledged that, "a positive and cooperative

MR. SNYDER: Doc—it's okay—really. I am pissed at the moment and shouldn't be a wise ass with my answers. I may be down, but I'm not going to do anything stupid. I mean Lorraine would be lost without me and my two boys would probably think that I was cursing them to the same fate … you know the "Snyder exit."

DR. NEAL: I am happy to hear that you have a number of people who care about you, and you they, and that they are good reasons to keep going.

MR. SNYDER: Yeah—and I am really busy with the Civic Association, leading the scholarship fund, and in the next two weeks I will be up to my ears in the Church Carnival, since they made me chair. So even if I was that down, I don't have time to do anything (smiling).

DR. NEAL: It does sound like you are really involved and respected by your community and church members. And yes, I know that at any one moment we can be angry enough or upset enough to say … and sometimes do … silly things. I wonder, until we meet next week, would you allow your eldest son to hold on to your guns temporarily? I think it would give him a sense of relief.

MR. SNYDER: Doc, really I'm not going to do anything stupid. But, if you think it will take the pressure off Lorraine and the boys, then sure. Also, I got to tell you, I thought this was going to be a bunch of mumbo-jumbo, but I enjoyed talking to you and would like to come back.

DR. NEAL: That's great—I've enjoyed meeting you. I am wondering in the time before we meet again if you would … (*Counselor presents ideas about homework including engaging in pleasurable activities, journaling thoughts, and eliminating the drinking, all of which the client agreed to try*).

psychotherapeutic relationship can be an invaluable and even life-sustaining force for suicidal patients" (p. 30). A therapeutic alliance enables clinicians to better comprehend clients' understanding of their suicidal behaviors, which is key to creating viable alternatives for problem solving and coping (Jobes, 2000).

Working together, the counselor and client will need to identify situational factors (e.g., fired from a job, death of loved one, argument) and/or distal factors (e.g., family history of suicide, depression, or anxiety) that were temporally connected to the crisis. Once identified, these will become the targets for reduction and development of the client's ability to cope with such conditions in the future.

Addressing Issues and Developing Coping Skills

A systematic review of controlled studies examining the effects of treatment for deliberate self-harm concluded there is insufficient evidence on which to make definitive recommendations regarding the most effective treatment for individuals who have engaged in deliberate self-harm (Hawton et al., 2002). While the specific theoretical orientation employed by the counselor should be tailored to that which best serves the client, research supports the value of problem-solving therapy, including: cognitive/behavioral-based treatments, Dialectical Behavior Therapy (DBT), and Solution-Focused Therapy (Bilsker & Forster, 2003).

Regardless of the approach employed, goals often involve: a) the resolution of intense emotions, b) the confrontation of self-destructive behaviors and the development of alternative response and coping skills, c) the development of problem solving and rational thinking, and d) the development of engagement and positive personal identity.

Before proceeding to the next section, it is suggested you review Exercise 4.2 as a way to apply what you have learned.

Specific Client Assessment: Risk of Homicide

While there is no single, reliable way of predicting client violence or risk of homicide, there are a number of factors, both static and dynamic, which have been associated with client dangerousness (Schoener, 2016).

Static Factors

The one static variable most often identified to be correlated with client violence is a history of past violence (Petit, 2005). Further, the risk of future violence increases linearly with the number of past violent acts (Buckley et al., 2003). Other static risk factors include history of impulsivity, substance misuse, male gender, younger age, lower intelligence, history of head trauma or neurological impairment, dissociative states, history of military service, weapons training, history of abuse, and diagnoses of major mental illnesses (Buckley et al., 2003; Cooper et al., 2005).

While identifying such static risk factors is important, it is also important to include dynamic factors, which focus on intra-individual variability in violence potential (Skeem & Mulvey, 2002).

Dynamic Risk Factors

Dynamic risk factors include persecutory delusions, command hallucinations, non-adherence with treatment, impulsivity, depression, hopelessness, suicidality, feasibility of a homicidal plan, and access to weapons (Buckley et al., 2003). Perhaps the most frequently cited dynamic risk factor is substance abuse or dependence (Cooper et al., 2005).

Instruments

One measure that combines several elements of risk assessment, including short-term dynamic risk factors, is the Short-Term Assessment of Risk and Treatability (START) (Nicholls et al., 2011; Webster et al., 2006). A less structured tool for danger assessment is one created by Hoff, L.A., Brown, L., & Hoff, M.R. (2009) and is found in Table 4.6. Similar to predicting suicide, the scale highlights the degree to which the client not only has a history of past violent behaviors, but also has a detailed plan of violent action and the means to engage the plan.

Case Illustration 4.2, highlights some of the factors that need to be considered when assessing the potential for violence or homicidal behavior.

EXERCISE 4.2

APPLYING WHAT I HAVE LEARNED

Directions: Review the following case material. Using your understanding of the material presented in this section, along with a colleague or classmate, discuss your reaction to the reflection questions.

Case:

You have been working with a 36-year-old female client who you believe is moderately depressed. Through your intake interview, you discover that her developmental history included the fact that her father, physically abusive to his wife and children, committed suicide when she was 8-years-old. The client shared that she had difficulty making friends throughout her school years and blamed it on living with her alcoholic mother, whom she felt was "an embarrassment."

The client went away to college, where she engaged in promiscuous behavior, binge drinking, and what she called "minor cutting" behavior.

She explained that she had sought out professional help in response to feeling sad. She stated she "might be depressed" about the fact that her intimate partner of five years recently moved out of her house, and at the same time, she was demoted at work, because of "her inability to meet deadlines."

You are the third counselor this client has sought out over the course of the past eight months, and this is your fifth session. As you end your session, the client stands, shakes your hand and states: "I want to thank you for trying to help me. You are the best counselor I have seen, but I realize that this isn't working—probably nothing will. I won't be coming back. There are other things I need to do now, but I really wanted to let you know, you did the best you could. Goodbye." The client starts for the door to leave.

Reflection:

1. Placing yourself in that scenario, how would you feel?

2. What salient elements in the scenario stand out as clinically significant in determining risk?

3. What, if any, distal and/or situation factors are potentially contributing to her "depression" and risk?

4. What are your options? How would you respond?

CASE ILLUSTRATION 4.2

AN ANGRY YOUNG WOMAN

Working at a community-mental health outreach center, you are assigned to work with Cheryl N.

Cheryl is a 26-year-old, Army National Guard Sergeant who has been on extended leave following a one-year tour in Iraq. Cheryl served on over 150 combat patrols. She experienced mortar and rocket fire on numerous occasions and once had an improvised explosive device (IED) explode 15 feet in front of her truck. She reported no injury with the exception of temporary hearing loss.

Cheryl comes from a military family. Her two brothers, father, and grandfather all served in the Marines as career soldiers. She described her dad as loving, yet stoic and reserved. Her mother, whom she was reluctant to talk about, was eventually described as "too emotional" and somewhat emotionally fragile.

Prior to her enlistment, Cheryl was very engaged in school. She was bright, athletic, and provided evidence of clear leadership abilities, serving as captain on both the volleyball team and rifle club. Since coming home, she has been arrested twice for bar fights and has been kicked out of her house for arguing with her mother and threatening to hurt her. The argument, which was about Cheryl's drinking, ended with Cheryl damaging her bedroom and punching holes in the wall. When questioned about the incident, she admitted that she has been drinking a bit more than usual and feels like she is on edge and stated that sometimes "People piss me off." Asked to elaborate, Cheryl stated, "People around here are wimps! They worry about the stupidest shit. They should spend one week doing what I was doing for a year to get their perspectives in order."

She has found it difficult to engage with her previous civilian friends and does not stay in touch with any of the vets that she knows. She reports that sometimes she just feels as if she is going to explode.

When asked if there was anything or anyone in particular that seemed to be the target for her anger, she replied, "Not really ... just all those self-indulged, entitled little bitches that you see all over the place." When asked how she thought about expressing her anger, her response was, "Right now, by drinking and freaking at my family, but I'd love to send a fuckin' mortar into one of those sorority houses."

Intervention with Clients at Risk for Homicide

Violence, violent behavior, or violence risk, per se, cannot be treated, since these are not disorders (Otto, 2000). When possible, the counselor will want to target the underlying disorders and the distorted thinking pattern or behavior that is at the root of the homicidal urge. Working on a client's issues of impulsivity, anger control, emotional lability, and substance abuse may be effective targets for treatment and for the reduction of their homicidal risk. However, with elevated risk, the forms of intervention become less typical of those often employed by professional counselors. Sometimes, the level of risk demands that steps be taken to protect potential victims, perhaps via warning or notification. Clearly, this form of intervention is outside the counselor's typical modus operandi and invites violation of the rules of confidentiality. As such, it is important for the counselor to understand the ethics and legality of such disclosure in his or her circumstance (see Chapter 14 for detailed discussion of the limits of confidentiality). It is also possible that the client presents at such a high risk that the counselor may need to engage with others, specifically law enforcement, to incapacitate the client either through hospitalization or incarceration. Because this step does not address the factors underlying the threatened violence, it should be viewed only as a stopgap measure (Otto, 2000).

Table 4.6 Assault and Homicidal Danger Assessment Tool

Key to Danger	Immediate Dangerousness to Others	Typical Indicators
1	No predictable risk of assault or homicide	Has no assaultive or homicidal ideation, urges or history of same; basically has satisfactory support system; social drinker only.
2	Low risk of assault or homicide	Has occasional assault or homicidal ideation (including paranoid ideas) with some urges to kill; no history of impulsive acts or homicidal attempts; occasional drinking bouts and angry verbal outbursts; basically satisfactory support system.
3	Medium risk of assault or homicide	Has frequent homicidal ideation and urges to kill but no specific plan; history of impulsive acting out and verbal outburst while drinking, on other drugs, or otherwise; stormy relationships with significant others with periodic high-tension arguments.
4	High risk of homicide	Has homicidal plan; obtainable means; history of substance abuse; frequent acting out against others, but no homicide attempts; stormy relationships and much verbal fight with significant others, with occasional assaults.
5	Very high risk of homicide	Has current high-lethal plan; available means; history of homicide attempts or impulsive acting out, plus feels a strong urge to control and "get even" with a significant other; history of serious substance abuse; also with possible high-lethal suicide risk.

Reprinted from Hoff, L.A., Brown, L., & Hoff, M.R. (2009). People in Crisis. Routledge, New York: New York (page 439).

Summary

- When assessing the history of self-harm, the counselor needs to gather data reflecting age of onset, types of harm (e.g., cutting, burning, hitting, excoriation), duration of the problem, frequency of the behavior, number of wounds per episode, and level of physical damage.

- An effective suicide risk assessment will entail: a) gathering information related to risk factors, protective factors, and warning signs of suicide; b) identifying the client's ideation, planning, behaviors, desire, and intent; and c) the clinical formulation of risk based on the data collected and the formulation of an intervention plan.

- A comprehensive approach to intervening with clients at suicidal risk includes: a) providing for immediate client safety, b) identifying and targeting underlying risk factors, and c) addressing and developing coping skills.

- Static risk factors associated with increased risk of violence include history of impulsivity, substance misuse, male gender, younger age, lower intelligence, history of head trauma or neurological impairment, dissociative states, history of military service, weapons training, history of abuse, and diagnoses of major mental illnesses.

- The risk of future violence increases linearly with the number of past violent acts.

- The most frequently cited dynamic risk factor to increasing violent behavior is substance abuse or dependence.

- Working on a client's issues of impulsivity, anger control, emotional lability, and substance abuse may be, for some clients, effective targets for treatment and for the reduction of their homicidal risk. However, with elevated risk, the forms of intervention become less typical of those employed by counselors, including informing identifiable victims and or incapacitating the client (e.g., hospitalization, legal action).

Important Terms

Distal factors

Dynamic factors

History of self-injury

Models of crisis intervention

Nature of self-injury

Protective factors

Risk fssessment

Risk factors

Risk management

Safety plan

Self-injury

Situational factors

Stabilization

Static factors

Suicidality

Short-Term Assessment of Risk and Treatability (START)

The Triage Assessment Form

Therapeutic alliance

Additional Resources

In Print

Shea S. C. (2002). *The Practical Art of Suicide Assessment: A Guide for Mental Health Professionals and Substance Abuse Counselors*. New York, NY: John Wiley & Sons, Inc.

Otto, R. K. & Douglas, K. S. (eds.). (2011). *Handbook of Violence Risk Assessment*. New York, NY: Routledge.

James, R. K., & Gilliland, B. E. (2012). *Crisis Intervention Strategies* (7th ed). Belmont, CA: Brooks/Cole (Cengage).

On the Web

VA/DoD Clinical Practice Guideline for Assessment and Management of Patients at Risk for Suicide Assessment and Management of Risk for Suicide Working Group, Department of Veterans Affairs/Department of Defense: http://www.healthquality.va.gov/guidelines/MH/srb/VADODCP_SuicideRisk_Full.pdf

National Action Alliance for Suicide Prevention Identifying and Assessing Suicide Risk Level: http://zerosuicide.actionallianceforsuicideprevention.org

References

American Psychiatric Association. (2003). Practice Guideline for the Assessment and Treatment of Patients with Suicidal Behaviors. *American Journal of Psychiatry (Supplement), 160*(11): 1–60.

Bilsker, D., & Forster, P. (2003). Problem-solving intervention for suicidal crises in the psychiatric emergency service. *Crisis, 24*(3), 134–136.

Brown, G. K., Henriques, G. R., Sosdjan, D., & Beck, A. T. (2004). Suicide intent and accurate expectations of lethality: Predictors of medical lethality of suicide attempts. *Journal of Consulting and Clinical Psychology, 72*, 1170–1174.

Buckley, P. F., Noffsinger, S. G., Smith, D. A., Hrouda, D. R., & Knoll J. L. (2003). Treatment of the psychotic patient who is violent. *Psychiatric Clinics of North America 26*(1), 231–272.

Cavanagh, J., Carson, A., Sharpe, M., & Lawrie, S. M. (2003). Psychological autopsy studies of suicide: A systematic review. *Psychological Medicine, 33*, 395–405.

Cooper, J., Kapur, N., Webb, R., Lawlor, M., Guthrie, E., Mackway-Jones, K., & Appleby, L. (2005). Suicide after deliberate self-harm: a 4-year cohort study. *American Journal of Psychiatry, 162*(2), 297–303.

Fowler J. C. (2012). Suicide risk assessment in clinical practice: Pragmatic guidelines for imperfect assessments. *Psychotherapy, 49*(1),81–90.

Gratz, K. L. (2001). Measurement of deliberate self-harm: Preliminary data on the Deliberate Self-Harm Inventory. *Journal of Psychopathology and Behavioral Assessment, 23*, 253–263.

Haney, E. M., O'Neil, M. E., Carson, S., Low, A., & Peterson, K. (2012). Suicide Factors and Risk Assessment Tools: A systematic review. Washington, D.C.: Department of Veterans Affairs.

Retrieved from http://www.ncbi.nlm.nih.gov/books/NBK92671/?term=NBK92671 Retrieved May 31, 2016.

Hawton, K., Casanas, I., Comabella, C., Haw C., & Saunders, K. (2013). Risk factors for suicide in individual with depression: A systematic review. *Journal of Affective Disorders, 147*(1–3), 17–28.

Hoff, L. A., Brown, L., & Hoff, M. R. (2009). *People in crisis*. New York, NY: Routledge.

James, R. K., & Gilliland, B. E. (2012). *Crisis intervention strategies* (7th ed.). Belmont, CA: Thomson Brooks/Cole.

Jobes, D. A. (2000). Collaborating to Prevent Suicide: A Clinical-research Perspective. *Suicide and Life-threatening Behavior, 3*(1), 8–17.

Lambert, M. T. (2002). Seven-year outcomes of patients evaluated for suicidality. *Psychiatric Services, 53*(1), 92–4.

Lescano, C. M., Hadley, W. S., Beausoleil, N. I., Brown, L. K., D'eramo, D., & Zimskind, A. (2007). A brief screening measure of adolescent risk behavior. *Child Psychiatry and Human Development, 37*, 325–336.

Linehan, M. M., Comtois, K. A., Brown, M. Z., Heard, H. L., & Wagner, A. (2006). Suicide Attempt Self-Injury Interview (SASII): Development, reliability, and validity of a scale to assess suicide attempts and intentional self-injury. *Psychological Assessment, 18*, 303–312.

Lukomski, J., & Folmer, T. (2004). Self-Mutilation: Information and Guidance for School Personnel. *National Association of School Psychologists, 5*, 91–93.

Muzina, D. J. (2007). Risk factors cannot predict suicide, but evaluating risk helps you determine the next appropriate action. *Current Psychiatry, 6*(9), 1–2. Retrieved from http://www.currentpsychiatry.com/home/article/suicide-intervention-how-to-recognize-risk-focus-on-patient-safety/e658ed8cda637c5a63f265dc179166d4.html June 10, 2016.

Myer, R. A. (2001). *Assessment for crisis intervention: A triage assessment model.* Belmont, CA: Wadsworth, Brooks/Cole.

Myer, R. A., Williams, R. C., Ottens, A. J., & Schmidt, A. E. (1992). Crisis assessments: A three-dimensional model for triage. *Journal of Mental Health Counseling, 14,* 137–148.

Nicholls, T. L., Petersen, K. L., Brink, J., & Webster, C. D. (2011). A clinical and risk profile of forensic psychiatric patients: Treatment team STARTs in a Canadian service. *The International Journal of Forensic Mental Health*, *10*, 187–199.

Nock, M. K., Holmberg, E. B., Photos, V. I., & Michel, B. D. (2007). Self-injurious thoughts and behaviors interview: Development, reliability, and validity of a new measure. *Psychological Assessment, 19*, 309–317.

Nock, M. K., Joiner, Jr., T. E., Gordon, K. H., Lloyd-Richardson, E., & Prinstein, M. J. (2006). Non-suicidal self-injury among adolescents: Diagnostic correlates and relation to suicide attempts. *Psychiatry Research, 144,* 65–72.

Otto, R. K. (2000). Assessing and managing violence risk in outpatient settings. Retrieved from http://www.antoniocasella.eu/archipsy/Otto_2000.pdf Retrieved June 7, 2016.

Petit, J. (2005). Management of the acutely violent patient. *Psychiatric Clinics of North America, 28*(3), 701–711.

Pompili, M., Serafini, G., Innamorati, M., Kotzalidis, G. D., Serra, G., Girardi, P., Janiri, L., Taterellia, R., Sher, L, & Lester, D. (2010). Suicidal behavior and alcohol abuse. *International Journal of Environmental Research and Public Health, 7*(40), 1392–1431.

Rogers, P. (2011). *Understanding risk and protective factors for suicide: a primer for preventing suicide.* Retrieved from www.sprc.org/library_resources/items/understanding-risk-and-protective-factors-suicide-primer-preventing-suicide. June 8, 2016.

Rogers, J. R. (2001). Suicide Risk assessment. In E. R.Welfel & R. E. W. Ingersoll (eds.), *The mental health desk reference* (pp. 259–264). New York, NY: Wiley.

Rudd, M. D., Berman, A. L., Joiner, T. E., Nock, M. K., Silverman, M. M., Mandrusiak, M., … Witte, T. (2006) Warning signs for suicide: Theory, research and clinical applications. *Suicide and Life Threatening Behavior, 36*, 255–62

Shea, S.C. (2009). Suicide assessment: Part 1: Uncovering suicidal intent, a sophisticated art. *Psychiatric Times, 26*(12), 17–19.

Schoener, G. R. (2009). Dangerous clients and the threat of violence. Retrieved from http://www.walkin.org/sites/default/files/DutyToWarn_0.pdf

Simeon, D., & Hollander, E. (Eds.). (2001). *Self-injurious behaviors, assessment and treatment.* Washington, D.C.: American Psychiatric Publishing.

Skeem, J. L., Monahan, J., & Mulvey, E. P. (2002). Psychopathy, treatment involvement and subsequent violence among civil psychiatric patients. *Law and Human Behavior. 26*(6), 577–603.

Slee, N., Garnefski, N., van der Leeden, R., Arensman, E., & Spinhove, P. (2008). Cognitive-behavioural intervention for self-harm: Randomized control trial. *The British Journal of Psychiatry, 192*(3), 202–211.

Vanderllinden, J., & Vandereycken, W. (1997). *Trauma, dissociation, and impulse dyscontrol in eating disorders.* Philadelphia, PA: Brunner/Mazel

Walsh, B. (2007). Clinical assessment of self-injury: A practical guide. *Journal of Clinical Psychology: In Session, 63*(11), 1057–1068.

Webster, C. D., Nicholls, T. L., Martin, M. L., Desmarais, S. L., & Brink, J. (2006). Short-term assessment of risk and treatability (START): The case for a new structured professional judgment scheme. *Behavioral Sciences & the Law, 24*, 747–766.

Whitlock, J., Eckenrode, J., & Silverman, D. (2006). Self-injurious behaviors in a college population. *Pediatrics, 117*, 1939–1948.

CHAPTER 5

Symptom Development and the DSM: When Coping Fails

I knew the client had been through so much, but it seemed like he was coping pretty well. Yet as the weeks went on, it was pretty clear he wasn't coping as well as I had thought. He couldn't sleep, he was having terrible nightmares. He was constantly on guard and couldn't trust anyone. He had pretty much detached from everyone he knew and had given up on most of the things he cared about.

As we discussed in Chapter 1, experiencing a crisis doesn't necessarily lead to the development of negative psychological symptoms. Many people experience crises throughout their lifetimes and find effective means of coping and processing the experience. However, when an individual struggles to cope with a distressing event, the experience can lead to psychological distress, which manifests itself in symptoms that may meet the criteria for a mental health diagnosis.

This chapter will review the specific psychological diagnoses, as described in the *Diagnostic and Statistical Manual of Mental Disorders, Fifth Edition* (DSM-5) (APA, 2013), that are most often associated with the experience of traumatic events. Specifically, after reading this chapter, you should be able to

1. Understand the basic process of identifying psychological symptoms for the purpose of diagnosis;

2. Recognize the DSM-5 diagnoses that are most commonly associated with exposure to a crisis or traumatic event;

3. Identify the symptoms that are part of the criteria for assigning these diagnoses;

4. Recognize the prevalence and prognosis for recovery from these diagnoses.

A Note on Diagnosis

The purpose of this text is not to provide a thorough understanding of the process of developing diagnoses and treatment plans; there are a host of texts available that can assist in understanding these procedures (e.g., Zubernis & Snyder, 2016). However, any discussion of DSM-5 diagnosis would be remiss without a summary description of the purpose and process of diagnosis and symptomology.

The diagnostic process can be challenging, especially for new clinicians and those not familiar with the diagnostic criteria for the disorders identified in the DSM-5. A symptom is a manifestation (e.g., typically an affect, behavior, or cognition) that is reported by a client. We use symptoms to determine if a client meets the criteria for a diagnosis, which is a term used to describe a set of symptoms. Clients may present to counseling with a predetermined notion of their own diagnosis, which may cloud your clinical judgment. Some symptoms are common across several disorders, which can make choosing the appropriate diagnosis difficult. Clients may provide history that suggests one diagnosis, but through the course of treatment, may exhibit behaviors or symptomology that requires a revision of the original diagnosis. A client's functioning may improve (or worsen) through the course of therapy, which may necessitate a change in the diagnosis. Or sometimes, you may simply not know if assigning any diagnosis is even appropriate. Some clients will present with a few of the symptoms necessary to make a diagnosis, but not enough, referred to sometimes as sub-symptomatic.

Regardless of the diagnosis assigned, it is paramount to remember the purpose for developing a diagnosis. Sometimes the purpose may be practical, for example, a clinical

EXERCISE 5.1

UNDERSTANDING CO-OCCURRING DISORDERS

Directions: At this point in the chapter, you have not read much about the specific symptoms and diagnoses associated with crisis events and traumatic experience. Prior to continuing through the chapter, work individually (or with a classmate or peer) to develop a list of psychological concerns that you believe may occur simultaneously after a person experiences a crisis. After reading the chapter, review your list, and see if there are any changes you would make, such as removing or adding any co-occurring diagnoses.

diagnosis is most often required for third-party billing. More importantly, a diagnosis provides the beginning of a roadmap, and that map is critical in the development of a treatment plan that will effectively assist the client in overcoming challenges, coping better, and eventually meeting the goals of therapy, presumably to reduce negative symptoms and live a happier, healthier, life.

But the diagnosis is merely a term used to describe a collection of symptoms which may suggest potential challenges and possible treatment modalities. The diagnosis is not a label that should be worn by the client like a scarlet letter. Nor is the diagnosis something that the client must live with forever. Most importantly, a diagnosis is not a description of a person; it is a term used as shorthand to describe a collection of symptoms a person is experiencing. If you broke your leg, you would not expect you doctor to call you a "broken leg" when you went in for treatment, would you? A mental health diagnosis is no different. A person is not Post-Traumatic Stress Disorder (PTSD) or Social Phobia. A person is a human being struggling with the symptoms of a disorder, and that person is looking to you for help.

What follows are descriptions of a number of common diagnoses associated with crisis experiences and traumatic events. However, it should be noted that this list is not exhaustive, and each will include a brief overview of the symptomology and features associated with the diagnosis, the prevalence of the diagnosis, issues related to treatment and recovery, and other important factors associated with each.

A feature unique to the publication of the DSM-5 that was not present in previous editions of the *Diagnostic and Statistical Manual* is a section specific to "Trauma- and Stressor-Related Disorders" (APA, 2013). Specifically, this section of the DSM-5 includes "disorders in which exposure to a traumatic or stressful event is listed explicitly as a diagnostic criterion" (APA, 2013, p. 265). However, as the DSM-5 correctly explains, responses to traumatic and stressful events are varied and somewhat unpredictable. Some clients will exhibit angry or aggressive symptomology or, possibly, dissociative symptoms, rather than the fear-based symptoms found throughout this section of the manual. Also, co-occurring disorders are sometimes found in diagnoses related to trauma and crisis; that is, individuals may meet the criteria for multiple diagnoses (e.g., PTSD, as well as a substance abuse disorder as a means of attempting to cope with the negative symptoms of post-traumatic stress).

Exercise 5.1 invites you to better understand how psychological diagnoses may co-occur.

Post-Traumatic Stress Disorder (PTSD)

The main feature of PTSD is the experiencing and re-experiencing of a traumatic event. The type of event can vary, but includes the exposure to death or threatened death, serious injury, or sexual violence (APA, 2013). Some examples of events that may lead to PTSD include exposure to war, violent crime, sexual assault or rape, kidnapping, terrorism, environmental or man-made disasters, or car accidents. An individual can experience PTSD by experiencing the event first-hand, witnessing the event as it occurred to someone else, learning that the event afflicted a loved one, or exposure to details of a traumatic event experienced by another person (APA, 2013). For example, a therapist who hears the specific and graphic details of an attempted murder may begin to experience symptoms as if the event happened directly to the therapist.

The diagnostic criteria for PTSD are quite extensive and include eight different conditions, as well as two specifiers that must occur for more than one month. Also, the criteria are somewhat different for children, given the different ways young children re-experience traumatic events developmentally. In individuals older than six years, the re-experiencing of the traumatic event can occur in a myriad of ways. The client may have recurring involuntary and intrusive memories of the event, which may also manifest as distressing dreams (APA, 2013). The person may experience flashbacks, during which time the client may feel as if the event is actually occurring again. People will attempt to avoid stimuli that are associated with the initial event, and they will experience negative cognitions and/or mood, such as an inability to remember details of the event, distorted cognitions, a persistent state of fear, feelings of detachment, and an inability to experience positive emotions.

PTSD is marked by hyperarousal and reactivity that is related to the re-experiencing of the trauma. Clients experiencing PTSD may have inappropriately angry outbursts and may act in self-destructive ways. PTSD may manifest in an exaggerated startle response, such as being "jumpy" or easily agitated. People experiencing PTSD may have difficulty sleeping or concentrating, and are often hypervigilant, excessively worrying about the potential threats in their environments (APA, 2013).

According to the DSM-5, the projected lifetime prevalence of PTSD in the United States is 8.7% of the population by age 75, using criteria from the last edition of the DSM-5 (APA, 2013). Lower rates are found in other countries, as well as older adults, and higher rates are found among individuals in dangerous professions (e.g., law enforcement, military personnel, etc.). Developmental level and cultural background also appear to impact the prevalence of PTSD.

A number of studies have examined the prevalence of PTSD among various populations and across an assortment of critical events. For example, one study examined college student exposure to potentially traumatic events and PTSD development (Boyraz, Granda, Baker, Tidwell, & Waits, 2016). These researchers found that just over 12% of students who experienced a potentially traumatic event developed symptomology that met the criteria for PTSD.

CASE ILLUSTRATION 5.1

THE CASE OF MARK: AN EXAMPLE OF PTSD

Mark is a 47 year old male who is married and has two children. For many years, Mark has been living with a secret that he hasn't shared with anyone: friends, family, or other therapists, despite having been in therapy before for issues related to anger. During his initial session with you, Mark shares that he was sexually abused by a neighbor for about two years, from the ages of seven to nine. While the abuse was occurring, the neighbor told Mark that if he told anyone about it, the neighbor would kill Mark's family. For almost 30 years, Mark has been living with this, and it has now become more than he can bear.

Mark had repressed the memory of the abuse for a very long time, but recently, his son was approached by a stranger who attempted to abduct him. Since the incident, Mark has been having dreams where his abuser appears and threatens his current family. Mark also says that throughout the day, he will feel like he's eight years old again and like he's "back there, when it happened." Mark has been trying to ignore the thoughts that have been haunting him, and since the incident with his son, refuses to go and visit his parent's house, even though they live 20 minutes away, and Mark used to visit often.

Mark says he has trouble remembering anything specific about the abuse, even his neighbor's name. Mark also tells you he refuses to let his son leave the house to go anywhere but school, even forcing him to quit playing soccer, because Mark "doesn't trust the way the coach looks at the kids." Mark tells you that he finds himself scared constantly, has had difficulty finding happiness in just about anything, and has stopped doing anything other than going to work. Mark tells you he used to golf competitively but has quit altogether, and no longer exercises or plays in his recreational softball league. Mark explains that his inability to concentrate has caused him a great deal of trouble at work, and he was recently given a negative performance review, the first in his career.

Another study examined children who had been exposed to accidental, life-threatening injuries (De Young, Haag, Kenardy, Kimble, & Landolt, 2016). In their research, the authors found that 10–30% of children who experience these injuries eventually develop PTSD, while 25–45% of their parents develop the disorder as a result of the injury to their child. Schwarzer, Cone, Jiehui, and Bowler (2016) examined the development of PTSD in police officers who responded to the World Trade Center on September 11, 2001. Within two years of the attacks, 2.5% of those police officers studied developed PTSD, 6.3% developed PTSD within six years of the event, and 11% within 10–11 years of the attacks.

In examining PTSD resulting from motor vehicle accidents, researchers found that PTSD is a relatively rare development following a car accident, with only 2.5% of participants reporting PTSD symptomology following a car accident (Stein et al., 2016). Interpersonal violence is more likely to result in PTSD, with 19% of rape survivors and 11.7% of those who experience intimate partner violence developing PTSD symptoms (Stein et al., 2016). In examining natural disasters, Wenjie et al. (2016) found that 23.7% of those who survived earthquakes ranging from 4.3–9.0 on the Richter Scale developed PTSD symptoms. This was slightly greater than the prevalence among those who experience floods, at 15.74% (Wenjie et al., 2016).

A common conclusion from these data is that the majority of people who experience a crisis or traumatic event do not develop PTSD. Even in an event as horrific as the World Trade Center attacks, only 11% of those police officers who responded to the attack site developed the disorder, and many of those developed PTSD years after the event. With appropriate intervention, that number could have been significantly less. The studies here suggest that the significant majority of individuals who experience a crisis do not develop PTSD. However, that does not necessarily mean they do not struggle with the experience; instead they cope effectively with their subjective experience, develop a different disorder, or present as sub-symptomatic for PTSD or other mental health diagnoses.

One of the greatest factors related to effective prognosis after experiencing PTSD is the existence of social supports. Both the DSM-5 (APA, 2013) and a number of studies (Schwarzer et al., 2016) identify social support as one of the leading factors in preventing and/or recovering from PTSD. Prognosis is also improved through the use of empirically supported treatment for PTSD, including Eye Movement Desensitization and Reprocessing (EMDR) (Bisson et al., 2007), Trauma-Focused Cognitive Behavioral Therapy (TF-CBT) (Cohen, Mannarino, & Knudsen, 2005), and other empirically supported modalities (Foa, Keane, Friedman, & Cohen, 2008).

As Case Illustration 5.1 points out, PTSD is a complex and challenging diagnosis for both the client and the clinician. Clients can experience a host of negative symptoms that can make it difficult to function at work, at school, and with friends and family.

> When Mark talks about the abuse, he states "I know it sounds crazy, but I almost feel like it was my fault somehow. I should have avoided the guy, but I didn't for some reason." Mark tells you that he has started drinking heavily and has considered having an affair, something he has never done before. Mark has had trouble falling asleep and staying asleep, waking several times a night, almost on schedule. He tells you that he has been having angry outbursts at family and co-workers, often without provocation. Mark says "I'm at the end of my rope here. I forgot this ever happened but now I can't think about anything else — at work, at home, even in my sleep. What am I going to do?"

Acute Stress Disorder

The etiology of Acute Stress Disorder mirrors that of PTSD, and the symptomology is very similar. The difference between these two diagnoses is that the onset of Acute Stress Disorder occurs between three days and one month after the experience of the traumatic or distressing event. The descriptions of the types of events are the same for both Acute Stress Disorder and PTSD, as are the symptoms of re-experiencing the event through disturbing memories and dreams. Acute Stress Disorder is marked by negative mood, dissociative symptoms, avoidance, and arousal. In short, if PTSD cannot be diagnosed until a month has passed, Acute Stress Disorder can be diagnosed in the interim.

According to the DSM-5, Acute Stress Disorder occurs in less than 20% of cases that follow traumatic events that do not include interpersonal violence (APA, 2013). Rates of 20–50% are seen following acts of interpersonal assault, such as rape, murder, and assault. Acute Stress Disorder may lead to a diagnosis of PTSD; however, it does not necessarily have to, and early intervention may be effective in resolving symptoms prior to the one month criteria for PTSD.

Reactive Attachment Disorder

<table>
<tr>
<td>

THE CASE OF LISA: THE IMPACT OF ABUSE AND NEGLECT

Lisa is a six-year-old girl who was recently adopted by two loving parents. Lisa's new parents have two other children, a 12-year-old biological daughter and a nine-year-old adopted son. Lisa was adopted after living in a group home with approximately 30 other children. In her group home environment, she was safe, well fed, clothed, and cared for, which is more care than she had ever had prior to becoming a ward of the state.

Lisa's biological parents were both addicted to heroin at her birth, and Lisa's first experiences after birth involved detoxing under the care of physicians. After her birth, Lisa lived with her maternal grandmother while her biological parents entered a drug treatment facility. After release from the facility, Lisa's father immediately relapsed and left the family, but her mother remained sober, and Lisa began living with her at three months of age.

Lisa's mother relapsed shortly after. Her mother began dating someone new, who was also addicted to heroin. Lisa would often lie in her crib for hours crying, because she was hungry, needed to be changed, or simply needed to be held. However, the drug use became pervasive, and neither Lisa's mother nor her new boyfriend did much to comfort Lisa. Eventually, Lisa went to live with her father, who did not provide much more comfort than did her mother. Several months later, Lisa moved in with her paternal grandmother, who was very ill and died a few months later. Without any reliable adults to care for Lisa, she was placed in to the foster care system, where she changed homes several times over nine months and was eventually moved to a group home. In short, between her birth and being adopted at age six, Lisa lived in six different homes, where she received little or no care, comfort, or affection from adults.

Since being adopted, Lisa's new parents have been struggling to connect with her. When she is hurt, lonely, or sad, she will quietly cry to herself, but will actively avoid care or comfort from her adoptive parents or siblings. Her family will try to hold her, but Lisa

</td>
</tr>
</table>

Reactive Attachment Disorder is a childhood disorder that results from a failure to develop important attachments during infancy or early childhood. This may occur as a result of neglect or abuse, frequent changes in adult caregivers, or rearing in settings where attachments are difficult, such as group homes (APA, 2013). As a result of these experiences, the child has marked difficulty developing appropriate attachments with caregivers and other protective and nurturing people in the child's life. A diagnosis of Reactive Attachment Disorder must be made after reaching a developmental age of nine months, and symptoms must be evident prior to age five. The most significant feature of this disorder is the inability to form emotional bonds with caring adults.

The specific diagnostic criteria of Reactive Attachment Disorder include consistent patterns of behavior that indicate inhibited and emotional withdraw from adult caregivers marked by a lack of comfort seeking during distress and a lack of response when comfort is provided (APA, 2013). Children diagnosed with Reactive Attachment Disorder will have little social or emotional responsiveness to others, have limited positive affect, and will display unexplained episodes of anger, sadness, irritability, or fearfulness.

According to the DSM-5, Reactive Attachment Disorder is uncommon, occurring in less than 10% of children who have been placed in foster care or institutional settings after being neglected (APA, 2013). However, the literature indicates greater prevalence of this disorder. Hall and Geher (2003) argue that up to 80% of abused children display Reactive Attachment Disorder symptomology, and another study found 38% of neglected toddlers developed the disorder (Kay & Green, 2013).

Prognosis for recovery is mixed, as the DSM-5 indicates that it is a rare disorder that is unlikely to occur (APA, 2013). Effective recovery from Reactive Attachment Disorder is linked with the quality of the caregiving environment the child experiences following the episodes of neglect. Hanson and Spratt (2000) also argue that effective treatment should incorporate the positive adult caregiver and includes managing anxiety, positive coping, and psychoeducation around issues of neglect, abuse, and other trauma-related experiences.

will show no emotion, and will rarely even react. Lisa shows very little emotion at all, only crying softly when she's hurt. The only other emotion Lisa displays is fear, which happens often and sometimes for no apparent reason. She has no friends at school or in her neighborhood, and doesn't seem interested in making any.

As Case 5.2 illustrates, the psychological impact of abuse and neglect can be significant for children and negatively impact development during crucial periods.

Disinhibited Social Engagement Disorder

Disinhibited Social Engagement Disorder is, simply put, the opposite reaction to the etiological causes of Reactive Attachment Disorder. That is, children diagnosed with this disorder have typically experienced neglect or other forms of abuse, have had repeated changes in caregivers, or have been raised in institutional settings where attachments were not available.

However, for children diagnosed with Disinhibited Social Engagement Disorder, rather than developing the avoidance behaviors found in Reactive Attachment Disorder, children instead become overly familiar with relative strangers (APA, 2013). Children do not display with the normal reservation associated with meeting new people or interacting with new adults. The diagnostic criteria for this disorder include overly familiar verbal or physical behavior, a lack of checking back with adults after venturing away, and a willingness to leave with unfamiliar adults without hesitation (APA, 2013). It is important to note that in order for these behaviors to meet the criteria for the diagnosis, they must be inappropriate for the child's culture and must occur after the child has reached a developmental age of nine months.

The DSM-5 indicates that this diagnosis is rare (APA, 2013). Among children who have been severely neglected and placed in institutional settings or foster care, the prevalence rate is less than 20%. According to the DSM-5, the diagnosis is rarely seen elsewhere. Similar to Reactive Attachment Disorder, positive caregiving and nurturing environments improve the prognosis for children diagnosed with this disorder, although persistence through adolescence is common.

Adjustment Disorders

Adjustment Disorders occur when behavioral or emotional symptoms manifest following a stressful or traumatic event. These symptoms are either inconsistent with the severity of the stressors, or cause a significant decrease in social, occupational, or other functioning (APA, 2013). Adjustment disorders may include dysphoric mood, anxiety, or both, or may exhibit conduct-related behaviors, such as aggression, criminal activity, or school-based problems. The symptoms of these disorders must occur within three months of the onset of the stressor and do not last more than six months after the stressor has passed. Most importantly, adjustment disorders do not meet the criteria for another disorder and are not developmentally appropriate responses to stress, for example, typical bereavement.

Adjustment disorders are relatively common, and are cited in the DSM-5 as the most common diagnosis in psychiatric hospital settings (APA, 2013). Among outpatient settings, the frequency of adjustment disorder being the principal diagnosis is between 5–20%.

Anxiety and Depressive Disorders

The DSM-5 provides separate categories for anxiety-related disorders, as well as depressive disorders (APA, 2013). Anxiety disorders include diagnoses such as: Generalized Anxiety Disorder, Specific Phobias, Social Phobias, Social Anxiety Disorder, Panic Disorder, and Agoraphobia. While not classified as an anxiety disorder in the DSM-5, Obsessive Compulsive Disorder was classified as an anxiety disorder in previous versions of the *Diagnostic and Statistical Manual* and sometimes results from unresolved trauma after a crisis. Among the depressive disorders, the most common diagnosis found among those who have experienced a crisis is Major Depressive Disorder.

The literature does identify a number of these diagnoses that can be related to the experience of a crisis. One study examined the correlation between depression and childhood attachments and other forms of interpersonal trauma (Fowler, Allen, Oldham, & Frueh, 2013). This study found significant relationships between the severity of one's depression and experience with interpersonal trauma and issues of attachment in childhood. In another study, researchers found that following the tsunami and resulting nuclear accident at the Fukushima nuclear plant in Japan, over two-thirds of those sampled in a nearby town reported symptoms meeting the criteria for Major Depressive Disorder (Kukihara, Yamawaki, Uchiyama, Arai, & Horikawa, 2014).

Other studies have found links between trauma and depression. Negele, Kaufhold, Kallenbach, and Leuzinger-Bohleber (2015) found that over 75% of the respondents in their study who were experiencing significant depression had experienced a traumatic event in childhood. Another study examined the correlation between traumatic events in childhood and the onset of depression during adulthood (Vares et al., 2015). In their study, the researchers found a significant correlation between childhood trauma and the cognitive elements of depression. Research indicates that strong coping skills, healthy attachments, and early intervention can all lead to the prevention of depression development or reduction of severity (Fowler, Allen, Oldham, & Frueh, 2013; Morris, Kouros, Fox, Rao, & Garber, 2014; Negele et al., 2015; Sinclair, Wallston, & Strachan, 2016; Vares et al., 2015).

Regarding anxiety-related disorders, there is also a host of research linking traumatic experience with anxiety, which is a logical conclusion given the fear that often results following a crisis. One study examined the development of anxiety-related disorders among a sample of 1,200 adults in Sudan, which has experienced a long and costly war (Ayazi, Lien, Eide, Swartz, & Hauff, 2014). Of those sampled, 15.8% experienced Generalized Anxiety Disorder, 13.2% experienced Panic Disorder, 17.8% had Agoraphobia, 15.3% experienced Social Phobia, and 12.7% met criteria for Obsessive-Compulsive Disorder.

Another study sought to examine the link between childhood trauma and Generalized Anxiety Disorder. In this study, 103 adults who were diagnosed with Generalized Anxiety Disorder were given a screening tool for childhood trauma (Simon et al., 2009). The results found that 70% of those participants diagnosed with Generalized Anxiety Disorder had experienced at least one traumatic event in childhood. Wood, Salguero, Cano-Vindel, and Galea (2013) found significant relationships between the experience of terrorism and the development of Panic Disorder and panic attacks. Another study found that among 929 adults who were present at the attack site on September 11, 2001, 10.5% developed symptoms meeting the criteria for Generalized Anxiety Disorder (Ghafoori et al., 2009).

Substance-Related and Addictive Disorders

As discussed in Chapter 1, when people experience distress after a crisis, they will typically attempt to manage the distress through coping skills. While many coping skills are effective and powerful, others are ineffective and can make the situation worse. Some people will turn to drugs, such as alcohol or illegal narcotics, as a means of coping with the distress that sometimes follows a crisis. The category of the DSM-5 that addresses abuse and addiction related to drugs and alcohol is titled Substance-Related and Addictive Disorders (APA, 2013).

A number of research studies have examined the link between traumatic exposure and drug abuse and addiction. In one study of homeless women who self-identified as addicts, trauma histories were highly prevalent. Among the 146 participants, 69% reported childhood abuse, 39% reported sexual abuse, and 51% reported emotional abuse (Sacks, McKendrick, & Banks, 2008). Additionally, of those who entered treatment, outcomes were more positive for those who had not experienced a traumatic event. Valhov et al. (2006) found an increase in alcohol abuse in New York City following the September 11, 2001, terrorist attacks. Another study found that among 253 participants in an inpatient addiction treatment center, 80% had experienced at least one traumatic event throughout their lifetimes (Dore, Mills, Murray, Teesson, & Farrugia, 2012). These are just a few examples of the many studies linking traumatic experiences to substance abuse and addiction.

Personality Disorders

The DSM-5 defines a personality disorder as "an enduring pattern of inner experience and behavior that deviates markedly from expectations of the individual's culture, is pervasive and inflexible, has an onset in adolescence or early adulthood, is stable over time, and leads to distress or impairment" (APA, 2013, p. 645). As this definition suggests, personality disorders are a part of the individual's core self, and as such, are complex and challenging to diagnose and treat. In previous versions of the *Diagnostic and Statistical Manual*, these diagnoses were classified as Axis II diagnoses, indicating that they were different from the majority of the diagnoses contained within the *Diagnostic and Statistical Manual*. With the DSM-5, the use of axes was abandoned, but it is important to understand that personality disorders are unique in that they are stable, pervasive, and inflexible.

The DSM-5 identifies 10 specific personality disorders; the research suggests that those most commonly found among individuals who have experienced crisis and trauma are Borderline Personality Disorder (BPD), Obsessive Compulsive Personality Disorder (which should not be confused with Obsessive-Compulsive Disorder), and Antisocial Personality Disorder. Antisocial Personality Disorder is indicated by a pattern of disregard and violation of the rights of others. Obsessive-Compulsive Personality Disorder is a pervasive pattern of preoccupation with perfectionism, control, and order, and BPD is marked by instability in relationships, self-image, and affect, as well as significant impulsivity (APA, 2014).

One study used qualitative analysis to examine links between risk for personality disorders and previous experience of trauma (Gilbert, Farrand, & Lankshear, 2012). The researchers identified a number of themes that intersected between traumatic experience and traits related to personality disorders. Another study used qualitative analysis to examine the correlations between childhood trauma and the development of personality disorders (Berenz et al., 2013). The study found correlations between traumatic experience and Obsessive-Compulsive Personality Disorder, Antisocial Personality Disorder, and BPD. Other studies found quantitative links between traumatic experiences and the development of BPD (Carvalho Fernando et al., 2014; Masson, Bernoussi, Mience, & Thomas, 2013; Zhang, Chow, Wang, Dai, & Xiao, 2012).

Personality disorders are incredibly complex, and as the definition provided in the DSM-5 suggests, are ubiquitous as an element of the client's personality. The symptoms related to these diagnoses begin early in life and if untreated, can manifest in increasing significance. As such, treatment for these disorders is equally complex, and effectiveness is difficult to measure. For individuals struggling with these disorders, mood is often labile, behavior unpredictable, and consequences can be significant. For example, many individuals with Antisocial Personality Disorder may find themselves with legal challenges, and individuals struggling with BPD may find social supports difficult to maintain. Clinicians should be sure they are qualified and prepared to work with people who meet these diagnostic criteria and seek adequate supervision for the welfare of their client and themselves.

Somatic Symptom and Related Disorders

The DSM-5 also discusses disorders that are somatic in nature (APA, 2013). Somatic disorders are marked by physical manifestations of psychological trauma or preoccupation with physical symptoms that is incongruent with the severity or importance of those physical symptoms. For example, after a crisis incident, children may report stomach aches or headaches that cannot be explained through physiological evaluation. One study found that firefighters who experienced PTSD as a result of their work were more likely to experience symptoms related to cardiovascular, respiratory, gastrointestinal, neurological, and other physical functioning that could not be explained through physical examination (McFarlane, Atchison, Rafalowicz, & Papay, 1994).

Other studies have supported these findings. In a study of 161 foster children who had experienced abuse, 95% reported at least one somatic symptom, and 80% of their caregivers affirmed the children's reports (Kugler, Bloom, Kaercher, Truax, & Storch, 2012). Another study found correlations between somatic symptoms and exposure to violence among women (Eberhard-Gran, Schei, & Eskild, 2007). A different research study found significant somatic symptoms among children who had lived through floods in China; many of these children experienced symptoms such as sleep disturbances, low energy, stomach pain, and dizziness (Zhang, Zhang, Zhu, Du, & Zhang, 2015). Vieno et al. (2015) also found correlations between cyberbullying and somatic symptoms, such as headaches, stomach pains, and backaches.

Exercise 5.2 challenges you to consider how somatic symptoms may manifest after a crisis.

EXERCISE 5.2

CONSIDERING SOMATIC SYMPTOMS

Directions: The chapter has identified a few examples of somatic symptoms. Alone or with a partner, brainstorm as many examples of somatic symptoms as you can, considering which symptoms would be most likely to occur following the experience of a crisis. When you have completed the chapter, do some individual research to determine how many of the symptoms you developed are found in the literature related to post-crisis somatic experience.

Summary

- A diagnosis provides the beginning of a roadmap, and that map is critical in the development of a treatment plan that will effectively assist the client in overcoming challenges, enhancing coping skills, and in eventually meeting the goals of therapy.

- The diagnoses most often associated with the experience of crisis include: PTSD, Acute Stress Disorder, Reactive Attachment Disorder, Disinhibited Social Engagement Disorder, Adjustment Disorders, Anxiety Disorders, Depressive Disorders, Substance Abuse and Addictive Disorders, Personality Disorders, and Somatic Disorders.

- The main feature of PTSD is the experience, and re-experiencing of a traumatic event. The type of event can vary but include the exposure to death or threatened death, serious injury, or sexual violence. Symptoms of PTSD are varied but include avoidance of triggers of the traumatic event, intrusive thoughts or nightmares, negative cognitions or mood, and heightened arousal and reactivity.

- Acute Stress Disorder is similar to PTSD in etiology and symptomology but occurs prior to PTSD, between three days and one month after the event.

- Reactive Attachment Disorder is a childhood disorder that results when children have experienced trauma or neglect and, as a result, have difficulty making attachments to caregivers.

- Disinhibited Social Engagement Disorder also results from children experiencing trauma or neglect but results in opposite symptomology from Reactive Attachment Disorder; that is, children with this disorder will become overly attached to adults without just cause.

- Adjustment Disorders describe an array of behaviors (e.g., depression, anxiety, conduct issues, etc.) that are inconsistent with the severity of the stressor that initiated the behavior.

- Some individuals who experience a crisis will develop disorders related to anxiety (e.g., Generalized Anxiety Disorder, Panic Disorder, Specific or Social Phobias). Another possibility is that those in crisis may develop symptoms of depressive disorders (e.g., Major Depressive Disorder).

- As a means of ineffective coping after a crisis has occurred, some individuals will abuse alcohol or other drugs, which may become clinically significant if the behavior meets the criteria for a disorder related to substance use or addiction.

- Crisis events can sometimes result in the development of Personality Disorders. Personality Disorders are marked by a stable pattern of inner experience and behavior that is culturally inappropriate, pervasive, inflexible, stable, and causes distress. Common Personality Disorders that may result from traumatic experiences include BPD, Antisocial Personality Disorder, and Obsessive-Compulsive Personality Disorder.

- Finally, clients may experience somatic symptoms following a crisis event. Somatic Disorders are marked by physical manifestations of psychological trauma or preoccupation with physical symptoms that is incongruent with the severity or importance of those physical symptoms. Examples of somatic symptoms following a crisis may include unexplained headaches, stomachaches, backaches, and dizziness.

Important Terms

Acute Stress Disorder

Adjustment disorders

Antisocial Personality Disorder

Anxiety disorders

Borderline Personality Disorder

Co-occurring disorders

Diagnosis

Diagnostic and Statistical Manual of Mental Disorders

Disinhibited Social Engagement Disorder

Exaggerated startle response

Eye Movement Desensitization and Reprocessing (EMDR)

Hyperarousal

Major Depressive Disorder

Obsessive-Compulsive Disorder (OCD)

Obsessive-Compulsive Personality Disorder

Personality disorders

Post-Traumatic Stress Disorder (PTSD)

Reactive Attachment Disorder

Somatic symptom

Substance-related disorders

Symptom

Trauma-Focused Cognitive Behavioral Therapy (TF-CBT)

Additional Resources

In Print

American Psychological Association (2013). *Diagnostic and Statistical Manual of Mental Disorders (5th ed.).* Arlington, VA: Author.

Zubernis, L., & Snyder, M. (2016*). Case conceptualization and effective interventions: Assessing and treating mental, emotional, and behavioral disorders*. Thousand Oaks, CA: Sage.

On the Web

American Psychological Association DSM-5 website: www.dsm5.org

EMDR Institute: www.emdr.com

Trauma-Focused Cognitive Behavioral Therapy: https://tfcbt.musc.edu/

References

APA (American Psychological Association). (2013). *Diagnostic and Statistical Manual of Mental Disorders (5th ed.).* Arlington, VA: Author.

Ayazi, T., Lien, L., Eide, A., Swartz, L., & Hauff, E. (2014). Association between exposure to traumatic events and anxiety disorders in a post-conflict setting: A cross-sectional community study in South Sudan. *BMC Psychiatry, 14,* 1–22. doi:10.1186/1471–244X-14-6

Berenz, E. C., Amstadter, A. B., Aggen, S. H., Knudsen, G. P., Reichborn-Kjennerud, T., Gardner, C. O., & Kendler, K. S. (2013). Childhood trauma and personality disorder criterion counts: A co-twin control analysis. *Journal of Abnormal Psychology, 122,* 1070–1076. doi:10.1037/a0034238

Bisson, J. I., Ehlers, A., Matthews, R., Pilling, S., Richards, D., & Turner, S. (2007) Psychological treatments for chronic Post-Traumatic Stress Disorder: Systematic review and meta-analysis. *British Journal of Psychiatry, 190,* 97–104. doi: 10.1192/bjp.bp.106.021402.

Boyraz, G., Granda, R., Baker, C. N., Tidwell, L. L., & Waits, J. B. (2016). Posttraumatic stress, effort regulation, and academic outcomes among college students: A longitudinal study. *Journal of Counseling Psychology, 63,* 475–486. doi:10.1037/cou0000102

Carvalho Fernando, S., Beblo, T., Schlosser, N., Terfehr, K., Otte, C., Lowe, B., … Wingenfeld, K. (2014). The impact of self-reported childhood trauma on emotion regulation in borderline personality disorder and major depression. *Journal of Trauma & Dissociation, 15,* 384–401. doi:10.1080/15299732.2013.863262.x

Cohen, J.A., Mannarino, A. P., & Knudsen, K. (2005) Treating sexually abused children: 1 year follow-up of a randomized controlled trial. *Child Abuse & Neglect, 29,* 135–145. doi:10.1016/j.chiabu.2004.12.005

De Young, A. C., Haag, A., Kenardy, J. A., Kimble, R. M., & Landolt, M. A. (2016). Coping with Accident Reactions (CARE) early intervention programme for preventing traumatic stress reactions in young injured children: Study protocol for two randomised controlled trials. *Trials, 17,* 1–10. doi:10.1186/s13063-016-1490-2

Dore, G., Mills, K., Murray, R., Teesson, M., & Farrugia, P. (2012). Post-traumatic stress disorder, depression and suicidality in inpatients with substance use disorders. *Drug & Alcohol Review, 31,* 294–302. doi:10.1111/j.1465-3362.2011.00314.x

Eberhard-Gran, M., Schei, B., & Eskild, A. (2007). Somatic symptoms and diseases are more common in women exposed to violence. *Journal of General Internal Medicine, 22,* 1668–1673. doi:10.1007/s11606-007-0389-8

Foa, E. B., Keane, T. M., Friedman, M. J., & Cohen, J. A. (2008). *Effective treatments for PTSD: Practice guidelines from the International Society for Traumatic Stress Studies (2nd ed.).* New York, NY: Guilford Press.

Fowler, J. C., Allen, J. G., Oldham, J. M., & Frueh, B. C. (2013). Exposure to interpersonal trauma, attachment insecurity, and depression severity. *Journal of Affective Disorders, 149,* 313–318. doi:10.1016/j.jad.2013.01.045

Ghafoori, B., Neria, Y., Gameroff, M. J., Olfson, M., Lantigua, R., Shea, S., & Weissman, M. M. (2009). Screening for generalized anxiety disorder symptoms in the wake of terrorist attacks: A study in primary care. *Journal of Traumatic Stress, 22,* 218–226. doi:10.1002/jts.20419

Gilbert, T., Farrand, P., & Lankshear, G. (2012). Troubled lives: Chaos and trauma in the accounts of young people considered 'at risk' of diagnosis of personality disorder. *Scandinavian Journal of Caring Sciences, 26,* 747–754. doi:10.1111/j.1471-6712.2012.00991.x

Hall, S. E. K., & Geher, G. (2003). Behavioral and personality characteristics of children with Reactive Attachment Disorder. *The Journal of Psychology, 137,* 145–162. doi: 10.1080/00223980309600605

Hanson, R. F., & Spratt, E. G. (2000). Reactive Attachment Disorder: What we know about the disorder and implications for treatment. *Child Maltreatment, 5,* 137–145. doi: 10.1177/1077559500005002005

Kay, C. & Green, J. (2013). Reactive Attachment Disorder following early maltreatment: Systematic evidence beyond the institution. *Journal of Abnormal Child Psychology, 41,* 571–581. doi: 10.1007/s10802-012-9705-9

Kugler, B., Bloom, M., Kaercher, L., Truax, T., & Storch, E. (2012). Somatic symptoms in traumatized children and adolescents. *Child Psychiatry & Human Development, 43,* 661–673. doi:10.1007/s10578-012-0289-y

Kukihara, H., Yamawaki, N., Uchiyama, K., Arai, S., & Horikawa, E. (2014). Trauma, depression, and resilience of earthquake/tsunami/nuclear disaster survivors of Hirono, Fukushima, Japan. *Psychiatry and Clinical Neurosciences, 68,* 524–533. doi:10.1111/pcn.12159

McFarlane, A. C., Atchison, M., Rafalowicz, E., & Papay, P. (1994). Physical symptoms in Post-Traumatic Stress Disorder. *Journal of Psychosomatic research, 38,* 715–726.

Masson, J., Bernoussi, A., Mience, M. C., & Thomas, F. (2013). Complex trauma and borderline personality disorder. *Open Journal of Psychiatry, 3,* 403–407. doi:10.4236/ojpsych.2013.34044

Morris, M. C., Kouros, C. D., Fox, K. R., Rao, U., & Garber, J. (2014). Interactive models of depression vulnerability: The role of childhood trauma, dysfunctional attitudes, and coping. *British Journal of Clinical Psychology, 53,* 245–263. doi:10.1111/bjc.12038

Negele, A., Kaufhold, J., Kallenbach, L., & Leuzinger-Bohleber, M. (2015). Childhood trauma and its relation to chronic depression in adulthood. *Depression Research & Treatment, 2015,* 1–11. doi:10.1155/2015/650804

Sacks, J. Y., McKendrick, K., & Banks, S. (2008). The impact of early trauma and abuse on residential substance abuse treatment outcomes for women. *Journal of substance abuse treatment, 34,* 90–100.

Schwarzer, R., Cone, J. E., Jiehui, L., & Bowler, R. M. (2016). A PTSD symptoms trajectory mediates between exposure levels and emotional support in police responders to 9/11: a growth curve analysis. *BMC Psychiatry*, *16*, 1–7. doi:10.1186/s12888-016-0907-5

Simon, N. M., Herlands, N. N., Marks, E. H., Mancini, C., Letamendi, A., Zhonghe, L., … Stein, M. B. (2009). Childhood maltreatment linked to greater symptom severity and poorer quality of life and function in social anxiety disorder. *Depression & Anxiety (1091–4269)*, *26*, 1027–1032. doi:10.1002/da.20604

Sinclair, V. G., Wallston, K. A., & Strachan, E. (2016). Resilient coping moderates the effect of trauma exposure on depression. *Research in Nursing & Health*, *39*, 244–252. doi:10.1002/nur.21723

Stein, D. J., Karam, E. G., Shahly, V., Hill, E. D., King, A., Petukhova, M., & … Kessler, R. C. (2016). Post-traumatic stress disorder associated with life-threatening motor vehicle collisions in the WHO World Mental Health Surveys. *BMC Psychiatry*, *16*, 1–14. doi:10.1186/s12888-016-0957-8

Vares, E. A., Salum, G. A., Spanemberg, L., Caldieraro, M. A., Souza, L. d., Borges, R. P., & Fleck, M. P. (2015). Childhood trauma and dimensions of depression: A specific association with the cognitive domain. *Revista Brasileira De Psiquiatria*, *38*, 127–134. doi:10.1590/1516-4446-2015-1764

Vieno, A., Gini, G., Lenzi, M., Pozzoli, T., Canale, N., & Santinello, M. (2015). Cybervictimization and somatic and psychological symptoms among Italian middle school students. *European Journal of Public Health*, *25*, 433–437. doi:10.1093/eurpub/cku191

Vlahov, D., Galea, S., Ahern, J., Rudenstine, S., Resnick, H., Kilpatrick, D., & Crum, R. (2006). Alcohol drinking problems among New York City residents after the September 11 terrorist attacks. *Substance Use & Misuse, 41,* 1295–1311. doi:10.1080/10826080600754900

Wenjie, D., Long, C., Zhiwei, L., Yan, L., Jieru, W., & Aizhong, L. (2016). The incidence of post-traumatic stress disorder among survivors after earthquakes: A systematic review and meta-analysis. *BMC Psychiatry*, *16*, 1–11. doi:10.1186/s12888-016-0891-9

Wood, Salguero, Cano-Vindel, & Galea, S. (2013). Perievent panic attacks and panic disorder after mass trauma: A 12-month longitudinal study. *Journal of Traumatic Stress*, *26*, 338–344. doi:10.1002/jts.21810

Zhang, T., Chow, A., Wang, L., Dai, Y., & Xiao, Z. (2012). Role of childhood traumatic experience in personality disorders in China. *Comprehensive psychiatry*, *53*, 829–836.

Zhang, Y., Zhang, J., Zhu, S., Du, C., & Zhang, W. (2015). Prevalence and predictors of somatic symptoms among child and adolescents with probable Posttraumatic Stress Disorder: A cross-sectional study conducted in 21 primary and secondary schools after an earthquake. *Plos ONE*, *10*, 1–14. doi:10.1371/journal.pone.0137101

Zubernis, L., & Snyder, M. (2016). *Case conceptualization and effective interventions: Assessing and treating mental, emotional, and behavioral disorders*. Thousand Oaks, CA: Sage.

The Many Faces of Crisis

CHAPTER 6

Crisis: Individual or Family System

There is a me that was before ... and now there is a me that is after ... I will never be the same nor ever feel that same sense of peace of mind, of safety ... of certainty that once was.

T he sentiment, spoken by a 31-year-old sexual assault survivor, reflects the experience of many who have survived sexual and non-sexual traumas. The reflection speaks to the hope of survival and highlights the reality of the traumatic short-term and longer-term life changes that often result.

The following chapter reviews the nature and experience of the crisis and trauma experienced as result of: sexual assault, violence at the hands of an intimate partner or family member, and individual disasters. After reading this chapter, you should be able to:

1. Define sexual assault, intimate partner violence (IPV), and personal disaster.

2. Explain the immediate and longer-term impact of sexual assault, IPV, and personal disaster of the survivor of each.

3. Describe the goals and approaches employed by those working as both crisis interventionist and longer-term therapist to survivors of sexual assault, IPV, and personal disaster.

Sexual Assault

Sexual assault is not restricted to forced sexual contact with someone who does not or cannot consent (i.e., rape) but includes all non-consensual sexual contact, including attempted rape and behavior such as groping and any unwanted sexual touching. Exercise 6.1 invites you to reflect on data that may reveal the subtle yet damaging impact of sexual assault.

The trauma experienced by a sexual assault survivor includes disruptions to normal physical, emotional, cognitive, and interpersonal behavior.

Survivors of sexual violence will react in their own ways as a reflection of their personal style, culture, and context in which the assault was experienced. With this as a caveat, Table 6.1 provides a description of some of the more commonly reported reactions to sexual assault.

EXERCISE 6.1

SEXUAL ASSAULT? INTIMATE PARTNER VIOLENCE?

Directions: Below you will find a scenario in which you are asked to imagine yourself as the initial counseling contact for the person portrayed. The circumstances are complex and can arouse many feelings, not just in the survivor, but in the mental health care worker, as well. Your task is to discuss your reaction to the questions posed at the end of the scenario with a colleague, classmate, or supervisor.

Scenario: As an intern in an outpatient community mental health center, you are called to an interview room to meet with a young (22-year-old) woman who was a walk-in client.

In meeting with her, you find that she is in a relationship in which she "desperately loves" the man that she is with but has experienced, in her words, "violent love making." Her goal for coming to the center is to find ways that she can ask the man to "be more gentle."

As you continue to listen to the unfolding story you find that the "violent" love making to which she refers includes verbal abuse, biting (to cause blood), hair pulling, and at times, choking. She continues to explain that she really wants him to stop these behaviors and has tried to ask but to no avail. She reiterated that he is a "the love of her life" and that while this "love making" has increased in physical intensity, she doesn't feel that he is abusive or violent, just "too excitable."

Reflection:

1. What are your feelings about the "non-abusive," "non-violent," and just "too excitable" nature of the sexual acts the client has described? Does it qualify as sexual abuse?

2. Is there anything in the story which may lead you to conclude that there is intimate partner violence occurring?

3. What would your initial goal(s) be in working with this woman?

4. As you imagine the story unfolding, what feelings might you have for the client? Her lover? The relationship? How might these influence your interactions?

Table 6.1 Common Physical, Psychological, and Emotional Reactions to Sexual Assault

Physical	Behavioral	Psychological	Emotional
• Immediately after a rape, survivors often experience shock. They are likely to feel cold, faint, become mentally confused (disorientated), tremble, feel nauseous and sometimes vomit • Increased startle response • Gynecological problems. Irregular, heavier and/or painful periods. Vaginal discharges, bladder infections. Sexually transmitted diseases	• Eating disturbances. This may be not eating or eating less or needing to eat more than usual • Sleep disturbances. This may be difficulty in sleeping or feeling exhausted and needing to sleep more than usual • Substance use/abuse • Not wanting to socialize or socializing more than usual, so as to fill up every minute of the day • Relationship problems, with family, friends, lovers, and spouses • Suicide attempts and other self-destructive behavior such as substance abuse or self-mutilation	• Nightmares • Flashbacks • Depression • Difficulty concentrating • Post-Traumatic Stress Disorder (PTSD) • Concerns about physical safety • Being very alert and watchful • Lack of control • Numbness	• Guilt, shame, self-blame • Embarrassment • Fear, distrust • Anxiety • Sadness • Vulnerability • Isolation • Anger

Stages of Recovery

Those who have experienced sexual assault report intense physical and emotional reactions during and immediately following the assault and, for most, for considerable time thereafter. The specific road to recovery will vary in form and duration from individual to individual. Attempting to detail a person's reaction to being sexually assaulted is difficult given the fact that individuals vary along many critical pre-abuse dimensions, the nature of the sexual assault, and the presence of cotemporaneous and culturally mediating variables.

However, with the above as a caveat, one pattern of responses that has been presented as a model is the Rape Trauma Syndrome (Burgess & Holmstrom, 1974, 1979). This has been regularly cited and employed as a vehicle for understanding the recovery pattern exhibited by many who have been survivors of sexual assault. It should be noted that, since their original presentation, the Rape Trauma Syndrome has been criticized within the scientific community (e.g., O'Donohue Carlson, Benuto, & Bennett, 2014). It is important to note that our use of it here is not a support of the suggested "syndrome," but rather as an organizational vehicle to describe the road traveled by many recovering from sexual assault. Burgess and Holmstrom (1974, 1979) suggested that those experiencing the trauma of rape proceed through three stages toward recovery: the acute stage, the outward adjustment stage, and the renormalization stage.

The Acute Phase

During the first days following an assault, the individual may be shocked, dazed, stunned, and experience a sense of numbness. Some may actively try to block out the experience and associated feelings, but with time, suppression will be difficult, and distress will increase.

During this *Acute Phase*, the individual may experience fears about personal safety, experience intrusive thoughts and flashbacks, and have anxiety and mood swings. There may be feelings of guilt, self-blame, shame, and anger. There may be such a flood of symptoms that the individual may feel out of control and as if he or she were "losing it" (see Case Illustration 6.1).

While there is no single pattern in response to rape, the U.S. Rape Abuse and Incest National Network (RAINN) asserts that rape victims in the acute phase will often respond in one of three ways: *expressed*, where the individual appears agitated, anxious, and emotional; *controlled,* where the survivor presents with little emotion acting as if all is fine, or; *shocked/disbelief*, where the survivor appears disoriented, unable to concentrate, make decisions, or function (RAINN, n.d.).

The Outward Adjustment Phase

The second "phase" in recovery has been called the Outward Adjustment Phase. The survivor will most likely attempt to resume much of her/his "normal life" while, at the same time, experiencing internal turmoil. The individual may experience pervasive feelings of fear specific to the circumstances of the assault, such as fear of being alone.

The individual may attempt to adjust throughout this phase by use of minimizations ("everything's okay"), dramatization (obsessively talking about the incident), suppression (refusal to discuss), explanation (analyzing everything that happened), and flight (makes changes to self, job, lifestyle,

---

CASE ILLUSTRATION 6.1

AMELIA: CONFLICT ABOUT SEXUAL ASSAULT

Amelia is a 38-year-old computer programmer who experienced sexual assault by her manager following an office party. While initially attempting to forget the event as a "misunderstanding" and even questioning her own "participation" in the sexual advances, the continued sexual harassment by her manager made life unbearable.

Following the attack, the manager continued to grab and touch her inappropriately, send her lewd emails, and threaten to disclose photos that he had taken of her at the time of the assault. The pressure grew until she felt the need to consult with a co-worker who informed her that she was "pretty drunk that night" and that it might be best just to move on.

With this lack of support and fear that any disclosure may result in her dismissal, Amelia decided to "move on," but moving on was not possible. Within weeks of the event, she began to experience symptoms, including anxiety, hypervigilance, and insomnia. She began to withdrawal from her friends and social contact and showed clear signs of anxiety (i.e., trembling) when in a closed space with any male co-worker. With each passing day, her own guilt and sense of self-loathing increased and, with it, her use of alcohol as a self-medication.

The lack of sleep and experience of constant stress and anxiety resulted in her reaching out to a general practitioner for medication. It was during that meeting that she disclosed the details of the event and the impact that it was having on her. She shared her anxiety about "coming out," feeling that no one would believe her and that she would be forced to leave a job that she loved. With the physician's support, she connected with a therapist who helped her process the event and make decisions that would restabilize her life.

etc.). Throughout this phase, the victim may still experience many of the symptoms previously encountered, including continuing anxiety, moods swings, rage, depression, difficulty sleeping, adjusting lifestyles, etc.

The Renormalization Stage

It is at this point that the survivor begins to engage in adjustment. During the *Renormalization Phase*, the individual will transition from being a "victim" to being a "survivor." In this process, the individual will gain a sense of control over their own life, resolving feelings of shame or guilt, and integrate the experience into their life. With the attack deposed from its position as central focus in the individual's life, the survivor will typically develop strategies for engaging socially and occupationally. The most common long-term problems are fears about personal safety and intrusive recollections of the experience. These will become less frequent, and the survivor will find a new way to be in, and engage with, the world.

Intervention

Recovery from sexual assault is a slow process which does not come easily nor without challenges. The survivor must be heard, feel they are understood and believed, and find the ability to reconnect to a community. Recovery takes time. The survivor sets the pace.

In general, behavioral and cognitive treatments have been found to be effective in reducing symptoms associated with sexual assault. This is not to suggest that other treatments are ineffective. However, meta-analytic studies evaluating efficacy have supported interventions that are cognitive and behavioral in orientation (see Regehr et al., 2013; Taylor & Harvey, 2009).

Most treatments include goals such as: (1) preventing and reducing Post-Traumatic Stress Disorder (PTSD)/trauma symptoms and (2) improving social adjustment and self-esteem. In most modalities of psychotherapeutic treatment, therapists focus more on the current situation and its solution, concentrating on a person's views and beliefs about life. Typically, therapists attempt to help survivors make sense of their memories and reduce or eliminate PTSD symptoms, including: thoughts, flashbacks, guilt, and fears associated with the survivor's response to the assault. Furthermore, many teach sexual assault victims additional skills, including anger management, assertiveness, and communication.

Intimate Partner Violence

Intimate Partner Violence (IPV), which is the ongoing pattern of coercive control maintained through physical, psychological, sexual, and/or economic abuse, is a widespread and devastating phenomenon. Millions of women are assaulted by intimate partners and ex-partners (Black, 2011). Over one in five women (22.3%) and nearly one in seven men (14.0%) have experienced severe physical violence by an intimate partner at some point in their lifetimes. This translates to nearly 29 million United States women and almost 16 million United States men experiencing such intimate violence (Breiding et al., 2014).

In addition to the immediate impact, IPV has lifelong consequences. Black (2011) found that beyond injury and death, victims of IPV are more likely to report a range of negative mental and physical health outcomes that are both acute and chronic in nature. IPV is a form of trauma that can result in significant mental health distress for survivors. Rates of clinical depression and PTSD are higher among abused women versus non-abused women, particularly if survivors have experienced other lifetime trauma (Warshaw & Sullivan, 2013).

Ongoing abuse and violence can induce feelings of shock, disbelief, confusion, terror, isolation, and despair and can undermine a person's sense of self. These, in turn, can manifest as psychological symptoms (e.g., reliving the traumatic event, hyperarousal, avoiding reminders of the trauma, depression, anxiety, and sleep disruption). For those who have experienced multiple forms of victimization (e.g., childhood abuse; sexual assault; historical, cultural, or refugee trauma), adult partner abuse puts them at greater risk for developing post-traumatic mental health conditions, including depression, anxiety, and substance abuse (Warshaw, Brashler & Gill, 2009).

It is not unusual for those unfamiliar with the complexity of intimate partner violence to simply question why the survivor did not leave. The factors associated with the experience—including a false sense of hope, personal shame, and feelings of responsibility, to concerns about children, money, and family—often make the decision to seek help difficult.

CASE ILLUSTRATION 6.2

MALIKA: WHY DID YOU STAY?

As with many who have found themselves in an abusive and violent relationship, Malika's story starts out pretty innocuously. In the beginning, her husband was often verbally critical of things such as her cooking or house cleaning or even her hairstyle or choice of dress; the criticism was mild and infrequent. Sadly, as is often the case, the verbal criticism escalated with emphasis on personal attacks, and these were often accompanied by physical contact, such as pushing or poking.

Over a period of some 18 years, the verbal assaults increased in frequency, as did the physical contact. While never struck, on multiple occasions she was shaken and thrown to the ground and had numerous household items thrown at her.

She had considered and threatened to leave on more than one occasion, but the threats were never carried out. When asked, "Why didn't you just leave?" she noted, "the one thing that stopped me was my concern for my two boys. I wasn't sure that I would get custody if I left, and even if I did, I wasn't sure that I could support them." Beyond the practical concerns of finance and living arrangements, Malika also shared concerns about her own perceived involvement in the abuse and the hope that things would change. "There were times when he was really kind and loving—so I wondered what it was that I was doing to make him flip out. Also, and I know now how stupid this is ... I really believed he would change. After all, in between the abuse, we had a somewhat normal relationship."

The complexity of the experience and the confusion often felt by the "victim" is illustrated in Case Illustration 6.2.

Intervention

Treatment models focus on empowerment by way of strength-based interventions. The intent is to reframe the individual as survivor rather than victim (Warshaw & Sullivan, 2013). A special challenge occurs when those experiencing IPV continue to engage in the abusive relationship, because of fears of repercussion should they leave, or concerns for children.

There is not much research supporting efficacy of specific treatment modalities when addressing complex trauma such as that found in experiences of longstanding intimate violence. However, two specific approaches: Cognitive Trauma Therapy for Battered Women (Kubany et al., 2003) and, HOPE: Helping to Overcome PTSD through Empowerment (Johnson et al., 2011) have some degrees of proven effectiveness.

Cognitive Trauma Therapy for Battered Women (CTT-BW) includes modalities such as PTSD psychoeducation, incorporation of stress management techniques, and some elements of exposure therapy (Kubany et al., 2003, 2004). What makes CTT-BW unique is that it also includes elements that address specific concerns related to this type of abuse. Those elements include: (1) guilt specific to this form of trauma (e.g. guilt regarding divorce, choices to stay in the household, impact on children, etc.); (2) previous trauma history; (3) the stress of a continued relationship with the abuser as a result of co-parenting; and (4) increased risk for repeated traumatization.

The second intervention approach, *Helping to Overcome PTSD through Empowerment (HOPE)* provides sessions two times each week over an eight week period (Johnson et al., 2011). The purpose of these sessions is based on Herman's (1992) work on recovering from trauma and includes: (1) re-establishing safety and self-care, (2) remembering and mourning, and (3) reconnection. The safety and self-care element is built though a strong therapeutic alliance, focus on stress management, and emotional regulation (Classen, Pain, Field, & Woods, 2006). The remembering and mourning phase allows the survivor to reframe the experience and refocus energy away from the trauma in the past, with a new focus on the present and future (Courtois, 2008). The reconnection phase provides the survivor with an opportunity to create new meaning and purpose in life, meaning that is disconnected from the trauma of the past.

While CTT-BW and HOPE both have data to support their effectiveness, additional studies would serve to strengthen the empirical support of these approaches. This empirical support is especially important in cases where the survivor is still being actively abused, or is at high risk for re-traumatization.

Personal Disaster

For some, the experience of crisis and trauma comes at the hands of a natural or human-caused catastrophe. Events such as hurricanes, earthquakes, fires, floods, and explosions will affect lives and property and can impact individuals, families or even communities. The term *personal disaster* is often used to describe an individual's experience of horror in response to these events and others, such as traffic accidents, assaults, loss of property etc. (Raphael, 1981).

It's important to remember that each survivor is unique and that their personal history, as well as psychological strengths or deficits, will influence their response to a given disaster. For example, Norwood et al. (2000) found that event factors, such as physical and emotional proximity to the disaster, contribute to one's crisis response to said disaster. Thus, while one can be traumatized by watching an event unfold on television, such as the terrorist attacks of September 11, 2001, the impact is magnified as one becomes physically engulfed by the crisis or has a loved one who is a victim of that disaster. Other individual factors can contribute to the nature and severity of one's crisis, such as: genetic vulnerabilities and capacities, prior history of a constant stress or exposure to past disasters, history or presence of a psychiatric disorder, health issues or psychopathology within the family, the presence or absence of family and social support structures, and the age and developmental level of the individual.

Signs of Trauma-Related Distress

An individual's response is a reflection of many factors, including one's physical and emotional proximity to the event, biological stress defense, past learning and adaptation to similar situations, the presence of social support, the possibility of separation or loss from loved ones, and the degree and type of system disruption or chaos surrounding the event (Norwood et al., 2000).

Most people experience some signs or symptoms of trauma-related stress after natural or personal disasters. As noted in Chapter 2, those

---

CASE ILLUSTRATION 6.3

ONE PERSON'S STORY OF IMMEDIATE AND LONG-TERM IMPACT OF KATRINA

Diane's story starts with Hurricane Katrina making landfall in Louisiana on August 29, 2005, leaving 1,826 dead. She fled her home in New Orleans prior to Katrina making landfall and watched, in "paralyzed horror," as the events unfold on the television. When she did return, she found the city destroyed and her own neighborhood deserted. Houses, trees, cars, and boats were thrown about as if toys discarded by a giant. Her own house, sans roof, was coated with mold.

Even though not physically present during the height of the storm, the impact of viewing both the destruction and the aftermath was significant. The shock she initially experienced wore off after about six months, and it was replaced by a sense of numbness, as if she were "dead, like a plug disconnected from a socket." She felt disconnected, at times enraged, and often anxious. Her sleep was disrupted, and her dreams brought images of the flooded and destroyed city. She reported feeling "as if ... I was dead, suspended in a kind of posthumous existence in which everything appeared to be real but was a hallucination."

The trauma was severe, and while she reported getting better over several years, she noted that "there would be relapses."

EXERCISE 6.2

RESPONDING AT THE TIME OF A DISASTER

Directions: While you have most likely lived (either directly or vicariously) through major human-caused disasters such as the terrorist attacks of September 11, 2001, or natural disasters, such as Hurricane Katrina, there are other more personal disasters that one may encounter including: house fires, car accidents, or maritime or aircraft accidents. For those who have encountered such a personal disaster, working with others in similar situations may elicit memories, images, and emotional responses. It is suggested you discuss the following with a colleague or supervisor.

Reflection:

If you imagined yourself in the role of first responder at a time of personal disaster, what type of situation (human-caused or natural disaster) do you feel may cause you a personal-emotional challenge?

As you envision yourself working with an individual immediately following the experience of personal disaster, what professional issue(s) or concern(s) would you set as a priority?

In providing Psychological First Aid to a victim of a personal disaster, what approach would you employ in order to connect and create a working alliance?

exhibiting a traumatic response following the personal experience with a disaster will experience a neuro-physiological dysregulation that renders the usual cognitive and behavioral responses less effective than normal. The victim of a personal disaster may experience difficulty breathing, feelings of terror or panic, feelings of being out of control and helpless, and even sensations as if one's heart is about to burst. Data from those who have intervened at times of major disasters suggest that victims of disasters often show symptoms of anger, depression, despair, generalized distress, hyperarousal, and PTSD that dissipate over time (Perilla, Norris, & Lavizzo, 2002). The immediate and long-term impact of personal disaster was vividly portrayed in an article by Susannah Breslin "After Hurricane Katrina, Years of Post-Traumatic Stress" (Breslin, 2011) (see Illustration 6.3).

For most victims, the initial reactions of shock, surprise, anger, helplessness, and confusion will subside over time (Bonanno, Westphal, & Mancini, 2011; Norris, Tracy, & Galea, 2009). However, epidemiological evidence clearly shows that substantial numbers of people suffer from serious mental health problems in the wake of disasters (Crabtree, 2012, 2013). For some, a more serious response in the form of Acute Stress Disorder or PTSD can appear immediately after the disaster or up to four weeks after a traumatic event. Such a condition requires the meeting of specific diagnostic criteria and individualized therapeutic intervention (see Chapter Five).

The impact of trauma can leave an indelible mark on one's psyche. This is true even for those caretakers who themselves have experienced personal trauma and are now called to serve and support others in crisis. Exercise 6.2, Responding at the Time of a Disaster, invites you to reflect on your own experience and the potential impact on your ability to support others in need.

Intervention

Most survivors in the emergency and early post-impact phase of a disaster exhibit mild to moderate stress reactions, which are most often proportional and functional given the danger in the disaster. For most individuals, recovery from even moderate stress occurs within 6 to 16 months of the event (Raphael & Newman, 2000).

As with other forms of trauma and crisis intervention, there is no one approach to intervention that has proven effective for all individuals experiencing personal disaster. Circumstances mandate a short, flexible, creative, adaptable approach compared to the usual organized, systematic, clinical approach (Cohen, 2002). While there is no one single therapeutic approach to post-disaster crisis counseling, the most commonly held goal for post-disaster crisis counseling is to restore the individual's capacity to cope with the conditions in which they find themselves. Specifically, most agree that post-disaster crisis counseling should target: a) restoring capacity of the individuals; b) reordering and organizing their new world; and c) helping the victims to deal with the bureaucratic relief emergency program (Cohen R., 2000). The focus of the interventions moves from psychological first aid through triage to recovery. For more information on the various stages of recovery from disasters, see Chapter Seven.

Summary

- Sexual assault includes all non-consensual sexual contact including attempted rape and behavior such as groping and any unwanted sexual touching.

- During the first days following a sexual assault, the individual may feel in shock, dazed, stunned, and a sense of numbness.

- The individual may experience pervasive feelings of fear specific to the circumstances of the assault, such as fear of being alone.

- During the renormalization phase, the individual will transition from being a "victim" to being a "survivor." In this process, the individual will gain a sense of control over his/her own life.

- Most treatments for survivors of sexual assault include goals such as: (1) preventing and reducing PTSD/trauma symptoms and (2) improving social adjustment and self-esteem.

- IPV is the ongoing pattern of coercive control maintained through physical, psychological, sexual, and/or economic abuse.

- Survivors of IPV are more likely to report a range of negative mental and physical health outcomes that are both acute and chronic in nature.

- Treatment models employed are typically strengths-based and empowerment-focused, viewing individuals as survivors, rather than as victims, and promoting therapeutic collaboration and choice.
- Two specific approaches (i.e., Cognitive Trauma Therapy for Battered Women (Kubany, Hill, & Owens, 2003) and, HOPE: Helping to Overcome PTSD through Empowerment (Johnson, Zlotnick, & Perez, 2011)) have found research support for their effectiveness.
- The term "personal disaster" is often used to describe an individual's experience of horror to these events and others, such as traffic accidents, assaults, loss of property, etc.
- While for most, the initial reactions of shock, surprise, anger, helplessness, and confusion that characterize feelings and behaviors will subside over time, epidemiological evidence clearly shows that a substantial number of people suffer from serious mental health problems in the wake of disasters.
- There is no one approach to intervention that has proven effective for all individuals experiencing personal disaster. The reality circumstances mandate a short, flexible, creative, adaptable approach, compared to the usual organized, systematic clinical approach.

Important Terms

Acute stage

Cognitive Trauma Therapy for Battered Women (CTT-BW)

HOPE: Helping to Overcome PTSD through Empowerment

Intimate Partner Violence (IPV)

Outer adjustment stage

Personal disaster

Renormalization stage

Post-Traumatic Stress Disorder (PTSD)/trauma symptoms

Psychological First Aid (PFA)

Sexual assault

Strengths-based and empowerment-focused intervention

The Rape Trauma Syndrome

Additional Resources

In print

Domestic Abuse Intervention Project (2002). *A guide for conducting domestic violence assessments*. Duluth, MN: Author.

Dass-Brailsford, P. (Ed.) (2010). *Crisis and disaster counseling: Lessons learned from Hurricane Katrina and other disasters*. Los Angeles, CA: Sage.

Hilton, N. Z., Harris, G. T., & Rice, M. E. (2010). *Risk assessment for domestically violent men*. Washington, D.C.: American Psychological Association.

On the Web

APA (American Psychological Association), Reclaiming hope in a changed world: www.apa.org/pubs/videos

Domestic Abuse Intervention Project, Power & control: A woman's perspective: www.theduluthmodel.org

Domestic Abuse Intervention Project, Power & control: The tactics of men who batter: www.theduluthmodel.org

The Domestic Violence Initiative for Women with Disabilities. www.dviforwomen.org

Rape, Abuse, & Incest National Network (RAINN): www.rainn.org

References

Black, M. C. (2011). Intimate partner violence and adverse health consequences: Implications for clinicians. *American Journal of Lifestyle Medicine*, 5, 428–439.

Bonanno, G. A., Westphal, M., & Mancini, A. D. (2011). Resilience to loss and potential trauma. *Annual Review of Clinical Psychology*, 7, 511–535.

Breiding, M. J., Smith S. G., Basile K. C., Walters M. L., Chen, J., & Merrick M. T. (2014). Prevalence and characteristics of sexual violence, stalking, and intimate partner violence victimization in the United States—National Intimate Partner and Sexual Violence Survey, United States, 2011. *MMWR*, 63(No. SS-8), 1–18.

Breslin, S. (2011). After hurricane Katrina, Years of Post-Traumatic Stress. *The Atlantic*. Retrieved July 2016 from http://www.theatlantic.com/national/archive/2011/08/after-hurricane-katrina-years-of-post-traumatic-stress/244029/

Burgess, A. W., Holmström, L. L. (1974). Rape Trauma Syndrome. *American Journal of Psychiatry*, 131(9), 981–986.

Burgess, A.W., & Holmstrom, L.L. (1979). Adaptive strategies and recovery from rape, *American Journal of Psychiatry*, 36(10), 1278–1282.

Classen, C. C., Pain, C., Field, N. P., & Woods, P. (2006). Posttraumatic personality disorder: A reformulation of complex posttraumatic stress disorder and borderline personality disorder. *Psychiatric Clinics of North America*, 29(1), 87–112.

Cohen, R. E. (2002). Mental health services for victims of disasters. *World Psychiatry*, *1*(3), 149–152.

Cohen R. (2000). Mental health services in disasters. Workers and instructor's guide. Washington, DC: Pan American Health Organization.

Courtois, C. A. (2008). Complex trauma, complex reactions: Assessment and treatment. *Psychological Trauma: Theory, Research, Practice, and Policy, 8*(1), 86–100.

Crabtree, A. (2013). Questioning psychosocial resilience after flooding and the consequences for disaster risk reduction. *Social Indicators Research, 113*, 711-728.

Crabtree, A. (2012). Climate change and mental health following flood disasters in developing countries, A review of the epidemiological literature: What do we know, what is being recommended? *The Australasian Journal of Disaster and Trauma Studies, 1*, 21–29.

Herman, J. L. (1992). *Trauma and Recovery*. New York, NY: Basic Books.

Johnson, D. M., Zlotnick, C., & Perez, S. (2011). Cognitive behavioral treatment of PTSD in residents of battered women's shelters: Results of a randomized clinical trial. *Journal of Consulting and Clinical Psychology, 79*(4), 542–551.

Kubany, E. S., Hill, E. E., & Owens, J. A. (2003). Cognitive trauma therapy for battered women with PTSD: Preliminary findings. *Journal of Traumatic Stress, 16*(1), 81–91.

Kubany, E. S., Hill, E. E., Owens, J. A., Iannce-Spencer, C., McCaig, M. A., Tremayne, K. J., Williams, P.L.(2004). Cognitive trauma therapy for battered women with PTSD (CTT-BW). *Journal of Consulting and Clinical Psychology, 72*(1), 3–18.

Norris, F. H., Tracy, M., & Galea, S. (2009). Looking for resilience: Understanding the longitudinal trajectories of responses to stress. *Social Science and Medicine, 68*, 2190–2198.

Norwood A. E., Orsano, R. J, & Fullerton, C. S., (2000). Disaster Psychiatry: Principles and Practice, *Psychiatric Quarterly, 71*(3), 207–226.

O'Donohue, W., Carlson, G.C., Benuto, L.T. & Bennett, N.M. (2014). Examining the scientific validity of rape trauma syndrome. *Psychiatry, Psychology and Law, 21*(6), 858–876.

Perilla, J. L., Norris, F. H., & Lavizzo, E. A. (2002). Ethnicity, culture and disaster response: Identifying and explaining ethnic differences in PTSD six months after Hurricane Andrew. *Journal of Social and Clinical Psychology, 22*(1), 20–45

RAINN. (n.d.). *After sexual assault.* Retrieved from www.RAINN.org

Raphael, B. (1981) Personal Disaster. *Australian and New Zealand Journal of Psychiatry, 15*, 183–198.

Raphael, B., & Newman, L. (Ed.) (2000). *Disaster Mental Health Response Handbook. Disaster Mental Health Response Handbook.* Centre for Mental Health, 1–170. Retrieved July 2016 from http://faculty.uml.edu/darcus/47.474/nswiop_Disaster_Handbook.pdf

Regehr, C., Alaggia, R., Dennis, J., Pitts, A., & Saini, M., (2013). Interventions to reduce distress in adult victims of sexual violence and rape: A systematic review. *Campbell Systematic Reviews, 3.*

Taylor, J. E., & Harvey, S. T. (2009). Effects of Psychotherapies with people who have been sexually assaulted: A meta-analysis. *Aggression and Violent Behavior, 14*, 273–85.

Warshaw, C., Brashler, P., and Gill, J. (2009). Mental health consequences of intimate partner violence. In C. Mitchell and D. Anglin (Eds.), *Intimate partner violence: A health based perspective.* New York, NY: Oxford University Press.

Warshaw, C., & Sullivan, C. M. (2013). A systematic review of trauma-focused interventions for domestic violence survivors. *National Center on Domestic Violence, Trauma & Mental Health.* Retrieved June 2016 from http://www.nationalcenterdvtraumamh.org/wp-content/uploads/2013/03/NCDVTMH_EBPLitReview2013.pdf

CHAPTER 7

Crisis: Community and Large-Scale Events

We'd been through hurricanes before; when you live on the coast, you know they're going to happen. And every time, the news makes it sound like it's the end of the world; that this is going to be the one that wipes everything out. But they're always wrong, and it never happens, so we stay, and we ride it out, and everything is fine. But this time, they were right, and everything wasn't fine. It's been six months now and we're still picking up the pieces, literally and emotionally.

T his description of how people prepare for and cope with large-scale disasters is all too common. Some community-based crises, like hurricanes, come with a warning and provide the opportunity to prepare. Other events, like terrorist attacks and spontaneous natural disasters, do not provide for the same kind of preparation. Regardless of the type of event, people's responses to large-scale disasters follow somewhat predictable patterns, which allow the crisis interventionist the opportunity to prepare and plan appropriate interventions.

The following chapter describes the common stages experienced by individuals and communities after large-scale crisis events, as well as information about specific types of community-based crises. After reading this chapter, you should be able to:

1. Identify the stages that individuals and communities experience before, during, and after a large-scale crisis;
2. Recognize the major incidents that can impact large groups of people, such as disasters, terrorism, shootings, and hostage-taking events;
3. Identify specific forms of intervention for each of the large-scale crises identified above.

Stages of Disaster Recovery

When a community-wide crisis occurs, such as a natural or man-made disaster, terrorist attack, mass shooting, or so forth, individuals and communities tend to follow a somewhat predictable pattern of response. Typically, this response follows six stages: (1) the Pre-Crisis Stage (2) the Impact Stage, (3) the Rescue Stage, (4) the Recovery Stage, (5) the Return to Life Stage, and (6) the Reconstruction Stage. There are different expected behaviors of those in crisis at each of these stages, and consequently, the crisis interventionist must consider different goals and interventions at each stage.

Stage 1: The Pre-Crisis Stage

As suggested by the title, the Pre-Crisis stage occurs prior to the occurrence of the event. The duration of this stage varies given the type of event. The Pre-Crisis stage typically consists of some sort of warning or threat that the crisis is imminent. This stage may or may not be known to the individuals in crisis at the time but, instead, may only be obvious after the crisis has occurred. For example, in the vignette provided at the beginning of this chapter, the Pre-Crisis stage was known to the community; weather forecasters indicated that a hurricane was approaching. However, in other situations there may not be obvious warning signs that the threat is developing. For example, in the case of the shootings at Sandy Hook elementary school, the shooter did indicate some signs of emotional distress and had amassed weapons and ammunition but obvious, visible signs of the threat were lacking, as compared to a forecasted weather event like a hurricane.

The goals of individuals at the Pre-Crisis stage typically include preparation and vigilance. For example, in the case of a predictable disaster, such as a hurricane or flood, people may take precautions, such as evacuating the affected area, or in lieu of evacuation, may instead stockpile necessities such as food, water, or batteries. They may take physical precautions, such as boarding windows, sandbagging areas that flood, and moving valuables to higher floors in a home. In cases where the crisis may not be as predicable, people may try to remain vigilant to possible emergencies. An example of this is the "See Something, Say Something" campaign designed to alert authorities to possible terror attacks.

The role of the crisis interventionist at the Pre-Crisis stage is preparation and mobilization. Those who provide crisis intervention services should be participating in continuing education to ensure they are prepared with the most recent knowledge and skillsets that have empirical support through research. Additionally, in the case of predictable large-scale disasters and crises, counselors can begin to prepare for travel to the affected areas, and local agencies can begin amassing human and other resources that may be necessary to help people survive a disaster or other crisis.

Stage 2: The Impact Stage

The Impact stage is when the crisis occurs. Depending on the type of crisis, this stage may last from a few hours to a few days. At this stage, the goals of those impacted by the crisis tend to be based in survival. People will typically respond through behaviors that follow the fight/flight/freeze modality, and will do whatever is necessary to survive the initial impact of the crisis. While those in the crisis will do their best to survive, another important goal of people in this stage is communication. Safety comes from being able to make contact with others, especially loved ones who are also impacted by the crisis. Ensuring one's safety and knowing that others are safe provide a sense of security during the Impact stage. As described in Chapter Three, the American Red Cross and others have developed websites where people can let others know they are safe after a crisis.

At this stage, we often witness and document acts of significant heroism. For example, during floods we often hear stories of people working together to go in to raging floodwaters to rescue those trapped in a swollen river. When mass shootings occur, we hear stories of people covering others with their bodies to protect them from the flying bullets. These acts of heroism often provide a glimmer of hope during the Impact stage, which is otherwise marked by fear, confusion, and hopelessness.

The role of the crisis interventionist at this stage is to provide basic needs to assist individuals with survival and communication. Providing resources for medical and Psychological First Aid (PFA; see Chapter Three) are critical during this phase. While crisis interventionists are not necessarily trained in medical procedures, some basic first aid training can be helpful during a crisis event. Other roles the crisis counselor can assume include monitoring the environment, as well as providing technical assistance and consultation to first responders on the scene.

The implementation of PFA during the Impact stage is critical, because it provides services that can be important during recovery from the crisis event. For example, the crisis interventionist can provide support, as well as a presence, during the Impact stage. One important task is to assist in reducing the psychological arousal that typically occurs during a crisis. Interventionists can assist in reuniting families and loved ones, whether in person or via telephone, Internet, or other means. Intervention may also include disseminating information to those affected and protecting individuals from further harm that might be caused by media or predators who come to the crisis site in order to take advantage of those in need.

Stage 3: The Rescue Stage

During the Rescue stage, individuals in the community begin the process of coming to terms with the crisis that has occurred, as well as beginning the process of assessing the impact of the event. This stage typically lasts for a week or less and is marked by a sense of community cohesion, which is often followed by disillusionment and exhaustion. As the crisis ends, people will often come together to help one another and provide assistance and support, which can create a sense of unity. However, as exhaustion sets in and the severity of the event becomes clear over time, community members may find themselves angry, confused, lost, scared, or otherwise discouraged.

The goal at this stage of the crisis is for people to adjust to the outcome of the crisis and begin the process of recovery. The behavior of individuals at this stage is typically a fusion of resilience and exhaustion. Crisis interventionists can assist at this stage by assessing the needs of individuals and of the community and begin to work with available resources to try to meet those needs. For example, those assisting during the crisis may be best served to meet the most basic needs of those in crisis: food, water, shelter, securing medications, and providing other safety and physiological needs. Helpers at this stage can also begin to triage mental health needs, assessing those who are most immediately impacted by the event and securing mental health services for those individuals. The crisis counselor can also amass resources for those who are not yet experiencing distress but may be in the days, weeks, and months to come. Finally, crisis interventionists can provide a source of accurate information, while dispelling the rumors that so often begin to spread through a community in crisis.

Stage 4: The Recovery Stage

At this stage, the work of recovering from the crisis event takes place. Communities are challenged to appraise the damage left by the critical incident and assess what needs to be done to recover. Planning for the future marks this phase, which can last for several weeks. Individuals who experienced the crisis may begin to present with mental health issues during this phase, such as processing grief and loss, experiencing

CASE ILLUSTRATION 7.1

SAM'S EXPERIENCE FOLLOWING HURRICANE SANDY

Sam lived along the New Jersey coast for almost 30 years when the forecasts for Hurricane Sandy began to surface in October, 2012. Sam had been warned of many hurricanes during the time he lived in his small, coastal town, and had heeded many warnings to evacuate over the years. The forecasts were usually far more dire than the actual storm, and the evacuation process was long, tedious, and expensive. In recent years, Sam had decided that it simply wasn't worth the time and expense to evacuate, especially given the relative weakness of hurricanes that make landfall in the Northeast United States. In fact, one year earlier, Hurricane Irene made landfall, and there was almost no damage and certainly no need to evacuate.

As the winds and rain began to pummel the town on October 29, Sam began to think he had made a very serious mistake by deciding to ride out this storm. The power went out early, and the streets began flooding overnight. Sam and his wife decided to move to the second floor of their small cottage home, since the basement was completely flooded, and the water was starting to inch toward the first floor. Shingles flew off the roof, and water began to come in through the windows. Without power, their cell phones eventually stopped working, which didn't matter much, because there was no cell service anyway.

When the storm finally passed, it was clear the entire town was flooded and everything would be a total loss. Sam and his wife were trapped in their home, but as the day went on, neighbors began coming by in small boats, rescuing one another and transporting people to local shelters. The community came together to ensure one another's safety, and donations began to pour in from unaffected towns. Sam realized that his elderly neighbor Betty was still at home, but no one could locate her, and she hadn't checked in to the local shelter. Neighbors continued to search, as did local first responders, but no one was able to find her. Sam had to make the difficult decision to leave his two dogs

intrusive memories, and forming the narrative story to describe the crisis and how it unfolded.

For those who are providing mental health services, this stage can be challenging. The crisis has passed, and basic needs, such as food, water, and shelter, are being met. However, the psychological needs of those who experienced the crisis are now beginning to emerge. Crisis interventionists at this stage should be working to identify individuals who are having difficulty processing the experience and who may be developing inaccurate narratives of how the events unfolded. Active listening and attending skills are critically important during this phase of the crisis, and the helper can not only monitor the community for those who may be struggling emotionally, but can also be attentive to internal and external threats that may be introduced in the community. These threats may include individuals who enter the community to prey on those in need, or who may try to meet their own needs at the expense of others.

An additional concern for the mental health responder is identifying and engaging with those people who may have an existing trauma history. As described in Chapter One, people who are unsuccessful at resolving past events are more prone to develop negative outcomes when faced with a new crisis. Mental health responders should be attentive to all those impacted by the crisis, but especially to those who were struggling to process a trauma before the most recent crisis occurred. Case Illustration 7.1 provides an example of the impact a crisis can have on someone with a history of trauma.

Stage 5: The Return to Life Stage

After the initial impact of the crisis has passed, members of the community are faced with the challenge of returning to "normal." The term normal is placed in quotes for two reasons: first, normal is a subjective term that is nearly impossible to define, but more importantly, normal is rarely possible after a crisis has occurred. After a crisis, people will often say, "I just want things to go back to normal." What that statement often means is that they want things to be as if the crisis never happened. But the crisis *did* happen, and denying the event will make moving on all the more difficult. That's why in crisis work, we often refer to this process as returning to a *new normal*. A new normal acknowledges that the crisis happened, and that it had an impact. However, that impact does not have to have to last forever, and people can recover, and even grow, following a catastrophe.

The Return to Life stage can last for several months or even several years. A number of important events typically take place during this stage. The goal is for individuals to reintegrate in to the community, and to begin to develop the definition of the *new normal*. People begin to work through their grief and will often experience the various stages of grieving as described by Kubler-Ross (2009): denial, anger, bargaining, depression, and acceptance. The Return to Life stage is marked by anniversary reactions, which are the psychological reactions that may take place when an anniversary of a crisis occurs. For example, as a society, we solemnly recognize the anniversary of the September 11, 2001, terrorist attacks with memorials in New York; Washington, D.C.; and other cities around the country. This stage is also marked by trigger events, or those events that cause individuals to re-experience the anxiety and stress of the original crisis.

During this stage, individuals may develop mental health diagnoses associated with the crisis, such as Post-Traumatic Stress Disorder (PTSD), adjustment disorders, specific phobias, depression, anxiety, and so forth (See Chapter 5). At this stage, the mental health professional's role is to provide treatment to those in distress in order to ameliorate symptoms and improve functioning. This may occur in individual, group, or family counseling, but typically occurs in more formal settings than the PFA employed at earlier stages of the disaster. For individuals who are experiencing significant distress, psychopharmacology may be indicated, or in severe cases, hospitalization may be necessary.

behind, since he had heard that the shelters weren't allowing animals.

As the water receded, Sam and others in his community became despondent. Their homes were destroyed, the local infrastructure was a total loss, and it didn't seem that help was coming. The shelters remained open, but no one wanted to stay there if they didn't have to. Sam and his wife decided to stay with family in New York State, but the commute back and forth to attend to issues at home began to take an emotional and financial toll. Eventually, Betty was located (she had decided at the last minute to evacuate and had gone inland to stay with a friend), but Sam's dogs were never found. Another neighbor, whom Sam knew casually, had also died in the storm.

Eventually, little by little, people began to rebuild their homes and the town began to repair the damage caused by Sandy. Sam noticed, though, that whenever a big storm was forecasted, he became angry and short tempered. He would sometimes stay on the second floor during heavy rainstorms, and purchased a large, expensive generator for his home. As time went on, Sam and the rest of his community did rebuild, but no one forgot those days in October 2012. Every year at the end of October, Sam and his neighbors gather and talk about those difficult days, weeks, and months when Sandy tore through their town.

Stage 6: The Reconstruction Stage

During this stage, the crisis has ended, and members of the community have moved on to the new normal discussed previously. People have come to terms with the event or events that precipitated the crisis and have processed the emotions associated with the event. This stage is not without its challenges, as people may experience setbacks as they progress through the new normal, but these setbacks are typically brief, and the individual possesses the requisite skills and knowledge to overcome these challenges and continue moving forward. Emotional functioning at the Reconstruction stage may be equal to where it was pre-crisis, may be slightly below where it was, or may even be greater than where it was prior to the crisis. Often referred to as Post-Traumatic Growth (PTG), emerging research suggests that individuals can grow and becoming stronger, healthier, and better functioning as a result of successfully processing a traumatic event (Calhoun & Tedeschi, 2014). For a more detailed explanation of PTG, see Chapter 12.

Exercise 7.1 invites you to examine how a community may progress through the stages of crisis.

Now that we have identified the various stages that people experience during and after a crisis, we will examine four specific types of large-scale crises: natural disasters, terrorism, mass shootings, and hostage situations.

Natural Disasters

According to the Centre for Research on the Epidemiology of Disasters (CRED), a disaster is defined as "a situation or event which overwhelms local capacity, necessitating a request to a national or international level for external assistance; an unforeseen and often sudden event that causes great damage, destruction, and human suffering"

(Guha-Sapir, Hoyois, & Below, 2014, p.7). CRED identifies a number of natural disaster types: geophysical, hydrological, meteorological, climatological, biological, and extra-terrestrial. In additional to natural disasters, CRED also classifies another type of disaster, a technological disaster, which is generally man-made. Table 7.1 provides examples of each of these types of disasters.

Table 7.1 Examples of Natural and Technological Disasters

Examples of Natural Disasters	Examples of Technological Disasters
Geophysical • Earthquakes • Volcanic activity	• Biological threats • Chemical emergencies or threats • Computer attacks/hacking • Explosions • Oil spills • Mass transit accidents • Nuclear power accidents • Power failures • Terrorist acts
Hydrological • Floods • Landslides • Tsunamis	
Meteorological • Storms • Fog • Extreme temperatures	
Climatological • Drought • Wildfires	
Biological • Epidemics • Insect Infestations	
Extra-terrestrial • Meteor impact • Space weather events	

In order to be recorded as a natural disaster by CRED, one of the following criteria must be met: 10 or more people must be reported killed, 100 or more people must be affected, a state of emergency must be declared, or a call for international assistance must be placed (Guha-Sapir et al., 2014). The psychological impact of natural disasters is well established in the literature. Specifically, researchers have found a host of mental health diagnoses that are associated with the experience of a natural disaster, including: PTSD, anxiety, depression, and other stress-related disorders (Davis, Grills-Taquechel, & Ollendick, 2010; Kukihara, Yamawaki, Uchiyama, Arai, & Horikawa, 2014; Sprague et al., 2015).

One study examined the impact of Hurricane Katrina on college students in the New Orleans region (Davis, Grills-Taquechel, & Ollendick, 2010). The study examined the impact of the hurricane on the psychological well-being of college students who attended schools where individuals were displaced, verses those who attended schools where students were not displaced. The findings indicated that those students whose lives were impacted more significantly by the hurricane reported significantly higher levels of depression and traumatic response (Davis et al., 2010). Similar results were found in studies of those who survived the earthquake and resulting tsunami in Japan during 2011 (Kukihara et al., 2014).

Sprague et al. (2015) investigated the psychological responses of young people who experienced the massive California wildfires that occurred during 2008–2009. The researchers found that those who lost their homes reported significantly higher levels of stress than did those who were forced to evacuate but did not experience property damage. Also, those who had support from peers and reported deriving from resilient families of origin indicated lower levels of stress than those who did not have those mitigating factors.

The Hurricane Katrina disaster has provided researchers with the opportunity to evaluate the effectiveness of a number of intervention strategies following a natural disaster. Ronan et al. (2008) found significant positive impact of PFA on the mental health outcomes of those who survived the Katrina disaster. Ursano et al. (2007) found similar results in their study of the survivors of Hurricane Katrina. Dass-Brailsford and Thomley (2015) found that the provision of walk-in mental health counseling centers provided significant reduction of stress-related symptoms after the hurricane. Finally, Nelson (2008) examined the resiliency of adolescents who had experienced the events that followed Katrina's landfall. This study found that negative outcomes could be mitigated through the development of emotional regulation and positivity.

Terrorism

As this book is being written, acts of terrorism are occurring faster than they can be researched and written about, especially in a textbook. Of course, the attacks of September 11, 2001, were the most influential in the recent history of the United States; however, there have been terrorist attacks occurring across the globe for centuries. This is surely not a new phenomenon, but it is one that has struck the consciousness of citizens of the United States in recent years.

For the purposes of this discussion, terrorism will be defined as acts of *domestic terrorism* and *international terrorism*. Domestic terrorism is defined in the United States as those acts that violate federal or state law, are intended to coerce civilians or influence government, and occur primarily within the jurisdiction of the United States. Conversely, international terrorism meets the first two criteria of domestic terrorism but occur primarily outside the jurisdiction of the United States (18 U.S.C. § 2331).

The impact of terrorism on individuals has been reported extensively in the literature. A number of researchers examined the psychological effects of the September 11 terror attacks on individuals living and working in New York City. One study found that close to 10% of those who lived near the World Trade Center experienced PTSD, but that number increased to 20% for those who lived closer to the site of the attacks (Galea et al., 2002). McArdle, Rosoff, and John (2012) conducted longitudinal research to determine the impact of the attacks on individuals across the United States. They found differences in psychological impact across gender, age, and geographic location. Greater impact was found among women, older adults, and those who lived closer to the attack sites.

Studies of terrorist attacks in other countries support the assertion that those impacted by terrorism are likely to experience greater levels of distress. Rubin et al. (2005) examined psychological reactions of those who experienced the coordinated bombings of the mass transit system in London in 2005. The researchers found that 31% of London residents reported significant stress and 32% reported an intent to travel less. This study also found that women, individuals with lower socio-economic statuses, and those from an ethnic or religious minority group had greater risks of psychological distress (Rubin et al., 2005). Vázquez, Pérez-Sales, & Matt (2006) found similar results after studying the impact of the 2004 train bombings in Madrid, Spain.

One might assume that mental health intervention would be critical after a terrorist attack, especially given the findings of the studies described here. However, the research suggests that counseling services are not adequately deployed following a terrorist event (Fairbrother, Stuber, Galea, Pfefferbaum, & Fleischman, 2004). Chongruksa, Parinyapol, Sawatsri, and Pansomboon (2012) do provide a list of empirically supported treatment modalities for addressing the trauma that can occur following an act of terrorism including:

- Trauma-focused cognitive behavioral therapy (TF-CBT)
- Stress management/relaxation—any psychological intervention that helps the client to mitigate the high stress that can result from terror-related events
- TF-CBT Group Therapy
- Cognitive Behavior Therapy (CBT)
- Eye Movement Desensitization and Reprocessing (EMDR)
- Non-trauma-focused CBT groups
- Other psychological interventions (e.g., non-directive counseling, psychodynamic therapy, and hypnotherapy)
- Psychoeducation

EXERCISE 7.2

INTERVENTION WITH A SURVIVOR OF TERRORISM

Directions: Read through the following case presentation, and then consider the questions that follow.

Case Illustration:

Diane is a long distance runner who has run over a dozen marathons in recent years. She was running in the Boston Marathon in 2013 when explosions ripped through the finish line. While Diane wasn't hurt, she was just approaching the area when the bombs exploded. She witnessed the injured people and remained near the finish line as first responders arrived to care for the wounded.

Diane has come to counseling, because she has recently had difficulty sleeping, has found herself very sad and despondent, and started experiencing panic attacks. She has not done any running since the 2013 marathon. Diane tells you that some of her symptoms have been occurring since the attacks: she will have nightmares and flashbacks to the day of the bombings. She finds herself constantly on guard, especially in public places and in large crowds. But recently, she was watching the news and saw a documentary on TV about the Boston bombings, and things have gotten worse since then.

Since she saw the TV program, she has found herself irritable and depressed. Her relationship with her spouse is worsening, and she finds herself yelling at her children for "no good reason." She has begun drinking heavily and has been missing work, because she's drunk or too hungover to go. She says, "I'm always on guard. I can never rest, and I'm always afraid something bad is going to happen. I KNOW something bad is going to happen. I will freak out for no reason and just start shaking and feel like I'm going to pass out. My hands shake, I feel like I can't breathe, my chest hurts, and I feel really hot. I can't keep focused, and I can't sleep. This has been going on for about three months now and I'm afraid I can't keep it together anymore. My kids are afraid of me, my marriage is falling apart, and I'm going to lose my job."

Mass Shootings

The definition of a mass shooting had long been considered an event when four or more people were shot and injured or killed, without a cooling off period (Follman, 2015). However, the United States Congress recently enacted legislation that defines a mass killing as an event where three or more people are killed in a single event (6 U.S.C. § 455). Regardless of the specific definition used, mass shootings have reached a point of prevalence in our society such that crisis interventionists must understand how these events unfold and how best to intervene following a mass shooting or killing event.

Mass shootings happen throughout society, and according to one source, there were 333 mass shootings across the United States in 2015 (Gun Violence Archive, 2016). Of course, many mass shootings have reached prominence in media, including the shootings at Columbine High School in Colorado in 1999, where 12 students and one teacher were killed and another 21 were injured. Another 2007 attack at Virginia Tech University claimed the lives of 32 and saw another 17 injured. At Sandy Hook Elementary School in Connecticut, 20 children and 6 teachers were killed, and at Pulse Nightclub in Orlando, Florida, 49 were killed and more than 50 others wounded. In 2012, the United States experienced one of the worst years in history relative to mass shootings. Table 7.2 provides examples of a few of the more significant mass shootings of 2012.

According to the U.S. Federal Bureau of Investigation (FBI), an active shooter is someone who is killing or trying to kill people in a populated area (Active Shooter Resources, 2016). There is no one profile of an active shooter, but 97% of the time, the shooter is male. In almost half the cases (43%), the crime is over before law enforcement arrives, while the other 57% of the time, police officers arrive during the event. The presence of law enforcement often stops the shooting, and the shooter may turn that aggression toward police officers. In one third of the events, when law enforcement arrives, the shooter is shot by police (Active Shooter Resources, 2016).

Active shooting incidents often occur in smaller communities where police departments are limited by resource restraints (Active Shooter Resources, 2016). The average length of an active shooter incident is 12 minutes and 37% of these crimes last less than five minutes. In 98% of the cases, there is only one shooter, and in 10% of the cases, the shooter simply stops and walks away. Two percent of shooters also bring explosive devices.

Diane reports that this is her first time in counseling.

Reflection:

1. What are Diane's presenting concerns? Do they meet the criteria for a principal diagnosis?

2. What are your short-term goals for treatment with Diane?

3. From a Cognitive-Behavioral Approach, what cognitive interventions could you use to begin reducing Diane's symptoms immediately?

4. What are your long-term goals for treatment with Diane? What intervention strategies might you consider employing to meet these long-term goals?

Table 7.2 Mass Shootings of 2012

Location	Injured and Killed
Health Spa; Norcross, GA	5 killed (including shooter)
High School Cafeteria; Chardon, OH	3 killed, 2 injured
Psychiatric Hospital; Pittsburgh, PA	2 killed (including shooter), 7 injured
University Classroom; Oakland, CA	7 killed, 3 injured
Coffee Shop; Seattle, WA	6 killed (including shooter), 1 injured
Movie Theater; Aurora, CO	12 killed, 58 injured
Sikh Temple; Oak Creek; WI	7 killed (including shooter), 3 injured
Sign Company; Minneapolis, MN	7 killed (including shooter), 3 injured
Spa and Salon; Brookfield, WI	4 killed (including shooter), 4 injured
Shopping Mall; Happy Valley, OR	3 killed (including shooter), 1 injured
Elementary School; Newtown, CT	28 killed (including shooter), 2 injured

Many individuals who commit mass shootings indicate observable behaviors prior to the attack, such as stockpiling weapons and ammunition, purchasing body armor, and acting out against those who the shooter perceives to be a threat. Most mass shooters experience a real or perceived grievance, and their ideation for resolving that grievance involves violence (Active Shooter Resources, 2016). Most of these events can

ANDERS BEHRING BREIVIK: THE ANATOMY OF A PLANNED MASS MURDER

Anders Behring Breivik killed 77 people and injured 319 in Norway on July 22, 2011. First, he detonated a bomb inside a van in Oslo, killing eight. He then donned a police officer's uniform and traveled to a youth camp on the island of Utoya, where he shot 67 people, most of whom were children. One 17-year-old died falling off a cliff in an attempt to dodge bullets; another drowned trying to escape. It might be easy to assume that these were the actions of someone who just snapped and went on a killing spree, but nothing could be further from the truth.

By his own accounts, Breivik spent over five years planning his horrific attack. He had lived with his mother until 2006, when he moved to a sugar beet farm. He claimed he was taking time off to play the video game, *World of Warcraft*. It didn't seem that farfetched, as Breivik had been a video game player for many years. During his trial, he said that he expected to die during his attack, so he wanted to have no regrets and thought that playing the game nonstop for a while would satisfy one of his goals before he died.

During the five years that led up to the attacks, Breivik traveled to various countries, stockpiling weapons and ammunition. He played first-person shooting video games, such as *Call of Duty,* to hone his shooting skills. He studied various terror attacks, with specific focus on the 1995 Oklahoma City bombing at the federal building there. His decision to move to a farm was pre-meditated, because he could then purchase the fertilizer necessary to build the bomb he eventually detonated in Oslo.

He carefully calculated the size of the farm he would need in order to purchase quantities of fertilizer necessary to build the bombs. Breivik refused to accept visits from friends after he moved to the farm, because had they visited, they may have found him in a chemical warfare suit, grinding ammonium nitrate pills using four different blenders. They may have also found him training with heavy weights on

be prevented through intervention by bystanders before any violence is perpetrated, including by recognizing warning signs and contacting law enforcement. However, exclusionary interventions, such as school expulsion or employment termination, do not stop the pathway to violence and may serve to exacerbate the situation.

We often hear that someone who commits a mass shooting "just snapped" and "lost it" one day, but this is rarely the case. Most often, those who commit mass shootings meticulously plan the details of their attacks in the weeks and months leading up to the shooting. The following case illustration provides an example of this type of planning.

These events are certain to impact the psychological well-being of those who are wounded, who witness the violence, or who are otherwise associated with a mass shooting. Hughes et al. (2011) studied the prevalence of PTSD symptoms among college students after the 2007 shooting at Virginia Tech. The researchers sampled 4,639 students and found that over 15% of those surveyed indicated a likelihood of having developed PTSD. A similar study examined the impact of a shooting at Northern Illinois University in 2008. Of those surveyed, 95% indicated some degree of PTSD symptomology, which decreased to 80% after eight months (Littleton, Kumpula, & Orcutt, 2011). Similar results were found in other studies of the impact of mass shootings on communities. A study by Sequin et al. (2013) found a significant incidence of psychological disorders and exacerbation of pre-existing psychological disorders within 18 months following a mass shooting at Dawson College in Canada.

Regarding intervention following a mass shooting, Jordan (2003) identified a stage model for intervention following a mass shooting event. While this model is specific to school shootings, its utility could be employed for other mass shooting events, as well. This model examines interventions for both primary victims (e.g., students, school staff, etc.), as well as secondary victims (e.g., witnesses, parents, siblings, community members, etc.). The model examines the impact and interventions for both primary and secondary victims at various stages of the shooting event: (1) The Traumatic Disaster Event (e.g., when the shooting occurs), (2) The Displacement and Separation Stage, when the threat to personal safety has passed but primary victims and families have not yet been reunited, and (3) The Reunification or Loss of Loved Ones Stage. At this stage, either primary victims are reunified with their loved ones, or those who have been killed are identified. Following each of these possibilities, a fourth stage, (4) Recovery, begins. For more on this model, see the resources listed at the end of this chapter.

his chest and back so he could be better prepared to carry out the attack with the bulk of numerous weapons and pounds of ammunition.

Breivik built a number of test bombs on the property, and would wait for thunderstorms so he could set off test charges without raising suspicion. He ordered a police uniform so that after the bomb exploded, he could call the youth camp and tell them that the police were sending an officer to keep the children safe, in case someone would come there to do harm. On the day of the attack, the camp sent a ferry to transport Breivik to protect the children there. Once he arrived, he opened fire.

As the details emerged about the planning that went in to the Breivik's attacks, it became clear that this was not someone who "just snapped."

Hostage Situations

Alexander and Klein (2010) define hostage-taking as "a lay term and refers to the detention of an individual, against their will and without legal authority, for a particular motive" (p.176). Santifort and Sandler (2013) expand this definition to include kidnapping, skyjacking, barricade missions, and the takeover of ground-based transportation, such as buses, trains, and ships. This definition specifies kidnappings as unique, because the victim and assailant can move quickly and freely from location to location.

Documented history of hostage taking dates back to ancient Roman and medieval times; however, more recent events have seen the taking of hostages as a means to a political end or for the purpose of extorting ransoms from families or governments (Alexander & Klein, 2010). The research on the impact of being taken hostage is limited given the ethical and practical challenges of obtaining data on these types of events. However, the limited research does indicate that being taken and held hostage can result in a traumatic response, including negative impact on cognitive, emotional, and social functioning (Alexander & Klein, 2009).

The symptomology that hostages often experience after the event has ended are indicative of a PTSD-like reaction. For example, those who have been taken hostage will experience impairment of concentration, as well as flashbacks and intrusive memories (Alexander & Klein, 2009). Victims of hostage situations often experience anxiety, numbness, dissociation, anger, and anhedonia. Individuals may also experience depression and guilt, especially if they survived when others did not. Finally, survivors of hostage-taking events may withdraw socially, avoid others, and experience significant irritability (Alexander & Klein, 2009).

There is a need for further research regarding the therapeutic features of hostage victims (Alexander & Klein, 2010). The current research is limited, because of the difficulty in following up on those taken as hostages (Alexander & Klein, 2009). For example, it may be inappropriate to conduct research studies with those who have been taken as hostages due to the risk of re-traumatizing individuals by asking them to relive highly emotional experiences that may include humiliation, sexual abuse, or torture (Alexander & Klein, 2010). Also, the sample size in these events is usually limited, sometimes involving only a single participant. Therefore, it may be best to consider interventions often utilized in general trauma exposure when working with those who have experienced a hostage situation.

Summary

- The Pre-Crisis stage occurs prior to the occurrence of the event. The duration of this stage varies, given the type of event. The Pre-Crisis stage typically consists of some sort of warning or threat that the crisis is imminent. This stage may or may not be known to the individuals in crisis at the time but, instead, may only be obvious after the crisis has occurred.

- The Impact stage is when the crisis occurs. Depending on the type of crisis, this stage may last from a few hours to a few days. At this stage, the goals of those impacted by the crisis tend to be based in survival.

- During the Rescue stage, individuals in the community begin the process of coming to terms with the crisis that has occurred, as well as beginning the process of assessing the impact of the crisis event. This stage typically lasts for a week or less and is marked by a sense of community cohesion, which is often followed by disillusionment and exhaustion.

- At the Recovery stage, communities are challenged to appraise the damage left by the critical incident and assess what needs to be done to restore the community. Planning for the future marks this phase, which can last for several weeks. Individuals who experienced the crisis may begin to present with mental health issues during this phase.

- The Return to Life stage can last for several months or even several years. A number of important events typically take place during this stage. The goal is for individuals to reintegrate into the community and to begin to develop the definition of the *new normal*.

- During the Reconstruction stage, the crisis has officially ended, and members of the community have moved on to the new normal discussed previously. People have come to terms with the event or events that precipitated the crisis and have processed the emotions associated with the event.

- According to CRED, a disaster is defined as "a situation or event which overwhelms local capacity, necessitating a request to a national or international level for external assistance; an unforeseen and often sudden event that causes great damage, destruction, and human suffering." (Guha-Sapir, Hoyois, & Below, 2014, p. 7). CERD defines disasters in two categories: natural and technological.

- Terrorism is defined as *domestic terrorism* and *international terrorism*. Domestic terrorism is defined as those acts that violate federal or state law, are intended to coerce civilians or influence government, and occur primarily within the jurisdiction of the United States. Conversely, international terrorism meets the first two criteria of domestic terrorism but occurs primarily outside the jurisdiction of the United States.

- The definition of a mass shooting had long been considered an event when four or more people were shot and injured or killed, without a cooling off period. However, the United States Congress recently enacted legislation that defines a mass killing as an event where three or more people are killed in a single event. Most often, those who commit mass shootings meticulously plan the details of their attacks in the weeks and months leading up to the shooting.

- Hostage-taking is defined as detaining an individual against one's will, without legal authority, and with motive. The research on the impact of being taken hostage is limited given the ethical and practical challenges of obtaining data on these types of events. However, the limited research does indicate that being taken and held hostage can result in a traumatic response, including negative impact on cognitive, emotional, and social functioning.

Important Terms

Active shooter

Anniversary reactions

Disaster

Domestic terrorism

Hostage taking

Impact Stage

International terrorism

Mass killing

Mass shooting

Natural disasters

New normal

Post-Traumatic Growth (PTG)

Pre-Crisis Stage

Primary victim

Reconstruction Stage

Recovery Stage

Rescue Stage

Return to Life Stage

Secondary victim

Technological disaster

Trigger events

Additional Resources

In Print

Calhoun, L.G. & Tedeschi, R. G. (2014). *Handbook of Posttraumatic Growth: Research and practice.* New York, NY: Psychology Press.

Jordan, K. (2003). A trauma and recovery model for victims and their families after a catastrophic school shooting: Focusing on behavioral, cognitive, and psychological effects and needs. *Brief Treatment & Crisis Intervention, 3*(4), 397–411.

Zakour, M. and Gillespie, D. (2013). *Community disaster vulnerability: Theory, research, and practice.* New York, NY: Springer.

On the Web

Active Shooter Resources: www.FBI.gov/activeshooter

Centre for Research on the Epidemiology of Disasters: http://www.cred.be

Inside the Warped Mind of Anders Breivik: http://www.telegraph.co.uk/news/2016/07/22/anders-breivik-inside-the-warped-mind-of-a-mass-killer/

References

Federal Bureau of Investigation (2016). Active Shooter Resources. Retrieved from https://www.fbi.gov/about/partnerships/office-of-partner-engagement/active-shooter-resources

Alexander, D. A., & Klein, S. (2009). Kidnapping and hostage-taking: A review of effects, coping and resilience. *Journal of the Royal Society of Medicine, 102*(1), 16–21. doi:10.1258/jrsm.2008.080347

Alexander, D. A., & Klein, S. (2010). Hostage-taking: motives, resolution, coping and effects. *Advances in Psychiatric Treatment, 16*, 176–183. doi: 10.1192/apt.bp.108.005991

Kubler-Ross, E. (2009). *On death and dying: What the dying have to teach doctors, nurses, clergy, and their own families.* New York, NY: Routledge.

Calhoun, L.G. & Tedeschi, R. G. (2014). *Handbook of Posttraumatic Growth: Research and practice.* New York, NY: Psychology Press.

Chongruksa, D., Parinyapol, P., Sawatsri, S., & Pansomboon, C. (2012). Efficacy of eclectic group counseling in addressing stress among Thai police officers in terrorist situations. *Counselling Psychology Quarterly, 25*(1), 83–96. doi:10.1080/09515070.2012.666424

Dass-Brailsford, P., & Thomley, R. H. (2015). Using walk-in counseling services after Hurricane Katrina: A program evaluation. *Journal of Aggression, Maltreatment & Trauma, 24*(4), 419–432. doi:10.1080/10926771.2015.1022287

Davis, T. E., III, Grills-Taquechel, A. E., & Ollendick, T. H. (2010). The psychological impact from Hurricane Katrina: Effects of displacement and trauma exposure on university students. *Behavior Therapy, 41*(3), 340–349. doi:10.1016/j.beth.2009.09.004

Fairbrother, G., Stuber, J., Galea, S., Pfefferbaum, B., & Fleischman, A. (2004). Unmet need for counseling services by children in New York City after the September 11th attacks on the World Trade Center: Implications for pediatricians. *Pediatrics*, 113(5), 1367–1374.

Follman, M. (Dec 3, 2015). How many mass shootings are there, really? *The New York Times.* Retrieved from www.newyorktimes.com

Galea, S., Ahern, J., Resnick, H., Kilpatrick, D., Bucuvalas, M., Gold, J., & Vlahov, D. (2002). Psychological sequelae of the September 11 terrorist attacks in New York City. *The New England Journal of Medicine, 346*(13) 982–987. doi: 10.1056/NEJMsa013404

Guha-Sapir, D., Hoyois, P., & Below, R. (2014). Annual Disaster Review 2014: The numbers and trends [Review]. Center for Research on the Epidemiology of Disasters (CRED), 1–54.

Gun Violence Archive (2016). Mass Shootings. Retrieved from http://www.gunviolencearchive.org/reports/mass-shootings/2015

Homeland Security Act, 6 U.S.C. § 455 (2013).

Hughes, M., Brymer, M., Chiu, W. T., Fairbank, J. A., Jones, R. T., Pynoos, R. S., & ... Kessler, R. C. (2011). Posttraumatic stress among students after the shootings at Virginia Tech. *Psychological Trauma: Theory, Research, Practice, And Policy, 3*(4), 403–411. doi:10.1037/a0024565

Jordan, K. (2003). A Trauma and recovery model for victims and their families after a catastrophic school shooting: Focusing on behavioral, cognitive, and psychological effects and needs. *Brief Treatment & Crisis Intervention, 3*(4), 397–411.

Kukihara, H., Yamawaki, N., Uchiyama, K., Arai, S., & Horikawa, E. (2014). Trauma, depression, and resilience of earthquake/tsunami/nuclear disaster survivors of Hirono, Fukushima, Japan. *Psychiatry and Clinical Neurosciences*, 68(7), 524–533.

Littleton, H., Kumpula, M., & Orcutt, H. (2011). Posttraumatic symptoms following a campus shooting: The role of psychosocial resource loss. *Violence & Victims, 26*(4), 461–476. doi:10.1891/0886-6708.26.4.461

McArdle, S. C., Rosoff, H., & John, R. S. (2012). The dynamics of evolving beliefs, concern emotions, and behavioral avoidance following 9/11: A longitudinal analysis of representative archival samples. *Risk Analysis: An International Journal, 32*(4), 744–761. doi:10.1111/j.1539-6924.2012.01814.x

Nelson, L. P. (2008). A resiliency profile of Hurricane Katrina adolescents: A psychosocial study of disaster. *Canadian Journal of School Psychology, 23*(1), 57–69.

Ronan, K. R., Crellin, K., Johnston, D. M., Finnis, K., Paton, D., & Becker, J. (2008). Promoting child and family resilience to disasters: Effects, interventions, and prevention effectiveness. *Children, Youth & Environments, 18*(1), 332–353.

Rubin, J. G., Brewin, C., R., Greenberg, N., Simpson, J., Wessely, S. (2005). Psychological and behavioural reactions to the bombings in London on 7 July 2005: Cross sectional survey of a representative sample of Londoners. *BMJ*, 1–7. doi: 10.1136/bmj.38583.728484.3A

Santifort, C., & Sandler, T. (2013). Terrorist success in hostage-taking missions: 1978–2010. *Public Choice, 156*(1/2), 125–137. doi:10.1007/s11127-012-0008-z

Séguin, M., Chawky, N., Lesage, A., Boyer, R., Guay, S., Bleau, P., ... Roy, D. (2013). Evaluation of the Dawson College shooting psychological intervention: Moving toward a multimodal extensive plan. *Psychological Trauma: Theory, Research, Practice, and Policy, 5*(3), 268–276. doi:10.1037/a0027745

Sprague, C., Kia-Keating, M., Felix, E., Afifi, T., Reyes, G., & Afifi, W. (2015). Youth psychosocial adjustment following wildfire: The role of family resilience, emotional support, and concrete support. *Child & Youth Care Forum, 44*(3), 433–450. doi:10.1007/s10566-014-9285-7

Terrorism, 18 U.S.C. § 2331 (2015).

Ursano, R. J., Fullerton, C. S., Benedek, D. M., & Hamaoka, D. A. (2007). Hurricane Katrina: Disasters teach us and we must learn. *Academic Psychiatry, 31*(3), 180–182. doi:10.1176/appi.ap.31.3.180

Vázquez, C., Pérez-Sales, P., & Matt, G. (2006). Post-traumatic stress reactions following the March 11, 2004 terrorist attacks in Madrid community sample: a cautionary note about the measurement of psychological trauma. *The Spanish Journal of Psychology, 9*(1) 61–74.

CHAPTER 8

Crisis and Trauma: Impact Across the Lifespan

Thank God she is only four. I know she doesn't realize how close we were to burning up with the house—and hopefully, she will soon forget the chaos of this night.

The parent, quoted in our introduction, is certainly hopeful when it comes to her daughter's reaction to the experience of watching her house burn to the ground. Sadly, her implied optimism and hope that her daughter will simply "forget the chaos" of that night and sidestep any disruption to her functioning and development, as a result of her age, is not borne out in the research.

The impact of a traumatic experience and the resulting level of psychological distress and disruptions depend upon factors such as the severity of the trauma, proximity to the traumatizing event, previous trauma exposure, and preexisting problems (APA, 2008). In addition, the extent and nature of the impact incurred as a result of trauma will also be affected by the individual's age and level of development at the time of the event (Ronen,

2002). From a developmental perspective, stress and traumatic experiences will have a differential impact as a function of emotional, cognitive, and behavioral maturity (Scott, Poulin, & Silver, 2012).

While individuals at each stage of development encounter unique challenges and sensitivities to the potential impact of crisis and trauma, those in the early stages of development (i.e., childhood and adolescence), as well as those navigating later life (i.e., later adulthood) appear to be most vulnerable to the detrimental impact of crisis and trauma. These developmental periods will serve as the target of our discussion within this chapter. After reading this chapter, you should be able to:

1. Explain the factors that make children, adolescents, and the elderly vulnerable to the impact of crisis and trauma;
2. Describe the neurophysiological, behavioral, and social-psychological consequences of traumatic experiences for children, youth, and the elderly;
3. Describe treatment approaches that have been demonstrated effective with children, youth, and the elderly who exhibit lasting effects of trauma; and
4. Explain the special challenges confronting therapists when attempting to work with children, youth, and older adults who have experienced trauma.

Children and Adolescents

Trauma and traumatic events are not restricted to those of adult status. Whether the event was one of abuse, violence, accident, or disaster, crisis affects all within its grasp, regardless of age.

According to the National Survey of Children's Health (NHCS, 2012), almost half of the nation's children have experienced at least one or more types of serious childhood trauma. In addition to the traumatic stressors encountered by adults, children and adolescents are also at risk of trauma related to bullying and embarrassment in school, violence in the home and community, experimentation with drugs, and other risky situations (Shaw, 2000).

In their review of the literature, Saunders and Adams (2014) found that, depending on the specific definition used for trauma, "8–12% of American youth have experienced at least one sexual assault; 9–19% have experienced physical abuse by a caregiver or physical assault; 38–70% have witnessed serious community violence; one in 10 has witnessed serious violence between caregivers; one in 5 has lost a family member or friend to homicide; 9% have experienced Internet-assisted victimization; and 20–25% have been exposed to a natural or man-made disaster" (p.1). These data support the sad reality that trauma, in various forms, impacts our children. In fact, risk of exposure to potentially traumatic events (PTEs) has been shown to peak in adolescence, with approximately two thirds of United States teens having been exposed to at least one PTE (McLaughlin et al., 2013).

In addition to these data, it should be noted that there is substantial research demonstrating that exposure to multiple forms of trauma in childhood is very common (Saunders & Adams, 2014). Depending on the type of trauma and victimization measured, incidents of multiple exposures has been reported to range from 20% to 48% of all youth victimized (Finkelhor, Turner, Shattuck, & Hamby, 2013; Saunders, 2003). These data are particularly concerning given the research regarding the impact on children's functioning after experiencing cumulative forms of victimization (Ford, Fraleigh, Albert, & Connor, 2010).

While these data are alarming, they are quite likely underestimates of the actual number of children and youth impacted by crisis and trauma. Measuring prevalence and incidence of child and adolescent trauma is difficult and affected by numerous factors, including the definition of trauma, the composition of the sample, and the measures employed. Further, the very secretive and stigmatizing nature of some types of traumatic events (e.g., physical and sexual abuse) can lead to the underreporting of prevalence and incidence (Gilbert, Widom, Browne, Fergusson, Webb, & Janson, 2009; Saunders & Adams, 2014).

Impact of Traumatic Experience

Like the parent illustrated at the beginning of this chapter, it would be comforting to assume that children, especially those under the age of five, are simply too young to know what is happening during a crisis, or if they do know, that their memories will soon fade. Sadly, that is not the case. Children and adolescents bring a unique vulnerability to crises and traumatic events and often experience impact to their neurological, behavioral, and emotional functioning (Ronen, 2002). A growing body of research has documented the detrimental effects of trauma exposure in early development. The experience of childhood trauma has been shown to be associated with impairments in multiple developmental processes, including: neurological development, emotion regulation, attachment formation, and autobiographical memory development; the latter has been linked to the ability to form a coherent sense of self (Goodman, Quas, & Ogle, 2010). Case Illustration 8.1 provides a clear example of the widespread and devastating impact that trauma can have on the functioning and normal development of a child.

Neurophysiological Effects

As clearly illustrated in Case Illustration 8.1, the stressors that a child or adolescent encounters will help to shape his or her growth and perspective and can have long-lasting impacts (Crane & Clements, 2005). There is evidence that the stress associated with traumatic events can change major structural components of the central nervous system and the neuroendocrine system (Green, 2012; Lanius, Vermetten & Pain, 2010). Severe traumatic stress affects the chemicals in the brain and can change brain structures, leaving a lasting effect (Spear, 2000).

Experiencing trauma can cause a reduction in the size of the brain's cortex, resulting in higher or lower responses to sensory stimuli (Moroz, 2005). Early exposure to adversity can alter the sensitivity of stress-response systems (e.g., hypothalamic-pituitary-adrenal axis), which in turn, enhances the risk of negative outcomes, including Post-Traumatic Stress Disorder (PTSD), following later stressors (McLaughlin et al., 2013).

In addition to impacting the stress response system, childhood trauma has been found to initiate long-term changes in neurobiology (Champagne, 2010; Fox, Levitt, & Nelson, 2010), affecting the basic regulatory processes in a youth's brain stem, limbic system, and neocortex, which can result in impairment of memory and emotional regulation (Heim, Mletzko, Purselle, Musselman, & Nemeroff, 2008).

Affect Dysregulation

The changes to the neurological structure and neuroendocrine systems in the body as a result of early trauma can impact cortisol levels, which can then impact the flight or fight response. For example, research shows that, as a result of these changes, traumatized youth may have difficulty in regulating emotions. They may exhibit exaggerated startle reactions, night terrors, and difficulty with mood swings (van der Kolk, Pelcovitz, Roth, Mandel, MacFarlane, & Herman, 1996). Other manifestations of affective or emotional dysregulation include emotional lability, anhedonia, flat or numbed affect, explosive or sudden anger, and incongruous

---

CASE ILLUSTRATION 8.1

TRAUMA IMPACTING ONE CHILD'S DEVELOPMENT

Andrea is a seven-year-old who was seen in the emergency room following a car crash in which she saw her older brother and mother killed. The car in which she was riding was "t-boned" by a delivery truck, and her brother who had been sitting in the seat next to her (without a seatbelt) was projected through the side window and decapitated.

While suffering only a few minor cuts and bruises, Andrea sat covered by her brother's blood, silently looking down and picking at the dried blood on her dress. When the therapist approached to sit next to her, she exhibited an exaggerated startle response, leaping to her feet and attempting to run down the hall. The nurse standing there gently guided her back to the chair next to the therapist. She sat and resumed her "dress-picking" behavior. The therapist sat in silence.

After a few minutes, the therapist introduced herself and asked Andrea if she wanted something to drink. In response to the inquiry, she screamed and once again began to run toward the emergency room exit. When the therapist attempted to gently restrain her, Andrea screamed "it's all my fault," and she began to cry hysterically. She fell into the therapist arms becoming completely limp, almost as if she were a rag doll. The therapist held her for a few moments in silence, and then Andrea broke the silence—looking at her dress—and crying, asked, "Why did Robert (her brother) ruin my dress? Mom is going to be angry." She began to sob and once again fell quiet.

In the weeks that followed, the exaggerated startle response, the uncontrollable wailing, and the focus on her blood stained dress began to recede, but her father noted that her sleep and eating patterns were disrupted and that on more than one occasion, he found her "spanking" her doll and proclaiming that she was bad.

CASE ILLUSTRATION 8.2

SEEKING SELF-REGULATION AND CONTROL

Lorraine, a 19-year-old college freshman, came to therapy because a "minor" habit of picking at the skin on her hands had become a major point of concern. The hand picking, a behavior she has had since her early elementary school years, had recently escalated in terms of frequency and intensity to the point where the tops of her hand would bleed and others began noticing the scaring.

In therapy, Lorraine noted that the behavior had begun in elementary school and that, at the time, her parents, teachers, and school counselors identified the behavior as a manifestation of anxiety. When she entered Middle School the hand scratching intensified, and she reported that it would sometimes wake her from sleep. At these times, she would note that the scratching had actually drawn blood. She also shared that it was at this point in her development that she began to have nightmares about cutting her hands and wrists, nightmares that evolved into daytime fantasies. While there was not an active attempt at suicide, the engagement in these fantasies led her parents to elicit professional help. Lorraine went to therapy for a year and began to employ relaxation strategies and thought-stopping interventions that seemed to help. The hand scratching behavior was unremarkable through high school but, now, had re-emerged as a significant disruption to her functioning.

Working with the college counselor, Lorraine identified that the behavior and the intrusive self-harming thoughts seemed to re-appear in concert with a recent development of a sexual relationship with a classmate. Noting that, while she really cared about the relationship, she simply "was not interested in sex" and engaged with him "out of love."

In reviewing the relationship and her feelings about the intimacy, Lorraine revealed that she had memories of being sexually assaulted by an older cousin on a number of separate occasions. While unclear about the specific timing or even the frequency of these assaults, she knew it was during the period of

or inappropriate affect (D'Andrea, Ford, Stolbach & Spinazzola, 2012). Finally, given developmental challenges, such as the evolving sense of self and the development of worldviews, some children and youth who have experienced traumas may develop anxiety disorders, depression, acute stress disorders, PTSDs, and even dissociative disorders (Carlson, Dalenberg, & McDade-Montez, 2012; McLaughlin et al., 2013). See Chapter Five for a more detailed discussion of these mental health diagnoses.

Trauma-Based Response Patterns

Given the changes in their ability to regulate emotions and impulses, it is not unexpected to find that children and teens who have experienced trauma tend to overreact to minor situations, are unable to calm down, or are unable to control their behavior. Behavioral dysregulation may represent affective overload, as well as attempts to dispel, reduce, or recover from negative affect states (Cicchetti & Rogosch, 2007; Ford et al., 2010).

In response to their inability to regulate emotions, children and adolescents may turn to alternative methods of self-regulation, including withdrawal, aggression, oppositional behavior, high-risk sexual behavior, self-injury, eating disorders, and substance abuse (Muehlenkamp, Peat, Claes, & Smits, 2012; Rajappa, Gallagher, & Miranda, 2012; Weiss, Tull, Viana, Anestis, & Gratz, 2012). The impact of early trauma on one's ability to self-regulate is clearly seen in Case Illustration 8.2.

Impact on Self and Worldview

Children and youth exposed to interpersonal trauma have often developed distorted attributions about themselves and the world. Shame, guilt, low self-esteem, poor self-image, poor self-efficacy, and a distorted locus of control are common among children with complex trauma histories (Gibb & Abela, 2008; Kim & Cicchetti, 2006; Valentino, Cicchetti, Rogosch, & Toth, 2008).

Not only can the child's sense of self be shaken, but one's core beliefs about the world in which they live can be shattered. A history of trauma can result in a child viewing the world as unsafe, with the anticipation that more pain is inevitable (Thompson et al., 2012). Such a worldview can result in the child having difficulty with trust, social affiliation, and attachment (Meaney, Brake, & Gratton, 2002; Heim et al., 2008).

time where her family held joint family vacations. This was a period of time when she was between the ages of three and six.

In discussing her memories of that time, she made a connection between being held down by her wrists during these encounters and her behavior, stating "I can remember that afterwards I would run into the bathroom, and I would scrub my belly and my wrists where he held me."

Enduring Effects

While many children and teens who encounter trauma in the early phases of development are resilient and return to normative functioning (APA, 2008), the truth is that, for many, the impact lasts well into adulthood. The Adverse Childhood Experiences (ACE) Study explored the long-lasting impact of childhood trauma into adulthood. Results from data collected on over 17,000 participants indicated a connection between childhood trauma exposure and adult high-risk behaviors; chronic illness, such as heart disease and cancer; and early death (Anda, Felitti, Brown et al., 2006). Also, early traumatic and crisis experiences have been linked to adult depression, PTSD, and substance abuse (Harris, Putnam & Fairbank, 2006), as well as academic/learning impairment (Holt et al., 2007).

Intervention

Children and adolescents tend to be resilient and return to previous levels of functioning within several weeks or months, especially those exposed to a single incident (APA, 2008). For those exposed to multiple traumas or who have a history of difficulty, the possibility of ongoing symptoms and the need for treatment is more likely.

A number of programs (e.g., Cohen, Berliner, & Mannarino, 2000) have emphasized a stage-based approach emphasizing the need to: 1) establish a sense of safety for the child, 2) foster an intact sense of self as safe, capable, and lovable by way of supporting remembrance and mourning, and 3) reconnecting and re-integrating the experience to move forward. In general, intervention models engaging in a step- or phase-based approach see the first phase as one in which the treatment goals include the establishment of a therapeutic alliance and the development of client symptom control, affect and impulse control, and understanding regarding symptoms and treatment processes.

EXERCISE 8.1

REFERRAL RESOURCE: ADDRESSING THE NEEDS OF CHILDREN AND YOUTH

Directions: Exercise 8.1 invites you to investigate the resources available within your community for addressing the needs of children and youth who have experienced trauma in their lives. It is helpful to not only gather data on the nature of these services, as well as the procedures for accessing them. In addition, it is helpful to contrast actual services offered in your community with those supported by research as effective. Gather the following data and, if possible, share, compare, and contrast to what a colleague or classmate found.

Resource Agency or Individual: _____

Contact Information (e.g., address, phone, email, fax, name of intake person, etc.): ___
_____
_____

Fee Structure and Payment Options (insurance? sliding scale?): _____
_____

Modality (individual, group, etc.): _____
_____

Theoretical Model(s) Approaches Employed:
_____

Supportive Services (e.g., housing, medical, etc.): _____
_____

As stability is achieved, the client will be assisted in processing the event and the traumatic memories and, later, aided in viewing themselves more accurately and less negatively (Green, 2012). It is at that stage that cognitive-behavioral interventions addressing cognitive distortions are often employed (Cohen et al., 2012). The final phase involves assisting the client to reconnect with productive activities and healthy relationships.

One of the most studied and empirically supported approaches to treatment of children and teens that have experienced various forms of trauma is Trauma-Focused Cognitive Behavioral Therapy (TF-CBT) (Cohen, Mannarino & Deblinger, 2006). TF-CBT incorporates elements of cognitive-behavioral, attachment, humanistic, empowerment, and family therapy models. While a complete presentation of this model is beyond the scope of this text, those interested are referred to Cohen, Mannarino, and Deblinger's book, *Treating Trauma and Traumatic Grief in Children and Adolescents* (Cohen, Mannarino, & Deblinger, 2006). In addition, information about this approach, along with training possibilities, can be found at: http://www.musc.edu/tfcbt.

Exercise 8.1 invites you to investigate the resources available within your community for addressing the needs of children and youth who have experienced trauma in their lives. It is helpful to gather data on both the nature of these services and the procedures for accessing them. In addition it is helpful to contrast actual services offered in your community with those supported by research as effective.

Later Life: Older Adult Experience with Crises and Trauma

The possibility that the older adult is more vulnerable to the immediate and long-term negative effects of trauma is not clear-cut. Some have suggested that older adults are more resistant to the negative effects of trauma, since they are less prone to fear and despair when contrasted to younger adults (Norris et al., 2002). Others have found older adults to be more vulnerable to distress and are at increased risk for experiencing negative and damaging consequences from traumatic events, as a result of their increased physical and emotional frailty and age-related changes in functionality, along with their reduced personal and social resources (Carballo et al., 2004; Cohen Silver, Holman, McIntosh, Poulin, & Gil-Rivas, 2002).

It is clear that the actual impact of crises and trauma varies both across, and within, developmental levels and, thus, all generalities need to be viewed with caution. However, with this caveat it is still important to review the literature that highlights those data pointing to the unique experiences of the older adult who has encountered trauma.

Age Increasing Vulnerability to Stress and Trauma

The older adult can be confronted by a number of crises that are unique to this developmental period, including: widowhood, negative impacts of retirement, fears of pain and disability, and problems caused by diminished sensory capacity. Factors such as increased health challenges, diminished cognitive abilities, and loss of loved ones and social support can facilitate the negative impact of trauma (Cook & Dinnen, 2015; Cook, Naseem & Thorp, 2015). In addition to these conditions, the very fact that many older adults find themselves more dependent on the care and support of others often places them in the vulnerable position of being abused. Some older adults find themselves the victims of elder abuse in the forms of: neglect, intimidation, physical force, threats, mistreatment, confinement, and punishment; these may result in injury, distress, deprivation, and even death (Karch & Nunn, 2011). More poignantly, according to the National Criminal Victimization Survey (Truman & Langton, 2015), this abuse most often occurs at the hands of the elder's children or grandchildren. The effects of this abuse can be devastating, resulting in a myriad of physical and mental health challenges (Fisher & Regan, 2006; Schofield, Powers, & Loxton, 2013).

Finally, the older adult who has had early life exposure to crisis and trauma may now exhibit the cumulative effect of that trauma over the course of their lifespan (Ogle, Rubin & Siegler, 2013, 2014). Numerous life changes can result in the older adult re-experiencing a previously negative and harmful life event and, as a result, overwhelm the individual's ability to cope at the moment (Lapp, Agbokou, & Ferreri, 2011). Case

CASE ILLUSTRATION 8.3

A REAWAKENING OF PAINFUL MEMORIES

Ramon is a 70-year-old Latino-American who lives with his wife of 45 years. He is a recently retired high school social science teacher. Ramon was involved in a multiple car accident while driving home from a vacation at the beach. While his car was totaled, neither he nor his wife were seriously injured. Two of the cars involved were engulfed in fire, but thankfully, all occupants escaped without serious injury. Ramon and his wife were transported to the hospital for evaluation and then released.

While the events of the week following the accident were unremarkable, Ramon began to have nightmares and anxiety specifically around the issue of riding in his car. In the weeks that followed the accident, Ramon experienced increasing sleep disturbance, irritability, and emotional outbursts (e.g., crying for no apparent reason, shaking, and yelling at minor irritants). He began to withdraw from social contact with friends and family and now refuses to get into a car, even as a passenger. The nightmares, emotional outbreaks, and withdrawal from friends and family seemed disproportionate to the actual events surrounding his recent accident.

Ramon initially attributed his response to simply "not feeling well" as a result of the accident. However, the fact that his symptoms continued to increase in frequency and disruption to his normal functioning motivated him to seek out professional counseling.

In the course of meeting with the therapist, Ramon revealed that, while serving in Vietnam, he witnessed a truck with four of his friends hit by enemy fire and burst into flames. All within the truck where killed as a result of the initial explosion and resulting fire. The event was traumatizing and, for close to a year, following his return stateside, Ramon experienced recurring nightmares about that event.

Ramon noted that he had not really thought about the event for well over 40 years. As a result of counseling, he began to realize that the recent accident reawakened the memories he felt he had put to rest.

Illustration 8.3 highlights the power of previous traumatic events and memories of those events on current functioning.

Increased Risk of Negative Consequences

With their personal resources challenged as a result of normative aging, many older people show higher levels of post-traumatic stress, as well as lower rates of recovery, than do young adults and adolescents (Carballo et al., 2004; Ohta et al., 2003). For many older adults, the trauma results in sleep problems, hyperarousal, and avoidance (Goenjian et al.,1994). For others, the impact can be more disruptive and include an experience of chronic or recurrent depression, compromised coping abilities, as well as somatic and health-related problems (Acierno et al., 2006; Fridman, Bakermans-Kranenburg, Sagi-Schwartz, & Van IJzendoorn, 2011).

While it is possible that the adaptation and resilience an older adult has developed over a lifetime can provide the coping resources needed to return them to functionality, for some, the disruption and negative effects require professional intervention.

Treatment

While research has identified a number of therapeutic approaches with robust support for their efficacy, most of the research has been targeted to young and middle-aged adults, rather than the older adult (Keane, Marshall, & Taft, 2006). Cognitive-behavioral therapies (CBT), for example, have been considered the preferred treatment modality with trauma survivors (APA, 2004; Keane, Marshall, & Taft, 2006). However, some have cautioned their use with the older adult due to age-related declines in cognitive capacity (e.g., Cook, Ruzek, & Cassidy, 2003; Flint, 2004). For example, Hyer & Sohnle (2001) point to the possible diminished capacity for comprehension, self-reflection, and memory as therapeutic challenges for those employing cognitive-behavioral approaches.

These concerns with CBT have been questioned in the literature, given the general support for the effectiveness of CBT in treating depression and generalized anxiety among older adults (Ayers, Sorrell, Thorp, & Wetherell, 2007). Clearly, large-scale studies on the efficacy of varied therapeutic approaches applied specifically to those experiencing the effects of trauma should be advanced.

Regardless of the theoretical model employed, it appears that treating the older adult presents a number of challenges that can confound the effectiveness of therapy. One issue that may reduce the likelihood of the older adult seeking psychotherapy is that their mental health needs may be masked by acute health demands or are compounded by higher rates of comorbidities of functional difficulties and chronic disease (Chung, Berger, Jones & Rudd, 2008). Further, when the issues identified are obviously of a psychological nature, many older adults resist such a presentation, being less psychologically minded and, thus, less responsive to psychosocial approaches to treatment (Burgmer & Heuft, 2004). This may be especially true when the original trauma occurred in the past. Under these conditions, the individual is more likely to identify the problems as attributed to a proximal issue or

---

EXERCISE 8.2

REFERRAL RESOURCE: ADDRESSING THE NEEDS OF THE OLDER ADULT

Directions: As with the previous exercise, you are now invited to investigate the resources available within your community for addressing the needs of older adults who have experienced trauma in their lives. It is helpful to not only gather data on the nature of these services, as well as the procedures for accessing them, but also to contrast what is being offered to what the research suggests is effective. Gather the following data and, if possible, share, compare, and contrast to what a colleague or classmate found.

Resource Agency or Individual: _____

_____

Contact Information (e.g., address, phone, email, fax, name of intake person, etc.): ___

_____

Fee Structure and Payment Options (insurance? sliding scale?): _____

_____

Modality (individual, group, etc.): _____

_____

Theoretical Model(s) Approaches Employed:

_____

Supportive Services (e.g., housing, medical, etc.): _____

_____

---

the aging process (Owens, et al., 2005), thus resisting revisiting the previous events and experiences.

As with the previous exercise (i.e., Exercise 8.1), you are now being invited to investigate the resources available within your community for addressing the needs of those older adults who have experienced trauma in their lives. It is helpful to not only gather data on the nature of these services, as well as the procedures for accessing these services, but also the unique challenges experienced when attempting to engage the elderly in such supportive services.

Summary

- The impact of a traumatic experience and the resulting level of psychological distress and disruptions depend upon factors such as the severity of the trauma, proximity to the traumatizing event, previous trauma exposure, preexisting problems, and individual's age and level of development at the time of the event.

- According to the NHCS (2012), almost half the nation's children have experienced at least one or more types of serious childhood trauma.

- In addition to the traumatic stressors encountered by adults, children, and adolescents are also at risk of trauma related to bullying and embarrassment in school, violence in the home and community, experimentation with drugs, and other risky situations.

- The experience of childhood trauma has been shown to be associated with impairments in numerous developmental processes, including neurological development, emotional regulation, attachment formation, and autobiographical memory development, which has been linked to the ability to form a coherent sense of self.

- The changes to the neurological structure and neuroendocrine systems in the body as a result of early trauma can impact cortisol levels and, as such, the flight or fight response, resulting in disruption to regulation of emotions.

- Childhood trauma has been found to have long-lasting effects into adulthood, including adult high-risk behaviors; chronic illness, such as heart disease and cancer; adult depression; PTSD; and substance abuse.

- Treatment programs targeting children and teens typically employ a stage-based approach emphasizing the need to: 1) establish a sense of safety for the child/youth, 2) fostering of an intact sense of self as a safe, capable, and lovable by way of supporting remembrance and mourning, 3) reconnecting and re-integrating the experience to move forward.

- Older adults can experience forms of crisis and trauma unique to their developmental stage, including: widowhood, negative impacts of retirement, fears of pain and disability, and abuse at the hands of caretakers.

- Older people show higher levels of post-traumatic stress, as well as lower rates of recovery, than do young adults and adolescents

- Numerous life changes can result in the older adult re-experiencing a previously negative and harmful life event and, as a result, overwhelm the individual's ability to cope at the moment.

- The older adult presents a number of challenges that can confound the effectiveness of the therapy, including: mental health needs may be masked by acute health demands; the exhibition of higher rates of comorbidities of functional difficulties and chronic disease; or the fact that many older adults are less psychologically minded and, thus, less responsive to psychosocial approaches to treatment.

Important Terms

Adverse Childhood Experience (ACE)

Affect dysregulation

Neuropsychological effects

Potentially Traumatic Event (PTE)

Trauma-Focused Cognitive Behavioral Therapy (TF-CBT)

Additional Resources

In Print

Cohen, J. A., Mannarino, A. P., & Deblinger, E. (2006). *Treating Trauma and Traumatic Grief in Children and Adolescents.* New York, NY: Guildford Press.

Hyer, L. A., & Sohnle, S. J. (2001). *Trauma among older people: Issues and treatment.* New York, NY: Brunner-Routledge.

Macleod, A. (2011). Reintegration takes teamwork, communication. Retrieved from http://www.army.mil/article/52897/Reintegration_takes_teamwork__communication/

Warner, E., Cook, A., Westcott, A., & Koomar, J. (2014). *SMART: Sensory Motor Arousal Regulation Treatment Manual.* Brookline, MA: The Trauma Center at JRI.

On the Web

The National Child Traumatic Stress Network: http://www.nctsn.org

Trauma-Focused Cognitive-Behavioral Therapy (Web-based learning course): http://www.musc.edu/tfcbt

SAMHSA Disaster Distress HELPLINE: http://www.samhsa.gov/find-help/disaster-distress-helpline

References

Acierno R., Ruggiero K. J., Kilpatrick D. G., Resnick H., Galea S. (2006). Risk and protective factors for psychopathology among older versus younger adults after the 2004 Florida hurricanes. *American Journal of Geriatric Psychiatry, 14*, 1051–1059.

American Psychiatric Association (2004). Practice guideline for the treatment of patients with acute stress disorder and posttraumatic stress disorder. Retrieved from http://www.psychiatryonline.com/pracGuide/loadGuidelinePdf.aspx?file=ASD_PTSD_05-15-06.

Anda R. F., Felitti V. J., Bremner J. D., Walker J. D., Whitfield C., Perry B. D., … Giles, W. H. (2006). The enduring effects of abuse and related adverse experiences in childhood. A convergence of evidence from neurobiology and epidemiology. *European Archives of Psychiatry and Clinical Neuroscience, 256*(3), 174–186.

Ayers C. R., Sorrell J. T., Thorp S. R., & Wetherell J. L.(2007). Evidence-based psychological treatments for late-life anxiety. *Psychology and Aging, 22*, 8–17.

Burgmer M., & Heuft G. (2004). Occurrence and treatment of post-traumatic stress disorder in an elderly patient after a traffic accident. *International Journal of Geriatric Psychiatry, 19*, 185–188.

Carballo, M., Smajkic, A., Zeric, D., Dzidowska, M., Gebre-Medhin, J., & Van Halem, J. (2004). Mental health and coping in a war situation: The case of Bosnia and Herzegovina. *Journal of Biosocial Science, 36*, 463–477.

Carlson, E. B., Dalenberg, C., & McDade-Montez, E. (2012). Dissociation in posttraumatic stress disorder: Part I: Definitions and review of the research. *Psychological Trauma: Theory, Research, Practice, and Policy, 4*, 479–489.

Cook, J. M., Ruzek J. I., & Cassidy E. (2003). Possible association of posttraumatic stress disorder with cognitive impairment among older adults. *Psychiatric Services, 2003, 54*, 1223–122.

Champagne, F. A. (2010). Early adversity and developmental outcomes: Interaction between genetics, epigenetics, and social experiences across the life span. *Perspectives on Psychological Science, 5*, 564–574.

Chung, M. C., Berger, Z., Jones, R. & Rudd, H. (2008). Posttraumatic stress and co-morbidity following myocardial infarction among older patients: The role of coping. *Aging Mental Health, 12*(1), 124–33.

Cicchetti, D., & Rogosch, F. A. (2007). Personality, adrenal steroid hormones, and resilience in maltreated children: A multilevel perspective. *Development and Psychopathology, 19*, 787–809.

Cohen, J. A., Berliner, L., & Mannarino, A. P. (2000). Treating traumatized children: A research review and synthesis. *Trauma, Violence, and Abuse, 1*, 29–46.

Cohen, J. A., Mannarino, A. P., & Deblinger, E. (2006). *Treating trauma and traumatic grief in children and adolescents.* New York, NY: Guilford Press.

Cohen Silver, R., Holman, E. A., McIntosh, D. N., Poulin, M., & Gil-Rivas, V. (2002). Nationwide longitudinal study of psychological responses to September 11. *JAMA: Journal of the American Medical Association, 288*, 1235–1244.

Cook, J. M. (2001). Post-traumatic stress disorder in older adults. *PTSD Research Quarterly, 12*, 1–7.

Cook, J. M., & Dinnen, S. (2015). Exposure therapy for late-life trauma. In P. A. Areán (Ed.), *Treatment of late-life depression, anxiety, trauma, and substance abuse* (pp. 133–161). Washington, D.C.: American Psychological Association.

Cook, J. Mf., Naseem, A., & Thorp, S. R. (2015). Treating PTSD in older adults. In N. C. Bernardy & M. J. Friedman (Eds.), *A practical guide to PTSD treatment: Pharmacological and psychotherapeutic approaches.* Washington, D.C.: American Psychological Association.

Crane, P. A., & Clements, P. T. (2005). Psychological responses to disaster: Focus on adolescents. *Journal of Psychosocial Nursing, 43*(8), 31–38.

D' Andrea, W., Ford, J., Stolbach, B., & Spinazzola, J. (2012). Understanding interpersonal trauma in children: Why we need a developmentally appropriate trauma diagnosis. *American Journal of Orthopsychiatry, 82*(2), 187–200.

Flint, A. J. (2004). Anxiety disorders. In Sadavoy, J., Jarvik, L., Grossberg, G., Meyers, B., (Eds.), *Comprehensive Textbook of Geriatric Psychiatry.* (pp687-699). New York: Norton.

Finkelhor, D., Turner, H.A., Shattuck, A., & Hamby, S.L. (2013). Violence, crime, and abuse exposure in a national sample of children and youth: an update. *JAMA Pediatrics, 167*(7), 614–621.

Fisher, B. S., & Regan, S. L. (2006). The extent and frequency of abuse in the lives of older women and their relationship to health outcomes. *Gerontologist, 46*(2), 200–209.

Ford, J. D., Fraleigh, L. A., Albert, D. B., & Connor, D. F. (2010). Child abuse and autonomic nervous system hyporesponsivity among psychiatrically impaired children. *Child Abuse & Neglect, 34*, 507–515.

Fox S.E, Levitt P, & Nelson C.A. (2010). How the timing and quality of early experiences influence the development of brain architecture. *Child Development, 81*, 28–40.

Fridman, A., Bakermans-Kranenburg, M. J., Sagi-Schwartz, A. & Vanljendoorn, M. H. (2011). Coping in old age with extreme childhood trauma: Aging Holocaust survivors and their offspring facing new challenges. *Aging and Mental Health, 15*(2), 242–242.

Gibb, B. E., & Abela, J. R. Z. (2008). Emotional abuse, verbal victimization, and the development of children's negative inferential styles and depressive symptoms. *Cognitive Therapy and Research, 32*, 161–176.

Gilbert R., Widom C. S, Browne K., Fergusson D., Webb E., & Janson S. (2009). Burden and consequences of child maltreatment in high income countries. *The Lancet, 3*(373), 68–81.

Goenjian, A. K., Najarian, L. M., Pynoos, R. S., Steinberg, A. M., Manoukian, G., Tavosian, A., & Fairbanks, L. A. (1994). Posttraumatic stress disorder in elderly and younger adults after the 1988 earthquake in Armenia. *American Journal of Psychiatry, 151*, 895–901.

Goodman, G. S., Quas, J. A., & Ogle, C. M. (2010). Child maltreatment and memory. *Annual Review of Psychology, 61*, 325–335.

Green, E. J. (2012). Facilitating resiliency in traumatized adolescents: Integrating play therapy with evidence-based interventions. *Play Therapy, 6*, 10–15.

Harris, W. W., Putnam, F. W. & Fairbank, J. A. (2006). Mobilizing trauma resources for children. In A. F. Lierberman & R. DeMartino (Eds.), *Shaping the future of children's health* (pp. 311–339). Calverton, NY: Johnson & Johnson Pediatric Institute.

Heim, C., Mletzko, T., Purselle, D., Musselman, D. L., Nemeroff, C. B. (2008). The dexamethasone/corticotropin-releasing factor test in men with major depression: Role of childhood trauma. *Biological Psychiatry, 63*, 398–405

Hiskey, S., Luckie, M., Davies, S., & Brewin C. R. (2008). The Emergence of Posttraumatic Distress in Later Life: A Review. *Journal of Geriatric Psychiatry and Neurology, 21*(4), 232–241.

Holt, M. K., Finkelhor, D., & Kantor, G. K. (2007). Multiple victimization experiences of urban elementary school students: Associations with psychosocial functioning and academic performance. *Child Abuse and Neglect, 31*, 503–515.

Hyer, L. A., & Sohnle, S. J. (2001). *Trauma among older people: Issues and treatment.* New York, NY: Brunner-Routledge.

Karch, D. & Nunn, K. C. (2011). Characteristics of elderly and other vulnerable adult victims of homicide by a caregiver: National Violent Death Reporting System–17 U.S. States, 2003–2007. *Journal of Interpersonal Violence, 26,* (1), 137–157.

Keane T. M, Marshall A. D., Taft C. T. (2006). Posttraumatic Stress Disorder: Etiology, epidemiology, and treatment outcome. *Annual Review of Psychology, 2,* 161–197.

Kim, J., & Cicchetti, D. (2006). Longitudinal trajectories of self-system processes and depressive symptoms among maltreated and non-maltreated children. *Child Development, 77,* 624–639.

Lanius, R. A., Vermetten, E., & Pain, C. (Eds.). (2010). *Impact of early life trauma on health and disease.* Cambridge, MA: Cambridge University Press.

Lapp, L. K., Agbokou, C. & Ferreri, F. (2011). PTSD in the elderly: The interaction between trauma and aging. *International Psychogeriatrics, 24*(6), 858–868.

Meaney, M. J, Brake W., Gratton A. (2002). Environmental regulation of the development of mesolimbic dopamine systems: A neurobiological mechanism for vulnerability to drug abuse? *Psychoneuroendocrinology, 27,* 127–138.

McLaughlin, K. A., Koenen, K. C., Hill, E. D., Petukhova, M., Sampson, N. A., Zaslavsky, A. M., & Kessler, R. C. (2013). Trauma exposure and posttraumatic stress disorder in a national sample of adolescents. *Journal of the American Academy of Child & Adolescent Psychiatry, 52,* 815–830.

Moroz, K. J. (2005). The Effects of Psychological trauma on children and adolescents. Vermont Agency of Human Serivces, Department of Mental Health. Retrieved from https://pdfs.semanticscholar.org/83c8/515628016bae47dfbcd2c9a6f96eeb564742.pdf

Muehlenkamp, J. J., Peat, C. M., Claes, L., & Smits, D. (2012). Self-injury and disordered eating: Expressing emotion dysregulation through the body. *Suicide and Life-Threatening Behavior, 42,* 416–425.

NSCH (National Survey of Children's Health). (2012). Data query from the Child and Adolescent Health Measurement Initiative, Data Resource Center for Child and Adolescent Health website. Retrieved July 25, 2016, from www.childhealthdata.org

Norris, F. H., Friedman, M. J., Watson, P. J., Byrne, C. M., Diaz, E., & Kaniasty, K. (2002). 60,000 disaster victims speak: Part I. An empirical review of the empirical literature, 1981–2001. *Psychiatry: Interpersonal and Biological Processes, 65,* 207–239.

Ogle, C. M., Rubin, D. C., & Siegler, I. C. (2013). The impact of the developmental timing of trauma exposure on PTSD symptoms and psychosocial functioning among older adults. *Developmental Psychology, 49,* 2191–2200.

Ogle, C. M., Rubin, D. C., & Siegler, I. C. (2014). Cumulative exposure to traumatic events in older adults. *Aging & Mental Health, 18,* 316–325.

Ohta, Y., Araki, K., Kawasaki, N., Nakane, Y., Honda, S., & Mine, M. (2003). Psychological distress among evacuees of a volcanic eruption in Japan: A follow-up study. *Psychiatry and Clinical Neurosciences, 57,* 105–111.

Owens, G. P., Baker, D. G., Kasckow, J., Ciesla, J. A., & Mohamed, S. (2005). Review of assessment and treatment of PTSD among elderly American armed forces Veterans. *International Journal of Geriatric Psychiatry, 20,* 1118–1130.

Rajappa, K., Gallagher, M., & Miranda, R. (2012). Emotion dysregulation and vulnerability to suicidal ideation and attempts. *Cognitive Therapy and Research, 36,* 833–839.

Ronen, T. (2002). Difficulties in assessing traumatic reactions in children. *Journal of Loss and Trauma, 7,* 87–106.

Saunders, B. E. (2003). Understanding children exposed to violence: Toward an integration of overlapping fields. *Journal of Interpersonal Violence, 18*(4), 356–376.

Saunders, B. E., & Adams, Z. W. (2014). Epidemiology of traumatic experiences in childhood. *Child and Adolescent Psychiatric Clinics of North America, 23*(2), 167–184.

Schofield, M. J., Powers, J.R. & Loxton, D. (2013). Mortality and disability outcomes of self-reported elder abuse. *Journal of the American Geriatric Society, 61*(5), 679–685.

Scott, S. B., Poulin, M. J., & Silver, R. C. (2013). A lifespan perspective in trajectories of response to 9/11. *Developmental Psychology, 49,* 986–998.

Shaw, J. A. (2000). Children, adolescents and trauma. *Psychiatric Quarterly, 71,* 227–243.

Spear, L. (2000). Neurobehavioral changes in adolescence. *Psychological Science, 9*(4), 111–114.

Thompson, R., Wiley, T. R. A., Lewis, T., English, D. J., Dubowitz, H., Litrownik, A. J., & Block, S. (2012). Links between traumatic experiences and expectations about the future in high-risk youth. *Psychological Trauma: Theory, Research, Practice, and Policy, 4,* 292–302.

Truman, J. L., & Langton, L. (2015). *Crime Victimization.* Retrieved from https://www.bjs.gov/content/pub/pdf/cv14.pdf

Valentino, K., Cicchetti, D., Rogosch, F. A., & Toth, S. L. (2008). True and false recall and dissociation among maltreated children: The role of self-schema. *Development and Psychopathology, 20,* 213–232.

van der Kolk, B. A., Pelcovitz, D., Roth, S., Mandel, F., MacFarlane, A., & Herman, J.L. (1996). Dissociation, affect regulation and somatization: The complex nature of adaptation to trauma. *American Journal of Psychiatry, 153* (Supplement), 8393.

Weiss, N. H., Tull, M. T., Viana, A. G., Anestis, M. D., & Gratz, K. L. (2012). Impulsive behaviors as an emotion regulation strategy: Examining associations between PTSD, emotion dysregulation, and impulsive behaviors among substance dependent inpatients. *Journal of Anxiety Disorders, 26,* 453–458.

CHAPTER 9

Specific Crisis Intervention Techniques in Various Settings

What happened? Church is a place of sanctity. Our church has always been a refuge for those in need, in pain ... those seeking solace and reconciliation. How could this become a target for such violence and hostility?

While it is tempting to dream of days gone by when churches were safe havens never to be accosted by the darker side of humanity, or when schools were simply places of play, excitement, stimulation, and growth, and communities were safe from threats, dangers, or crisis, such a world is a fantasy. The pastor quoted above stood watching the burning of her church and the surviving graffiti of hate still visible on the crumbling walls; she knows all too well that no one, no place, is immune from terror, crisis, or disaster.

The current chapter will review specific models and intervention techniques employed in our K–12 schools, our college campuses, and our communities' public settings. After reading this chapter, you should be able to:

1. Describe the elements involved in the PREPaRE Model of School Crisis Prevention and Intervention;

2. Describe the role and function of Threat Assessment Teams;

3. Describe the role and function of Behavioral Intervention Teams;

4. Explain what is meant by the term "Trauma Contagion"; and

5. Explain what is meant by Geographic, Psychological, and Social Proximity and how they are used to identify those at risk for trauma contagion

K–12 School Settings

For even in "days gone by," those working in schools encountered the unexpected death of a student, teacher, administrator, or parent; an accident of young drivers over the weekend; or damage done as a result of fire, hurricane or tornadoes. Schools are not environments that are immune to crisis and trauma. In addition to natural disasters, students experience violence and death related to suicide, gang activity, and even more dramatically, at the hand of snipers and hostage-takers.

Most of us are familiar with the "fire-drill" plan that saw us following a teacher to a designated spot outside of our building. In addition, many schools in vulnerable locations have plans and protocols in place in the event of a serious weather incident, such as a tornado. But given events of the past 20 years, schools have expanded their crisis plans to include protocols for responding to events such as: suicide, death, grief and loss, violence, weapons in school, school shootings, bomb scares, campus intruders, and community or national disasters.

These protocols direct all involved to address the question "What if … ?" The answer is one that will not only organize people and resources but will highlight lines of authority, communication and responsibilities. The proper handling of school crises is essential to minimizing negative impact, not so much on the academic achievement of the students but, instead, their very physical and psychological wellbeing.

Given the age of the population served within our school settings, the chaos and experience of instability and threat to one's safety that can be encountered at times of crisis can result in severe emotional responses and possible long-term psychosocial and educational problems. Therefore, it is important for schools to develop and employ a crisis plan that will provide order and establish stability for the community when shaken by crisis.

Planning for Crisis

The focus of a comprehensive crisis plan is to provide immediate assistance to those in crisis, minimize the distress and chaos experienced, and assist the school community in returning to a normal educational environment as quickly as feasible (Brown & Trusty, 2005). Such a plan will also address residual psychosocial problems and explore the development and implementation of preventive measures, reducing the possibility of crisis re-occurrence.

One model developed specifically for school-based mental health professionals is the PREPaRE Model of School Crisis Prevention and Intervention (Brock et al., 2009). The PREPaRE model incorporates best practice research, as well as the recommendations for crisis teams offered by the U.S. Department of Education (2003). It identifies a specific hierarchical and sequential set of activities that target: **P**reventing and preparing for psychological trauma, **R**eaffirming physical health and perceptions of security and safety, **E**valuating psychological trauma risk, **P**roviding interventions and **R**esponding to psychological needs, and **E**xamining the effectiveness of crisis prevention and intervention (see Table 9.1).

Table 9.1 PREPaRE Model of School Crisis Prevention and Intervention: An Outline

Stage	Description of Target	Sample Strategies
Crisis Prevention and Preparedness	Activities to ensure physical and psychological safety (Reeves et al., 2008)	Physical Safety: • Use of surveillance • Use of access control • Employment of screening devices • Development of crisis response procedures including evacuation and lockdown (Joshi & Lewin, 2004). Psychological Safety: • Provision of social-emotional interventions and support • Student guidance services • Positive behavioral supports • Developing student resiliency (Brock et al., 2009) • Immediate crisis intervention resources and longer-term psychotherapeutic resources
Reaffirmation	Convey stability and the reaffirmation of both objective physical safety and student perceptions of safety	Reaffirm Physical Health & Safety: • Respond to special and acute needs • Ensure student comfort (e.g., provide water, snacks, blankets, etc.) Reaffirm Psychological Health & Safety: • Recognizing the importance of adult reactions and behaviors (e.g., stay calm, direct, nurturing yet authoritative) • Reuniting/locating caregivers and significant others • Providing facts and adaptive interpretations • Providing opportunities to take action (e.g., student gatherings, engagement in reparation activities, and where possible, engage in efforts to restore equilibrium, etc.).
Evaluation	Evaluate psychological trauma: "crisis exposure, physical proximity, risk factors" (Brock et al., 2009) Evaluating psychological trauma: Internal vulnerability risk factors	Evaluate Student Internal Vulnerability (Brock et al., 2009): • Identify those with pre-crisis psychological challenges or history of trauma • Identify students with avoidance coping styles • Identify students with poor ability to regulate emotions

| Providing intervention and responding to psychological needs | Provide crisis interventions and respond to mental health needs, (Brock et al., 2009; Brymer et al., 2012) | Re-Establish Social Support:
• Reunite with primary caregivers
• Reunite with peers/teachers
• Facilitate community connection

Provide Psychological Education:
• Group/classroom guidance providing accurate information on "what" and "what to do"
• Provide students and caretakers information on what to expect and how to respond. Talk about emotional reactions and direct to avenues of support.
• Provide information about stress reactions and coping to reduce distress and promote adaptive functioning

Provide Psychological Interventions:
• Engage students/classroom discussions and activities that allow students to express and discuss feelings about the crisis.
• Individual crisis intervention (see psychological first aid)
• Longer term psychotherapeutic treatment
• To link students and staff with available services needed at the time or in the future. |
| Examination | Evaluate/examine the effectiveness of crisis response services provided | • Planners meet for a debriefing session to evaluate how procedures worked, what revisions are needed, and clarify preventive implications.
• Using a crisis planning team, assess what happened, what was done (prior to, during and after) and the outcomes of these procedures. |

Interventions

Table 9.1 provides both a guiding structure and illustrations of actions that can be taken at each stage of the process. Additional information and guidance can be acquired by going to the National Child Traumatic Stress Network and the National Center for Post-Traumatic Stress Disorder (PTSD). The Network has created the Psychological First Aid for Schools Field Operations Guide, along with handouts. These are all available at http://www.nctsn.org/content/psychological-first-aid-schoolspfa.

Psychological First Aid for Schools (PFA-S) employs brief interventions targeted to reducing the initial distress and development of coping strategies following school crisis, disaster or terrorism events. As noted in the Psychological First Aid for Schools Field Operation Guide (Brymer et al., 2012, p. 5), the basic objectives are:

• To establish a positive a non-intrusive, compassionate connection with students and staff members

• To provide for safety and physical and emotional comfort

• To calm those emotionally overwhelmed or distraught

• To help identify survivors' immediate needs and concerns

• To offer practical assistance for addressing these needs and concerns

- To connect survivors to social support networks

- To take a strength based approach, acknowledging the coping strengths of survivors and empower them to take an active role in their recovery

- To connect survivors to other relevant school or community resources[1]

It is helpful for schools to not only develop an extensive response plan, but also to develop a checklist that can serve as a reminder of tasks and responsibilities during times of crisis. The following resource for the development of such a checklist is available from the University of California Los Angeles' Center for Mental Health in Schools: http://smhp.psych.ucla.edu/pdfdocs/crisis/crisis.pdf.

Responding to College Campus Crises

Media images of the mass shootings at Virginia Tech (April, 2007) and Northern Illinois University (February, 2008) have raised our collective consciousness regarding the possibility of violence on college campuses. While incidents of campus shootings are dramatic and concerning, they are not the only, nor the most common, forms of violence being encountered on our college campuses. It is more common for the campus community to be shaken by incidents of aggravated assault, robbery, sexual assault, and other interpersonal violence. Given this, steps should be taken to prevent and intervene at times of all forms of campus violence.

Intervention/Prevention-System Level

When speaking of violence intervention, two unique, yet interrelated, focal points emerge. There are approaches that target prevention of violence on campus and those that remediate the negative effects of violence on survivors, should it occur.

Given the open access and general freedom experienced on our college campuses, it is not surprising that institutions of higher learning are vulnerable to intrusion and violence from those outside the college community, as well as those from within. Given this reality, many institutions have established teams (e.g., Behavioral Intervention Teams and Threat Assessment Teams) that are charged with assessing and managing risks (Pollard, Nolan & Deisinger, 2012). Central to the work of these teams is the creation of a culture of reporting and the facilitation of sharing information, as well as the engagement of prevention and intervention policies and procedures (Sokolow, Lewis, Schuster, 2011).

---

1 Lee Ann Hoff, Lisa Brown, and Miracle R. Hoff, "Assault & Homicidal Danger Assessment Tool," *People in Crisis: Clinical and Diversity Perspectives*, 6th ed., pp. 439. Copyright © 2009 by Taylor & Francis Group. Reprinted with permission.

Behavioral Intervention Teams (BITs) employ a formalized approach to addressing mental health issues and other behaviors that either pose a danger of harm to self or others or disrupt the learning environment. The goals of the BIT are: (a) to prevent crises before they occur through the provision of outreach and educational programming, consultation, appropriate assessment, and referrals; (b) to ensure that students whose behavior is of concern are contacted through follow-up processes and have access to the appropriate services needed to improve their welfare; and (c) to create a unified and accessible reporting and tracking system that will allow members of the BIT to observe patterns of behavior that may necessitate further assessment and provide documented responses to distressed students (Sokolow, Lewis, & Schuster, 2011; Sokolow & Lewis, 2009). Table 9.2 highlights a number of system-wide methods for fostering the creation of a culture of reporting, one that services prevention and intervention with potential dangers on campus.

Table 9.2 Creating a Climate of Reporting

1. Communicate that the campus is one of care and concern versus one of punishment and negative sanctions.

2. Employ and teach a common language for what constitutes danger, what to report, to whom, when, and how.

3. Establish communication feedback loops to ensure reporters feel heard and respected.

4. Involve those on campus who are trained in violence prevention.

5. Engage those on campus who have the power and authority to affect such things as the use of alcohol and drugs, hazing, etc.

6. Encourage a culture of reporting, employ policies of immunity for those who come forth with information.

7. Empower bystander intervention by offering training on identification of risks, available resources, and safe intervention strategies.

8. Promote the increased awareness and valuing of campus and community based mental health support service available to those in crisis.

9. Establish an anti-retaliation policy to protect those who report but also develop mechanisms to protect or at least minimize the risk of retaliation against a reporter.

Adapted from Sokolow, Lewis, & Schuster, 2011

Whereas BITs will have baseline data on individuals who are at risk, their focus is typically pre-crisis, whereas a Threat Assessment Team (TAT) will be called in when a threshold of severity is reached. Typically, the TAT is engaged when a behavior of concern is brought to their attention. The TAT is typically a multidisciplinary group of colleagues with the primary goal of identifying, preventing, and reducing the risk of violence on campus while promoting the safety and well-being of all members of the college community. The team will have the authority and capacity to engage university resources to assess and address specific incidents of threats. The goal is to identify concerns in their early phases and to engage constructively and collaborative with all parties before problems escalate into violent outcomes.

Sokolow and Lewis (2009) have expressed concerns about the possible inefficiency of a two-team model and suggest that the teams be combined in a way where threat assessment becomes a sub-set or sub-function of the behavioral intervention skills set. These authors feel that such a process would ensure efficient and effective communication and responding to potential threats on campus.

Responding to the Survivor(s)

While most colleges and universities provide counseling services to their students, some have also either created or trained behavioral health Trauma Response Teams or, by way of contract, have engaged the services of those within the community who have the knowledge and skills necessary to serve in that capacity.

When responding to a mass tragedy or attack, direction for intervention can be found in the post-event analyses and report to the Virginia Tech Review Panel developed by Heil et al. (2008). Table 9.3 provides what we feel are the generalizable principles extracted from the Heil et al. (2008) report. It is important to consider these as the response teams prepare their protocols for intervening at the time of a mass crisis.

In addition to employing principles learned from the experience and post-analyses from other universities (see Table 9.3), response teams need to be trained to employ evidence-based or evidence-informed practices. These would include interventions described in Chapter Three (e.g., Psychological First Aid) or therapeutic strategies, such as Prolonged Exposure (Nayak, Powers, & Foa, 2012) and Cognitive Processing Therapy (Chard, Schuster, & Resick, 2012).

Community Crisis

One does not have to search very far to find incidents and events resulting in crisis and trauma for entire communities. Natural disasters, such as Hurricane Katrina or the tragic events of 9/11 (for more information on these events, see Chapter 10), are dramatic illustrations of the reality that entire communities are subject to the experience of crisis and trauma. Real events point to the fact that places that were previously considered safe and neutral are no longer immune from crisis and tragedy; examples include: the

July 20, 2012 mass shooting that occurred inside a Century 16 movie theater in Aurora, Colorado; the Cascade Mall shooting rampage; and the shooting that took place at the Emanuel African Methodist Episcopal Church in downtown Charleston, South Carolina, on the evening of June 17, 2015.

Table 9.3 Guidance from a Review of the Virginia Tech Massacre

Emotional Equilibrium Begins with a Safe Place to be	The adverse effects of trauma are greatly reduced if victims receive comfort, reassurance, and a sense of safety from those they trust. This support from others who those in need trust counteracts the feelings of insecurity, helplessness, and meaninglessness that the victimized often experience (Walsh, 2007).	Provide a place where the survivor(s) can feel they are secure, have access to information, and can reunite with loved ones.
Accurate Information as Aid and Comfort	Accurate information provides the survivor(s) a way to define and understand the chaos and ultimately cope with the event and its consequences.	Provide information in a sensible way. Maintain the timeliness of the information, ensure that it is accurate and explain why information may be limited or missing. Accuracy and honesty is essential. Create an information network—a formal, reliable source of information to counteract rumor. Such a network not only provides accurate information but affords social support, which can mitigate the adverse effects of the event (Cohen, 2004).
Flexible Models of Therapy and Effective Interventions	Mental health services need to be flexible, adaptable and available (extended days and hours). Engage with other caretakers and step outside of the formal structure and processes of traditional counseling/psychotherapy.	Effective intervention rests on flexibility and spontaneity—as such, develop a comfort with service, which is less "traditional" in terms of place, time, length, etc. "Think Broadly" regarding scope of service (to include friends and family members).
The Importance of Core Counselor Core Qualities	Emotional support is communicating to a stressed person that he or she is valued and accepted despite the difficulties the stressful event creates.	While there is much to do it is important to remember to be that caring caretaker. Convey understanding, acceptance and valuing at a time when a survivor may feel abandoned and certainly devalued.
Care for the Caretaker	The events—the stories—the empathic experience from one and with one surviving trauma will not only provide an opportunity to serve but may bring with it an experience of sadness and vicarious trauma.	Be familiar with the indications of trauma contagion, secondary or vicarious traumatization, and empathy fatigue. Work with colleagues, supervisors, or personal therapist to regain perspective and develop and engage in wellness plans.

Clearly, entire communities can experience crisis and trauma that result in neighborhoods being in a state of shock. This is a reality and needs to be accepted if an effective program for community trauma response can be developed. Once crises and trauma are accepted as a possibility, communities will then need to develop trauma response plans and teams as an integral part of their emergency preparedness operations (Hajer & Walsh, 2005). Currently, there is no one empirically supported approach to community trauma response. While there may be an absence of a single, accepted model of response, there are principles that seem to be embraced and applied across a variety of natural and man-made disasters that place communities in crisis.

Responding to a Community Crisis and Trauma

When responding to communities in the wake of a major disaster or emergency situation, it is clear that life support and sustaining interventions are essential, including the provision of food, water, shelter, and medical resources. However, it is important to recognize that those impacted by a community crisis or disaster are anxious, stressed, and often experience the short- and long-term effects of trauma.

The American Psychological Association, in coordination with the American Red Cross, developed a Disaster Response Network (http://www.apa.org/practice/programs/drn/index.aspx). This Disaster Response Network is composed of state-organized groups of psychologists who are trained in crisis response and can be called upon in the event of a disaster. These specialists are trained to offer emotional and behavioral support, promote resilience and the development of resiliency skills, collect and share resource information, and offer psychoeducational programming regarding common challenges that occur months and years after disaster.

During the first hours and days following a disaster, responders generally engage in providing Psychological First Aid (PFA) (see Chapter Three). The interventions provided are designed to meet the immediate practical and stress-induced needs of survivors, rather than engaging in extensive psychological treatment. The interventions, while tailored to the unique needs of each individual involved, generally target eight core actions (see Table 9.4).

Table 9.4 Targets for Psychological First Aid

1. **Contact and Engagement:** Many disaster survivors will not use mental health services, so it is important to not only respond to contacts initiated by those affected but also reach out and, if appropriate, initiate contacts in a nonintrusive, compassionate, and helpful manner.
2. **Safety and Comfort:** Given the disruptive nature of crisis, it is important to enhance the immediate and ongoing safety of those affected and provide for their physical and emotional comfort.

3. **Stabilization:** Some victims may feel overwhelmed and distraught and, thus, need the emotional support necessary to regain emotional stability and calm. In addition, some may need time-limited brief (e.g., one to three sessions) crisis therapy providing emotional support and problem solving and providing information about expected "normal" reactions to disaster.

4. **Information Gathering:** Since everyone is unique in both needs and concerns, it is important to identify immediate needs and concerns and tailor psychological first aid interventions to those specific needs and concerns.

5. **Practical Assistance:** Going beyond that which is typically considered a psychological service, first responders providing psychological first aid will offer practical help to the survivor in addressing immediate needs and concerns.

6. **Connection with Social Supports:** Since social support has been found to serve as an important predictor of post-disaster outcomes, it is important to reduce distress by helping structure opportunities for contacts with primary support persons, as well as family members, friends, and community contacts.

7. **Information on Coping Support:** Information designed to provide survivors with an understanding about post-trauma responses, coping mechanisms, and circumstances that call for further support and treatment will help them better cope with the event and its aftermath.

8. **Linkage with Collaborative Services.** Understanding that there may be delayed or extended responses to the crisis event, it is important to connect survivors with services and resources that may be needed in the future.

Beyond addressing the immediate, short-term needs of those impacted via PFA, it is also known that some within the community will need more in-depth psychological services and, thus, may need to be referred to those trained in best practices in disaster mental health response.

Trauma Contagion

Trauma has been found to affect everyone that has close contact with a traumatized person or traumatizing situation (McClelland, 2013). It could be argued that trauma is truly a contagious condition, one that is a risk for all who engage with the traumatic narrative (Baird & Jenkins, 2003). This contagion of trauma can impact family members, friends, colleagues, acquaintances, and even therapists and take form in the development of symptoms similar to the survivor's own post-traumatic stress response. (See Chapter 13 for more information on the impact of crisis on the helper.)

CASE ILLUSTRATION 9.1

A NEIGHBOR'S FIRE

It was horrible. I heard the fire trucks and the Emergency Medical Technicians (EMT) yelling, so I woke up and walked down the block to see what was happening. The house was completely engulfed in flames. Fire fighters were having a difficult time getting into the house, and someone was on the front lawn screaming about Benny being inside.

I know I've seen her before, but I didn't really know her. I watched one of the fire fighters — came running out the front door, right before the roof collapsed. He was holding Benny. He ran right by me. Benny was some type of little dog, a terrier I think. He was limp in the fire fighter's arms, and the lady, I think her name is Mrs. Alberto, was screaming that Benny was dead.

I can't get that image out of my mind. I haven't slept in three days—I keep waking and imagining that I am smelling smoke. I feel like I'm on pins and needles thinking that something is going to happen. Not sure what ... but something. It is really getting to me.

At Risk

When attempting to identify those at particular risk for trauma contagion, a practitioner may do well to review the circles of vulnerability model of community assessment that has been developed at the Community Stress Prevention Center in Kiryat Shmona, Israel (Lahad & Cohen, 2006). While the model was developed with specific reference to suicide contagion, it is believed that it also provides a meaningful and useful framework from which to view the potential of contagion regardless of the nature of the specific form of trauma.

This model suggests that individuals who are at the greatest risk for contagion include those who witnessed the event or its immediate aftermath (geographical proximity), had a psychological connection to the deceased (psychosocial proximity), or had a social connection (social proximity).

Geographical Proximity

Geographical proximity refers to the physical distance a person is from the location of an incident. This would not only include individuals who directly witnessed the events but also those who were directly exposed to the immediate aftermath of the event, such as first responders (see Case illustration 9.1). Beyond the obvious group of individuals who had physical connection to the incident, research suggests that extensive and repetitive media coverage of crisis and traumatic events broadens this geographic proximity (Gould, 2001). This was clearly evident in the rise of emotional conflicts, PTSD-like symptoms, anxiety, and depression reported across the nation as a result of media coverage of the terrorist attacks of September 11, 2001 (see Chapter 10).

Psychological Proximity

The concept of psychological proximity refers to the degree to which another feels connected or can identify with the victim(s) (see Case Illustration 9.2).

This psychological proximity can be enacted by simply sharing a similar culture, sharing similar interests/activities, and even being perceived as having similar characteristics. This might be the case of an individual who was a life-long race car enthusiast who now experiences vicarious trauma upon hearing of the fatal accident of his favorite professional driver.

But perhaps the most noteworthy implication of psychological proximity has to do with its focus on the degree to which one may feel connected to the victim. Those experiencing crisis and trauma seek out emotional connection with those providing service. As such, it is easy to imagine the close psychological proximity that may be a regular companion for those who work as crisis counselors. While this emotional connectivity is of value to the survivors, it can serve as a source of trauma contagion for the helper. The voices and experiences of our clients become a part of our own stories, and while not all are negative, the point is that the stories change us regardless if they are inspiring or upsetting (Mahoney, 2003).

Social Proximity

The final element in the circles of vulnerability is social proximity. This refers to the relationship and assumed level of connectedness one has with the victim. It is suggested that social proximity can extend from those with an intimate connection to those who simply know the victim(s). Thus, a parent of a child who has committed suicide, or a spouse of someone who was raped, or the brother of someone lost in the terrorist attacks of September 11, 2001, would all have strong social proximity.

But, this element is also important when such intimacy or depth of relationship does not exist. Individuals who are social friends, acquaintances, or even simply members of the same social circle may experience some level of contagion. Exercise 9.1 invites you to apply these circles of vulnerability to predict the level of vulnerability for a number of individuals on the periphery of a community crisis.

CASE ILLUSTRATION 9.2

IT BECAME UNBEARABLE

The patient was a 13-year-old male named Timothy. He was brought to the emergency room after cutting his wrist and being discovered in the school's second floor bathroom. Talking with him, the social worker discovered that he had an extensive history of being bullied throughout middle school, and now during the first few days of his freshman year in high school, he was being teased by upperclassmen.

In sharing his story, he noted that, while he had previously thought about killing himself, he would dismiss the idea because of his concern for what it would do to his parents. He would always just say to himself, "Suck it up."

When asked why he attempted to kill himself now, he responded that it became unbearable and that he "just couldn't take it anymore." However, what the social worker soon discovered was that the actual degree of bullying that he was experiencing was actually much less than what happened in middle school. What made this unbearable appeared to be a vicarious traumatization as a result of psychologically identifying with another victim of bullying. Timothy shared that he had heard about a sophomore at the same school who over the past weekend committed suicide as a result of his own history of being a victim of bullying. Timothy stated that, for some reason, knowing that this student was bullied simply brought a flood of memories and pain, as well as extreme anxiety, which just became unbearable.

EXERCISE 9.1

PROXIMITY AND VULNERABILITY TO TRAUMA CONTAGION

Directions: The table below depicts conditions of trauma or crisis. In each situation, there are a number of people who will be in proximity to the event. Your task is to identify those not directly traumatized but who may, as a result of proximity, be vulnerable to trauma contagion. With a classmate or colleague, describe why you identified the forms of proximity for each of the following situations.

Condition of Trauma or Crisis	Individual or Role	Geographical Proximity	Psychological Proximity	Sociological Proximity
Example: A high school student commits suicide and is found at home.	Parents, Siblings in the house	X	X	X
	Classmates and Teachers		X	X
	School Counselor			
	Police on the scene	X	X	X
There was a shooter in the school hallway, so teachers and students had a lock down in place.				
A married woman in therapy working through issues of childhood sexual abuse.				
Evacuation of an office building following an explosion under the guidance of first responders.				
Terrorist attack of September 11, 2001.				

Reducing Potential of Contagion

The research around the issue of trauma contagion has typically focused on contagion as connected to suicide. The Center for Disease Control (CDC) has developed Recommendations for a Community Plan for the Prevention and Containment of Suicide Clusters (CDC, 1988). While the directives developed refer to suicide and its contagion containment, they appear to give direction to all responding to trauma and seeking to reduce the possibility of contagion, regardless of the nature of the incident or trauma. Table 9.5 provides a listing of directives adapted from the CDC's (1988, 1994) report.

Table 9.5 Reducing the Potential of Contagion

Focus	Directive
Communicating About the Incident/Event	• Confirm the facts • Confront sensationalized information • Do not speculate • Discuss the positive steps being taken, and try to get the media to help in the response by reporting where troubled persons can go for help
Mobilize Crisis Response Team	• Identify those at risk of contagion • Provide information about risk factors and warning signs • Interview persons at risk, refer for counseling or other services as needed • Identify relevant community resources
Engage in Psychoeducation Procedures	• Equip care providers with talking points, referral information • Inform all impacted by the incident about the importance of prevention and the specific warning signs • Let all know that help is available and provide direction on how to connect with helpful resources
Support Those Affected by the Event	• Provide small group and individual counseling • Provide outlets for grieving • Consider establishing hotlines or walk-in suicide crisis centers, even temporarily
Engage the Community	• Response to the crisis should involve all concerned sectors of the community • Communicate with all groups and services in impacted area providing accurate information on not just what happened but what services are available, if needed

Contagion and the Helper

When you consider the various forms of proximity that contribute to an individual's vulnerability for contagion, it should become obvious that those attempting to provide services and support at times of crisis and trauma are particularly vulnerable. Besides being within geographical proximity to both the event and the aftermath, crisis interventionists and trauma workers are, by definition, engaged at a psychological level. Trauma work can be emotionally difficult and taxing for counselors and caretakers. Pearlman and Saakvitne (1995) noted that caring about and caring for others can result in the "transformation in the inner experience of the therapist that comes about as a result of empathic engagement with the client's traumatic material" (p. 31).

Clearly, for trauma workers to remain healthy and effective, they must develop the knowledge, skills, and dispositions that allow them to experience concerns, while avoiding contagion. Chapter 13 will discuss this topic of caring for the caretaker while avoiding contagion.

Summary

The PREPaRE Model of School Crisis Prevention and Intervention identifies a specific hierarchical and sequential set of activities that target: **P**reventing and preparing for psychological trauma, **R**eaffirming physical health and perceptions of security and safety, **E**valuating psychological trauma risk, **P**roviding interventions and **R**esponding to psychological needs, and **E**xamining the effectiveness of crisis prevention and intervention

- Creating a culture of reporting and sharing information is critical in the engagement of prevention and intervention policies and procedures on college campuses.

- BITs employ a formalized approach to addressing mental health issues and other behaviors that either pose a danger of harm to self or others or disrupt the learning environment.

- TATs are typically a multidisciplinary group of colleagues with the primary goal of identifying, preventing, and reducing the risk of violence on campus while promoting the safety and well-being of all members of the college community.

- The Disaster Response Network is composed of state-organized groups of psychologists who are trained in disaster response and provide psychological first aid and offer emotional and behavioral support during times of community crisis.

- Trauma contagion has been found to affect those that have close contact with a traumatized person or traumatizing situation.

- Individuals who are at the greatest risk for contagion include those who witnessed the event or its immediate aftermath (geographical proximity) and had a psychological or social connection to the deceased (psychosocial proximity).

Important Terms

Behavioral Intervention Team (BIT)

Circles of Vulnerability

Comprehensive crisis plan

Culture of reporting

Disaster Response Network

Geographical proximity

National Child Traumatic Stress Network

PREPaRE Model

Psychological First Aid (PFA)

Psychological proximity

Social proximity

Threat Assessment Team (TAT)

Trauma contagion

Additional Resources

In Print

ASCA (American School Counselor Association) (2007). *Position statement: Crisis/critical incident response in the schools.* Alexandria, VA: Author

James, R. K., & Gilliland, B. E. (2013). *Crisis intervention strategies* (7th Ed.). Belmont, CA: Brooks/ Cole Cengage Learning.

Ritchie, E. C., Watson, P.J., & Friedman, M.J. (Eds.). (2006). *Mental health intervention following disasters or mass violence.* New York, NY: Guildford Press.

Sokolow, B. A., Lewis, W. S. & Schuster, S. K. (2011). Preventing the preventable. Retrieved November 10, 2016 from https://nabita.org/documents/PreventingthePreventable2011NaBITA Whitepaper_001.pdf

On the web

American Academy of Experts in Traumatic Stress: www.aaets.org

American Red Cross Building a Disaster-Resistant Neighborhood Program: www.tallytown.com/ redcross/drn.html

National Organization for Victim Assistance (NOVA): www.trynova.org

The International Critical Incident Stress Foundation, Inc.: www.icisf.org

References

Baird, S. & Jenkins, S. R. (2003). Vicarious traumatization, secondary traumatic stress, and burnout in sexual assault and domestic violence agency staff. *Violence and Victims, 16*(1), 71–86.

Brock, S. E., Nickerson, A. B., Reeves, M. A., Jimerson, S. R., Lieberman, R. A., & Feinberg, T. A. (2009). *School crisis prevention and intervention: The PREPaRE model.* Bethesda, MD: National Association of School Psychologists.

Brown, D., & Trusty, J. (2005). *Designing and leading comprehensive school counseling programs: Promoting student competence and meeting student needs.* Belmont, CA: Brooks/Cole.

Brymer M., Taylor M., Escudero P., Jacobs A., Kronenberg M., Macy R., … Vogel J. (2012). *Psychological first aid for schools: Field operations guide, 2nd Edition.* Los Angeles, CA: National Child Traumatic Stress Network. Retrieved from http://www.nctsnet.org/sites/ default/files/pfa/school/1-PFA_for_Schools_final.pdf

CDC (Center for Disease Control). (1988). CDC recommendations for a community plan for the prevention and containment of suicide clusters. *MMWR Supplements 37*(S-6), 1–12. Retrieved November 18, 2016, from https://www.cdc.gov/mmwr/preview/mmwrhtml/00001755.htm

CDC. (1994). Suicide contagion and the reporting of suicide: Recommendations from a national workshop. *Morbidity and Mortality Weekly, 43*, 9–18.

Chard, K. M., Schuster, J. L., & Resick, P. A. (2012). Empirically supported psychological treatments: Cognitive processing therapy. In J. Gayle Beck & D. M Sloan, *The Oxford Handbook of Traumatic Stress Disorders,* 439–448. New York, NY: Oxford University Press.

Cohen, J., Goodman, R. F., Brown, E. J., & Mannarino, A. (2004). Treatment of childhood traumatic grief: Contributing to a newly emerging condition in the wake of community trauma. *Harvard Review of Psychiatry, 12*, 213–216.

Gould, M. S. (2001). Suicide and the media. *Annals of the New York Academy of Science, 932*, 200–224.

Hajer, M., & Walsh, M. (2005). Coping with community trauma. *RM magazine.* Retrieved November 26, 2016, from http://webapps.icma.org/pm/8704/public/cover.cfm?author=marilyn%20 hajer%20and%20mary%20walsh&title=coping%20with%20community%20trauma

Heil, J., Johnson, L., Lewis, g., Gilbert, D. Inge-Messerchmidt, J., Salzbach, R., Smith, M., & Strosnider, S. (2008). Psychological intervention with the Virginia Tech shootings: Lessons learned and recommendations for the hospital setting. Retrieved November 25, 2016, from http://psychhealthroanoke.com/Resources/VTRepCircjohnheilfinal2.pdf

Joshi,P.T, & Lewin, S.M. (2004). Disaster, Terrorism & Children. *Psychiatric Annals, 34(9),* 710–716.

Lahad, M., & Cohen, A. (2006). *The community stress prevention center: 25 years of community stress prevention and intervention.* Kiryat Shmona, Israel: The Community Stress Prevention Center.

Mahoney, M. J. (2003). *Constructive psychotherapy: A practical guide.* New York, NY: Guilford.

McClelland, M. (2013). Is PTSD contagious? *Mother Jones, January/February.* Retrieved from http://www.motherjones.com/politics/2013/01/ptsd-epidemic-military-vets-families.

Nayak, N., Powers., M. B. & Foa, E. B. (2012). Empirically supported psychological treatments: Prolonged exposure. In J. Gayle Beck & D. M. Sloan, *The Oxford Handbook of Traumatic Stress Disorders* (pp. 427–438). New York, NY: Oxford University Press.

Pearlman, L. A., & Saakvitne, K. (1995). Helpers' responses to trauma work: Understanding and intervening in an organization. In B. H. Stamm (Ed.), *Secondary traumatic stress: Self-care issues for clinicians, researchers and educators* (pp. 65–79). Lutherville, MD: Sedran Press.

Pollard, J. W., Nolan J. J., & Deisinger, E. R. D. (2012). The practice of campus-based threat assessment. *Journal of College Student Psychotherapy, 26*(4), 236–276.

Reeves, M. A., Brock, S. E., & Cowan, K. C. (2008). Managing school crises: More than just response. Effective crisis management begins long before a critical incident occurs. *Principal Leadership: High School Edition, 8*(9), 10–14

Sokolow, B. A., & Lewis, W. S. (2009). 2nd *Generation Behavioral Intervention Best Practice.* Retrieved November 11, 2016, from https://www.ncherm.org/pdfs/2009NCHERMwhitepaper. pdf

Sokolow, B. A., Lewis, W. S. & Schuster, S. K. (2011). *Preventing the preventable.* Retrieved November 10, 2016, from https://nabita.org/documents/ PreventingthePreventable2011NaBITAWhitepaper_001.pdf

U.S. Department of Education. (2003). *Practical information on crisis planning: A guide for schools and communities.* Retrieved on February 15, 2009, from w.ed.gov/admins/lead/safety/ emergencyplan/ crisisplanning.pdf

Walsh, B. (2007). Clinical assessment of self-injury: A practical guide. *Journal of Clinical Psychology: In Session, 63*(11), 1057–1068.

CHAPTER 10

Brief Case Studies of Crisis Intervention

There are some words that simply arouse a gut wrenching response. Among those are Columbine, Hurricane Katrina, and 9/11.

The 21st century has seen more than its share of natural and man-made crises. The names identified above are but a few of those from which we could have sampled our case studies. Sadly, the challenge in writing a chapter such as this is that there are so many crisis events from which to choose. Crisis and trauma have been, and will most likely continue to be, our companion for years to come.

The current chapter will review the nature of crisis intervention as it took shape in three American crises: Columbine, Hurricane Katrina, and the terrorist attacks of September 11, 2001 (9/11). The selection is not intended to be exhaustive or all-inclusive. Rather, while each is unique in its own way, they collectively depict the impact of crisis on a large scale and the issues confronting the clients with whom we wish to intervene.

After reading this chapter, you should be able to:

1. Describe the salient characteristics of three major disasters: The Columbine High School shootings, Hurricane Katrina, and 9/11;

2. Explain the immediate and longer-term impact of each of three major disasters: The Columbine High School shootings, Hurricane Katrina, and 9/11; and

3. Describe the lessons learned from the analysis of the events leading up to and following the disasters: The Columbine High School shootings, Hurricane Katrina, and 9/11.

Case Study: What We Hope to Learn

When it comes to major crisis events, prevention is the ideal; however, to effectively intervene is the hope. Theories help guide our anticipatory planning, but it is the post hoc analyses of the what, the why, and the how of these events and our response to them that allow us to sharpen not just our theories, but also our practice. It is through case study analysis, within real-life context, that insight and direction can be gained. Analysis of the events defining a major disaster and the crisis response at the time can help us identify the elements that compounded the impact of that event and interfered with our response and interventions. For example, when reviewing the case of Hurricane Katrina, we find that the challenges of maintaining the existence and operation of communication systems, or addressing the need for public safety, security and health resources, and even understanding the essential nature and importance of infrastructure assessment and maintenance, all compounded the response during that disaster.

The value of such analyses rest not in finger pointing but in responding and adjusting our policies, procedures, training, and resources in preparation for future events. Similarly, as we will discuss, we have learned much in our review and study of the events leading up to and following the Columbine High School massacre. One valuable outcome has been the increased research and attention to both the identification of early warning signs of students at risk for such violence, as well as the development of both remedial and prevention services and programs within our schools. Finally, a post hoc look at the long-term impact of a tragedy such as 9/11 has further helped us to recognize and begin to respond to medical and psychological needs, not just of those victimized by the events, but of those who provided care to the victims of these tragedies.

The brief presentations of the events of the Columbine High School shootings, Hurricane Katrina, and 9/11 are intended to increase the reader's understanding not only of these events and the responses provided in support and care of those who are victimized, but also to stimulate thinking, researching, and testing of ideas that can serve to reduce the possibility of similar occurrences and sadly, when needed, ensure an increase in our ability to provide effective responses.

Columbine

The Event

For those in Littleton, Colorado, April 20, 1999, is a date that is not only etched in their psychic memories, but has and will continue to arouse reactions that range from disbelief to post-traumatic syndromes. This is the date that two young adults, Eric Harris (18) and Dylan Klebold (17), killed 13 people and wounded 20 in their assault on Columbine High School.

According to the general accounting of events (e.g., see Kohn, 2001) Eric Harris, working out of the garage at his home, filled duffel bags with bombs and rigged weapons within his trench coat. After picking up Dylan Klebold, the two drove to the high school, entered, and began shooting.

Within minutes of the first shots being fired, police arrived at the school. Sadly, by the time of their arrival, at least three people were dead and six were injured (Kohn, 2001). Students were reported to have been hiding under lunchroom tables.

With the police taking positions around the school, Harris and Klebold moved toward the library, shooting in the halls and throwing bombs into the cafeteria. Once in the library, they began shooting students. Leaving the library, they moved to what was identified as the school commons, lobbing a pipe bomb in the cafeteria and igniting a fire. After 47 minutes of siege, the assembled special weapons and tactics (SWAT) team entered. For two and half hours, the first SWAT team cleared classrooms, and a second team evacuated students and staff from the area around the cafeteria. It has been reported (Kohn, 2001) that it was nearly three hours after the first SWAT team entered that they knew that the gunmen were dead. Klebold and Harris committed suicide.

The entire traumatic event, which saw the assembly of over a thousand police officers and rescue personnel from 47 agencies and played out over a five-hour period, has been assessed as one of the worst mass shooting and deadliest episodes of school violence in United States history.

The Impact of Crisis

The immediate impact was clearly that which one would expect. The confusion and disbelief that accompanied the early moments of their experience gave way to terror and panic, and yet, within this context, illustrations of courage and the strength of the human condition emerged. The events and experience of that day are best understood through the eyes of the survivors. Case Illustration 10.1, provides an article written by Mark Obmascik of the *Denver Post*, that presents the experience of that day from the his point of view.

In the weeks that followed, the survivors found that their numbness gave way to strong negative feelings, such as guilt, anger, irritability, and general anxiety or nervousness (Norris, 2007). Many felt guilty about what they could have done, and others found themselves mired in rumination about the events of that day. For most, the need to connect with one another, to cling together, was primary (Austin, 2003).

While efforts to return the community to a semblance of normalcy continued, the strain of the day and the impact of the crisis continued to be evident. For the students, the memories stimulated by the environment of Columbine led many to transfer to other schools or to choose homeschool rather than return. The enduring impact was not confined to the students. While some teachers continued to teach at Columbine, some sought transfers to others schools, and others chose early retirement.

The impact of the assault on Columbine high school was felt well beyond the community of Littleton. Columbine generated the most intensive period of legislative activity on school violence to date (Lawrence & Birkland, 2004). In what has been termed "The Columbine Effect," (Cloud, 1999) many schools and communities shifted into a panic response and enacted very strong policies, including zero-tolerance policies that led to what may be seen as overreactions. For example, a seven-year-old boy in Cahokia, Illinois, was suspended for having a nail clipper at school, and in Minnesota, a high school omitted a picture of an Army enlistee in the senior class, because she posed atop of a cannon outside of a Veterans of Foreign Wars post.

While there was clear evidence of a nation in panic, perhaps overreacting, there have been a number of significant changes in our schools targeted at increasing security and decreasing the possibility of another such tragedy. Many schools have introduced measures to heighten means of security (e.g., cameras, metal detectors, electronic visitor clearances, etc.). Schools have also increased methods of communication, especially when experiencing violence, bullying, and weapons possession. Schools have enacted zero-tolerance policies regarding the possession or use of weapons, have enacted anti-bullying and violence programs, and perhaps most importantly, have increased their crisis planning processes and the availability of mental health counseling.

CASE ILLUSTRATION 10.1

FIRST-HAND ACCOUNTS: COLUMBINE

The Denver Post interviewed numerous survivors of the Columbine shootings and presented their findings in an article written by Mark Obmascik. The collective description paints a picture of a school in complete panic. Security strobe lights pulsating, alarms blaring, individuals running and screaming and with all … the sounds of bullets occupying halls where student laughter was once heard. Through their stories, one is able to not only feel the terror and chaos of that day, but the courage and the strength of the human condition exhibited by teachers, staff, and students. It is suggested that you go to http://extras.denverpost.com/news/shot0613a.htm and read their stories.

Responding to the Crisis

In the immediacy of the moment, the school district had to make many important decisions instantaneously. With students scattered throughout the area and frantic parents attempting to connect, the administration directed or bussed students to nearby Leawood Elementary, where they gathered in the cafeteria awaiting family members. As parents were united with their children, they were able to leave the premises. Lists of students sent to the hospital were posted on the walls (Austin, 2003).

While attempting to provide the social and emotional support called for in the shock and horror following the event, the district authorities connected with local agencies, including the American Red Cross, to provide food and water for those at Leawood Elementary. Provision was made for the gathering of students, school staff, and arriving parents, and mental health responders were on site to provide supportive services.

The following day, schools were closed, and a crisis center was established at a local church. When school resumed (at Chatfield High School), seven additional mental health counselors joined the Chatfield High School counseling and social work staff, and an additional 23 counselors provided services at other area schools. In addition, the community opened a one-stop resource center, the Columbine Connection, and created SHOUTS, a youth drop-in center.

For weeks to come, county and school district officials provided informational meetings and students and staff gathered in support of one another (Austin, 2003). The centers employed a multidisciplinary approach and provided information, victim assistance, group support, referral, and outreach mental health services (Johnson, 2000).

These services helped to support the family and connect all within the community. As noted in her address to the American School Counselor Association Conference (2002, as cited by Austin 2003), Betsy Thompson stated, "The most important learning for all of us as we've responded to the Columbine shootings is that the power of relationships is second to none. Whether it's the relationships with our community partners, the relationships that counselors had with students, the relationships that staff had with one another—the power of relationships is really a key to healing and recovery."

Hurricane Katrina

The Event

August 29, 2005, marked the unfolding of an event, a crisis that had a widespread and devastating impact on the people and environment of the Gulf Coast areas of Alabama, Louisiana, and Mississippi. In the span of five hours, Hurricane Karina wreaked havoc on approximately 90,000 miles of territory, displacing hundreds of thousands of people, and leaving New Orleans underwater for weeks to come. The cost in lives and property was enormous. There were over 1,600 deaths and 1,000 missing people (Markwell & Ratard, 2009). In terms of costs, the U.S. Department of Transportation (2006) estimated more than $80 billion in damages. But these are just the numbers, the statistics.

For millions of Americans, the horror of watching the unfolding disaster will be seared into their memories. Survivors were shown walking in waist-high water with debris and even human corpses washing by, while others were trapped on rooftops attempting to gain the attention of rescuers in boats and helicopters. The human tragedy continued to unfold for days to come, with thousands crowding into the Superdome and convention center in downtown New Orleans, finding a lack of sanitary conditions, food, and water. The images were surreal, and even veteran newscasters were presented as shaken and upset (Dass-Brailsford, 2010). Case Illustration 10.2 provides you with an opportunity to experience the depth and breadth of the destruction and human devastation that resulted from Katrina.

CASE ILLUSTRATION 10.2

THROUGH THE EYES OF SURVIVOR: KATRINA

Unlike other case illustrations depicted throughout this text, for this case, we invite you to go to https://www.youtube.com/watch?v=4FhcOoWxF1Q and review the documentary on Katrina. Moving from initial serge through the breaching of the levees, to the sad realities of individuals trapped and then relocated and displaced, the case of Katrina is worthwhile to understand as it will provide a foundation for the appreciation of the depth and breadth of the trauma encountered.

Beyond the challenges of establishing safe relocation and adequate food, clothing, and other necessities, survivors of Katrina experienced massive displacement, physically and psychosocially (Houston, Reyes, Pfefferbaum, & Wyche, 2010).

The Impact of Crisis

As might be expected, Katrina had both immediate and longer-lasting adverse effects. Prior to continuing with a description of the data reflecting those effects, we invite you engage with Exercise 10.1. We hope that your reflections on the questions posed in this exercise will help you see beyond the numbers, the data, the statistics, and "see" the experience of those victimized by this natural disaster.

As your reflected on the questions posed in Exercise 10.1, you may have gained some insight into some of the negative experiences that were presented to the survivors during and immediately following the grounding of the hurricane. But, the impact went well beyond that which was immediately experienced. The Center for Disease Control and Prevention (2006) reported that more than 50 percent of those responding to their needs assessment showed signs of a "possible" need for mental health treatment. Unlike the pattern that emerged from other major disasters, where the prevalence of negative impacts decreased with time, data collected for Hurricane Katrina suggested that the depth and breadth of negative experiences encountered by survivors actually increased with time (Kessler et al., 2008). In a study of close to 400 low-income parents exposed to Hurricane Katrina, the prevalence of probable serous mental illness doubled, and nearly half of those in the study exhibited probable Post-Traumatic Stress Disorder (PTSD) (Rhodes et al., 2010). The presence of PTSD symptoms was in evidence for up

WHAT WOULD I DO?

Directions: It is hard, if not impossible, to truly understand the stress experienced by those displaced by Hurricane Katrina. The video presentations show the waist-high water, the floating debris, and sadly, human corpses and give one a sense of the confusion, dismay, and sense of powerlessness experienced by those forced from their homes to take up residence on a cot at the Superdome. There is no way we can replicate that experience, nor would we want to. It is important, however, that you take a moment and try to imagine the disruption experienced.

Below, you are asked to reflect on a number of questions. You may find it insightful to share your reflections with a colleague, a classmate, a friend, or a family member. In reflecting upon each of these questions, you may gain a tiny glimpse of that which was experienced by those displaced during Hurricane Katrina.

The Situation:

There is a knock at your door, and two national guard members confront you. You are told that you must leave right now. You do not know where you are being taken or when you will be able to return.

Reflection:

1. What do you have on your person: money, clothes, etc.? Is it sufficient for you to survive, thrive, or even feel comfortable for one day, one week, or one month?

2. How would you connect with your family, friends, and loved ones if the roads are impassable, there is no transportation, there is no internet, cellular service, or even land lines?

3. Do you need medication? Did you have it at the time of your forced exit? If not, what would you do? If you do, do you have enough for a month?

4. Imagine that you now find yourself sitting on a cot, in a large indoor arena with over 20,000 people, mostly strangers. How comfortable are you resting your head and closing your eyes?

to two years after the incident (Chia-Chen Chen et al., 2007; Tucker et al., 2008).

A particularly vulnerable population, one for whom the negative impacts were particularly profound, was the children. In a survey taken 18 to 27 months after Katrina, McLaughlin et al. (2009) found that 20% of children who had experienced high levels of stress as a result of Katrina presented with social-emotional disturbances.

Responding to the Crisis

As noted, the long-term consequences of Katrina did not seem to follow the path of decline following other large-scale disasters. Research has suggested that the negative impact of such disasters is relatively short lived, with survivors recovering from the trauma and initial shock within a few months (e.g., Thienkrua et al., 2006). However, it appears that the widespread community disruption and protracted recovery that characterized Hurricane Katrina resulted in more sustained and enduring negative consequences (Rateau, 2009).

As is true for all natural disasters, with Katrina, there was a need and value of providing immediate support for basic needs. Addressing basic needs at times such as these has been well documented as a means of buffering against stress and the possibility of increased risk of PTSD (Galea, Tracy, Norris, & Coffey, 2008; Kaniasty & Norris, 2008). In addition to providing social support as a means of meeting the fundamental needs of these individuals, crisis counselors were also called upon to provide one-to-one crisis counseling to those overwhelmed by their own emotion. The focus, as is true for all crisis intervention, was to help restore a sense of power and control to both the client's internal and external environments and help mobilize their coping mechanisms, thus fostering a return to pre-crisis functioning (Dass-Brailsford, 2010).

The post-event analyses of both the impact of Katrina and the effectiveness of the interventions have led to some important conclusions. Specifically, in order to facilitate survival after a disaster such as Hurricane Katrina, crisis workers should: (a) create a disaster plan that includes specific action to take before, during and after the disaster; (b) create electronic records with back-up services outside the area of operation; (c) create disaster communication plans, and (d) develop collaborative relationships with other supportive agencies.

September 11, 2001 (9/11)

For those watching the NBC Today show on September 11, 2001, they were presented with what at first appeared to be a routine show with its predictive segments. The same sense of predictive routine was being played out by many Americans watching the show or preparing to start their day. The routineness of the day, however, ceased approximately 22 minutes into the show. It was at that point that viewers returned from a McDonald's commercial to see the first reports of a plane crashing into the North Twin Tower of the World Trade Center in New York City.

The horrific events, images, and reports that unfolded that day are seared in the memories of not just those directly involved but the millions who saw or have seen the video and reports of the attacks on the twin towers, the Pentagon, and the plane crashing into a field in Pennsylvania. The specifics of the events, the immediate consequences, and the continuing long-term effects of this day are described below.

The lessons we have learned go well beyond the socio-political adjustment made or the provision of long-term medical and psychological services for those touched by the events of that day. These lessons include the impact that such an event has on the collective psyche and individual world and self-views of all directly or vicariously impacted by crisis.

The Event

The world was changed at 8:45 a.m. on September 11, 2001, when an American Airlines Boeing 767 crashed into the north tower of the World Trade Center in New York City. Given the time of day and the location of this event, it is not surprising that millions of Americans were vicariously transported, via the morning news shows, from the safety of their home and morning routines to the unfolding events of the day (e.g., see https://www.youtube.com/watch?v=OtZKEjr-Sfg).

What was initially perceived as a tragic accident, one leaving a huge hole near the 80th floor of this 110-story skyscraper, was soon seen as something more nefarious and world-changing than first thought. It was a mere 18 minutes after the first plane hit the

North Tower that a second Boeing jet, Flight 175, crashed into the South Tower near the 60th floor. Massive explosions occurred, and smoke and debris filled the sky.

The shock and horror that was experienced during these 18 minutes was but the beginning. At 9:45 a.m. a third American Airlines jet, Flight 77, slammed into the west side of the Pentagon military headquarters. As with the events unfolding in New York, the jet fuel caused a massive fire and structural collapse.

As those who watched the attacks attempted to gain a collective breath, images of the collapse of the World Trade Center Towers, with its massive cloud of dust, smoke, debris, and human lives filled the television screen. While these events in Washington and New York were taking center stage in our news reporting, a fourth hijacked plane was being taken down, crashed by a group of courageous passengers. United Airlines Flight 93 was hijacked by four terrorists and, in an attempt by passengers and crew to regain control, the plane crashed at 10:10 a.m. into a field near Shanksville, Pennsylvania, killing all 44 people on board.

As the events of that day have been reviewed and analyzed, we now know that it was 19 militants associated with the Islamic extremist group Al-Qaeda who planned and carried out the hijacking of these four commercial airliners, directing them to suicide attacks upon the United States.

EXERCISE 10.2

AN EXPERIENCE BEYOND WORDS

Directions: The scale and devastating impact of the attack on the twin towers, New York City, on September 11, 2001, is clearly reflected in the following video. As noted at the beginning of the video, the voices and images presented within the documentary can be upsetting, and as such, you should consider reviewing the video only to the degree to it helps you to understand the breadth and depth of such a traumatic event.

Even though you might have watched this video when first introduced at the beginning of this chapter, we invite you to once again watch the video and this time reflect and record your thoughts and feelings, especially as you try to place yourself within the lived experience of those trapped and those serving as first responders.

https://www.youtube.com/watch?v=BFOTneNSy3g

The Impact of the Crisis

The attacks on September 11th resulted in the creation of a new socio-political order, one that continues to unfold even to this day. Operation Enduring Freedom was the American-led international effort to destroy the Taliban and Osama bin Laden's terrorist network. While that military operation lasted a couple of months, the active engagement of our country in the fight against terrorism took on full steam and remains at peak as of this date. While the events of that day changed our political climate, the greatest impact was on our social reality, the experience of which still continues.

The numbers are staggering. Close to 3,000 people died on that day in New York alone. This included those within the towers and immediate vicinity, as well as 343 firefighters and paramedics, 23 New York City police officers, and 37 Port Authority police officers, all first responders.

The numbers of deaths at the Pentagon totaled 125, plus the 64 people on board the airliner; 44

people died in the crash at Shanksville. Another 10,000 were treated for injuries. Overall, it has been estimated that more than 10,000 children lost parents or loved ones on September 11, 2001 (Cohen, Goodman, Brown, & Mannarino, 2004).

While these statistics, these numbers, are in and of themselves horrifying, they alone fail to accurately depict the level of trauma, tragedy, and crisis experienced that day. Exercise 10.2 invites you to review and reflect upon the images and voices of those directly experiencing the horror of the Twin Towers. The video can be upsetting and, therefore, you are cautioned prior to your decision to review.

The events of that day, graphically depicted across national television, had a significant impact on those watching from the safe confines of their homes. In a meta-analysis of 150 studies investigating the impact of 9/11, Perlman et al. (2011) found that while the actual attacks were confined to New York, Washington, and Pennsylvania, up to five days after, 44% of the adult United States population reported experiencing substantial stress, fear, and insecurity. As might be expected, it was the people directly victimized by the events, including first responders and volunteers, that encountered the largest negative impact. Research shows that the prevalence of PTSD in rescue and recovery workers two to three years after 9/11 ranged from 6.25% for police to 21.2% for unaffiliated volunteers (Perlman et al., 2011). These data point to the power of that day as a traumatizing experience. However, one can only imagine the depth of trauma and intensity of the psychological pain experienced by those directly victimized that day. Case Illustration 10.3 provides a glimpse into one survivor's experience.

Responding to the Crisis

For years prior to 9/11, an accepted approach to addressing large-scale traumatic events was to *go inside, it might not land there. So I turned and ran into the building, down into the mall, and that's when it hit. I dove to the ground, screaming at the top of my lungs, "Oh, no! Oh, no! Jenny and Ben! Jenny and Ben!" It wasn't a very creative response, but it was the only thing I could say. I was gonna die.*

The explosion was extreme, the noise impossible to describe. I started crying. It's hard for me to imagine now that when I was on the ground awaiting my doom, hearing that noise, thousands of people were dying. That noise is a noise thousands of people heard when they died.

When it hit, everything went instantly black. You know how a little kid packs a pail of sand at the beach? That's what it was like in my mouth, my nose, my ears, my eyes—everything packed with debris. I spat it out. I puked, mostly out of horror. I felt myself: Am I intact? Can I move? I was all there. There was moaning. People were hurt and crying all around me.

I'm alive, yeah. But I'm trapped beneath whatever fell on top of me and this place is filled with smoke and dust. This is how I'm gonna die—and this was worse. Because I was going to be cognizant of my death. I was going to be trapped in a hole and it was going to fill with smoke and they were going to find me like one of those guys buried in Pompeii.

I sat there thinking of my wife and son again. It wasn't like seeing the photos of Jenny and Ben that I had on my desk, though. The images I had were of them without me. Images of knowing that I'd never touch them again. As I sat there, thinking of them, I suddenly got this presence of mind: I gotta try to survive.

I tore off my shirt and wrapped it around my mouth and nose to keep some of the smoke out. I started crawling. It was absolutely pitch-black. I had no idea where I was crawling to, but I had to keep trying. It's haunting to think about it now.

I saw a light go on. I can't say I was happy, because I was horrified, but that light was hope."

engage in Critical Incident Stress Debriefings (CISD) (Everly & Mitchell, 1999). The focus of this approach is on facilitating the victims' sharing of their thoughts and feelings as a way of providing relief (Seery et al., 2008). This approach has been called into question.

Research since 9/11 has suggested that such an approach may not be as useful as first thought, being too brief to allow for adequate emotional processing. A meta-analysis by van Emmerik et al., (2002) shows that this approach does not significantly improve PTSD or other trauma-related symptoms, such as general anxiety and depression. In fact, a study by Sherman et al. (2005) found that those survivors who chose not to discuss their experience showed better mental health outcomes than those who did.

As a result of the research following 9/11, there has been a shift away from this CISD approach to a triage approach aimed at not only the immediate distress (i.e., "first aid") and stabilization but also the development of survivors' adaptive functioning (Ford & Courtois, 2009). The approach is one that targets promotion of a sense of safety, calm, self-efficacy, connectedness, and hope (Briere & Scott, 2013). Special attention is given to addressing practical needs, such as finding a safe place or reconnecting with loved ones. Meeting these basic needs is seen as a way of ensuring that these conditions do not exacerbate the trauma from the event itself.

In the case where additional psychological intervention is required, a cognitive behavioral approach has been identified as best practice. A human caused disaster, such as the attack of 9/11, creates conditions of uncertainty about the future and possibility of a reoccurrence. In turn, these conditions result in long-term enduring stress. Because of the elements of uncertainty and apprehensiveness, cognitive behavioral strategies have been employed to help the victims reprocess

the experience in order to extinguish the fear and to reframe the memories as just that—
historical memories.

Summary

- Case study analyses following a major disaster help those in crisis service to \adjust policies, procedures, training, and resources in preparation for future events.

- On April 20, 1999, Eric Harris and Dylan Klebold killed 13 people and wounded 20 in their assault on Columbine High School.

- One of the valuable outcomes to the Columbine High School attack has been the increased research and attention to both the identification of early warning signs of students at risk for such violent activity and the development of both remedial and prevention services and programs within our schools.

- Columbine generated the most intensive period of legislative activity on school violence to date. Many schools heightened means of security (e.g., cameras, metal detectors) and increased methods of communications, especially when experiencing violence, bullying, weapons possession, by engaging zero-toler-ance policies regarding possession or use of weapons, providing anti-bullying and violence programs, and perhaps most importantly by increasing crisis plans and the availability of mental health counseling.

- An important lesson emerging from the analyses of Columbine was that the power of relationships is a key to healing and recovery.

- On August 29, 2005, Hurricane Katrina wreaked havoc on approximately 90,000 miles of territory, displacing hundreds of thousands of people, and resulted in 1,600 deaths.

- An analysis of the impact of Katrina revealed that, unlike the pattern that emerged from other major disasters where the prevalence of negative impacts decreased with time, data collected suggested that the depth and breadth of negative experiences encountered by victims of Katrina actually increased with time.

- The world was changed at 8:45 a.m. on September 11, 2001, when an American Airlines Boeing 767 crashed into the north tower of the World Trade Center in New York City.

- We now know that it was 19 militants associated with the Islamic extremist group Al Qaeda who planned and carried out the hijacking of these four commercial airliners, directing them to suicide attacks upon the United States.

- Operation Enduring Freedom was the American-led international effort to destroy the Taliban and Osama bin Laden's terrorist network.
- As a result of the research following 9/11, there has been a shift away from the critical incident stress debriefings approach to a triage approach aimed at not only the immediate distress (i.e., "first aid") and stabilization, but also the development of victim's adaptive functioning.

Important Terms

Case study

Columbine High School

Columbine Connection

Columbine effect

Critical Incident Stress Debriefings (CISD)

First responders

Harris, Eric

Hurricane Katrina

Klebold, Dylan

Operation Enduring Freedom

Osama bin Laden

September 11, 2001 (9/11)

Shanksville

SHOUTS

Superdome

Taliban

Triage approach

Twin Towers of the World Trade Center

Zero tolerance

Additional Resources

In print

Dass-Brailsford, P. (2010). *Crisis and disaster counseling: Lessons learned from Hurricane Katrina and other disasters.* Thousand Oaks, CA: Sage Publications.

Office for Victims of Crime. (n.d.). *Responding to September 11 victims: Lessons learned from the states.* Washington, D.C.: Author. Retrieved October 23, 2016, from http://www.ovc.gov/publications/infores/911lessonslearned/ovcpost911.pdf

The Governor's Columbine Review Committee. (2001). The report of Governor Bill Owens: Columbine review commission. Retrieved October 23, 2016, from https://schoolshooters.info/sites/default/files/Columbine%20-%20Governor's%20Commission%20Report.pdf

On the Web

(*Warning:* The following are video accounts of the disasters discussed within this chapter, and they are often graphic).

Columbine High School Attack: Zero Hour Full Documentary: https://www.youtube.com/watch?v=TzvUTV2LSRM

Hurricane Katrina: Katrina, The New Orleans Nightmare: Documentary on the Devastation of Hurricane Katrina: https://www.youtube.com/watch?v=JEAedjLXw7Q

September 11, 2001 (9/11): Remembering 9/11. National Geographic Channel: http://channel.nationalgeographic.com/remembering-911/videos/the-911-attacks/

References

Austin, S. J. (2003). *Lessons learned from the shootings at Columbine High School.* The Human Side of School Crises–A Public Entity Risk Institute Symposium. Retrieved October 17, 2016, from https://www.schoolcounselor.org/asca/media/asca/Crisis/columbine.pdf

Briere, J. N., & Scott, C. (2013). *Principles of trauma therapy: A guide to symptoms, evaluation, and treatment* (2nd ed.). Thousand Oaks, CA: Sage Publications, Inc.

Centers for Disease Control and Prevention. (2005). *Assessment of health-related needs after Hurricanes Katrina and Rita—Orleans and Jefferson Parishes* (pp. 38–41). Morbidity and Mortality Weekly Report. Vol. 55. New Orleans area, Louisiana: Oct 17–22, 2006.

Chia-Chen Chen, A., Keith, V. M., Airiness, C., Li, W., & Leong, K. J. (2007). Economic vulnerability, discrimination, and Hurricane Katrina: Health among Black Katrina survivors in eastern New Orleans. *Journal of the American Psychiatric Nurses Association, 13*(5), 257–266.

Cloud, J. (1999). The Columbine Effect. *Time Magazine.* Retrieved October 17, 2016, from http://content.time.com/time/magazine/article/0,9171,35098,00.html

Cohen, J., Goodman, R. F., Brown, E. J., & Mannarino, A. (2004). Treatment of childhood traumatic grief: Contributing to a newly emerging condition in the wake of community trauma. *Harvard Review of Psychiatry, 12*, 213–216.

Dass-Brailsford, P. (2010a). Hurricane Katrina. In P. Dass-Brailsford, *Crisis and Disaster Counseling: Lessons Learned from Hurricane Katrina and Other Disasters* (pp. 17–32). Thousand Oaks, CA: Sage Publications..

Dass-Brailsford, P. (2010b). Effective Disaster and Crisis Intervention. In P. Dass-Brailsford, Crisis and Disaster Counseling: *Lessons Learned from Hurricane Katrina and Other Disasters,* (pp. 49–66). Thousand Oaks, CA: Sage Publications.

Everly, G., & Mitchell, J. (1999). *Critical incident stress management (CISM): A new era and standard of care in crisis intervention.* Ellicott City, MD: Chevron.

Ford, J., & Courtois, C. (2009). Defining and understanding complex trauma and complex traumatic stress disorders. In C. Courtois & J. Ford (Eds.), *Treating complex traumatic stress disorders* (pp. 13–30). New York, NY: Guilford.

Galea, S., Tracy, M., Norris, F., & Coffey, S. F. (2008). Financial and social circumstances and the incidence and course of PTSD in Mississippi during the first two years after Hurricane Katrina. *Journal of Traumatic Stress, 1,* 357–368

Houston, J. B., Reyes, G., Pfefferbaum, B. & Wyche, K. F. (2010). Provider perspectives on serving the needs of displaced disaster survivors following Hurricane Katrina. In P. Dass-Brailsford, *Crisis and Disaster Counseling: Lessons Learned from Hurricane Katrina and Other Disasters* (pp. 99–144). Thousand Oaks, CA: Sage Publications.

Johnson, K. (2000). *School Crisis Management* (2nd ed.). Alameda, CA: Hunter House Publishers.

Kaniasty K., & Norris F. H. (2008). Longitudinal linkages between perceived social support and posttraumatic stress symptoms: Sequential roles of social causation and social selection. *Journal of Traumatic Stress, 21,* 274–281.

Kessler, R. C., Galea, S., Gruber, M. J., Sampson, N. A., Ursano, R. J., & Wessely, S. (2008). Trends in mental illness and suicidality after Hurricane Katrina. *Molecular Psychiatry, 13*(4), 374–384.

Kohn, D. (2001). What really happened at Columbine. Retrieved October 10, 2016, from http://www.cbsnews.com/news/what-really-happened-at-columbine/

Lawrence, R. G., & Birkland, T. A. (2004). Guns, Hollywood, and school safety: Defining the school-shooting problem across public arenas. *Social Science Quarterly, 85,* 1193–1207.

Markwell, P. & Ratard, R. (2006). Deaths Directly Caused by Hurricane Katrina. Retrieved October 12, 2016, from http://dhh.louisiana.gov/assets/oph/Center-PHCH/Center-CH/stepi/special-studies/KatrinaDeath1.pdf

McLaughlin, K., Fairbank, J., Gruber, M., Jones, R., Lakoma, M., Pfefferbaum, B. Sampson, N.A.& Kessler, R.C. (2009). Serious emotional disturbance among youth exposed to Hurricane Katrina 2 years post disaster. *Journal of the American Academy of Child & Adolescent Psychiatry, 48*(11), 1069–1078.

Norris, F. H. (2007). Impact of mass shootings on survivors, families and communities. *PTSD Research Quarterly, 18*(3), 1050–1835.

Perlman, S. E., Friedman, S., Galea, S., Hemanth, P. N., Eros-Sarnyai, M, Stellman, S. D., … Greene, C.M. (2011). Short-term and medium-term health effects of 9/11. *The Lancet, 378*(9794), 925–934

Rateau, M. R. (2009). Differences in emotional well-being of hurricane survivors: A secondary analysis of the ABC news Hurricane Katrina anniversary poll. *Archives of Psychiatric Nursing, 23,* 269–271

Rhodes, J., Chan, C., Paxson, C., Rouse, C. E., Waters, M., & Fussell, E. (2010). The impact of Hurricane Katrina on the mental and physical health of low-income parents in New Orleans. *American Journal of Orthopsychiatry, 80*(20), 237–247.

Seery, M., Silver, R., Holman, A., Ence, W., & Chu, T. (2008). Expressing thoughts and feelings following a collective trauma: Immediate responses to 9/11 predict negative outcomes in a national sample. *Journal of Counseling and Clinical Psychiatry, 76*(4), 657–663.

Sherman, M., Zanotti, D., & Jones, D. (2005). Key elements in couples therapy with veterans with combat-related posttraumatic stress disorder. *Professional Psychology: Research and Practice, 36*(6), 626–633.

Thienkrua, W., Cardozo, B. L., Chakkraband, M. L. S., Guadamuz, T. E., Pengjuntr, W., Tantipiwatanaskul, P., ... Van Griensven, F. (2006). Symptoms of posttraumatic stress disorder and depression among children in tsunami-affected areas in southern Thailand. *Journal of the American Medical Association, 296,* 549–559.

Tucker, P., Pfefferbaum, B., Khan, Q., Young, M. J., Aston, C. E., Holmes, J., ... Thompson, J. (2008). Katrina survivors relocated to Oklahoma: A tale of two cities. *Psychiatric Annals,* 38(2), 125–133.

U.S. Department of Transportation (2006). Catastrophic hurricane evacuation plan: A report to Congress. Retrieved October 12, 2016, from http://www.fhwa.dot.gov/reports/hurricanevac-uation/chapter1.htm#ch103

SECTION 4

A Focus on the Helper

CHAPTER 11

The Helper at Times of Crisis: Needed Knowledge, Skills, and Disposition

I assumed that with my training as a mental health counselor and my experience in private practice, I would be effective in my helping of the victims of the hurricane. I don't think I did harm ... but I know ... I needed much more training than I had!

T he voice of the mental health practitioner reflecting on her experience while attempting to work in the crisis surrounding a hurricane highlights the unique demands of crisis and disaster work. Working at times of crisis and disaster is challenging and requires special knowledge, skills, and dispositions.

While the fundamentals of the helping relationship and the skills of effective counseling continue to serve as foundations for those engaged, the uniqueness of the demands encountered in crisis and trauma work renders the traditional training for mental health professional as insufficient. Traditional models and paradigms of counseling and therapy simply do not work at times of crisis or in provision of disaster and trauma relief.

In the aftermath of the attack on September 11, 2001 (see Chapter 10), it became quite clear that there was a need for readily available and appropriately trained mental health volunteers who could respond and serve at times of crisis and disaster (Webber & Mascari, 2005). However, the experience of that event revealed that not only were many mental health providers ill prepared to assist those affected by the events of that day (see Case Illustration 11.1), but that most counselor education programs failed to develop the special set of skills and disposition needed for one to be effective in providing service to those in crisis or traumatized by disaster (Smith, 2005).

Reviews of counselor preparation programs, for example, found them lacking in crisis counseling training (Morris & Minton, 2012; Minton & Pease-Carter, 2011). The 2016 Council for Accreditation of Counseling and Related Educational Programs (CACREP; 2015) standards lists the term "crisis" twice in the core curriculum and three times in the specialty areas of clinical mental health, clinical rehabilitation counseling, and marriage couple and family counseling. However, of the 654 CACREP accredited counseling programs reviewed by Guo, Wang, Lok, Phillips, and Statz (2016) only 192 (29.4%) required students to take a stand-alone crisis counseling course.

These data not only highlight the uniqueness of the knowledge and skills required of those serving at these times of crisis, but also the need for training that goes well beyond that traditionally provided. The current chapter will highlight the unique knowledge, skills, and dispositions required of those serving in the capacity of mental health providers during times of crisis, trauma, and disaster. Specifically, after reading this chapter, you will be able to:

1. Describe the unique demands of crisis, trauma, and disaster mental health services;

CASE ILLUSTRATION 11.1[1]

FEELING OVERWHELMED AND INADEQUATE

It was the anniversary of September 11, 2001, and we had planned a memorial service for our students and staff. Little did I realize the impact this reminder would have, not just on the students, but our faculty … and me.

We left the auditorium where, in addition to moments of reflection and songs, we read a list of names of those lost during the attacks on the Twin Towers. We know that many of our school student body, staff, and faculty had loved ones, friends, and neighbors either lost or directly impacted by that day, but we falsely assumed that the passage of a year would have resulted in some healing. Boy, were we wrong.

I returned to my office and within minutes I literally had over a dozen 1st through 5th graders at my door, crying hysterically, engaging in arguments with one another, all truly overwhelmed with anxiety and grief.

Look, I've been a practicing school counselor for over 11 years, and I am licensed as a mental health counselor in my state. I have more than 60 credits of graduate training and thousands of hours of practice, but nothing prepared me for this.

The circumstances called for a quick response—true crisis intervention—and I felt both overwhelmed and inadequate. It was not just the number of students converging on my office, nor even the intensity of their grief and anxiety, although these did throw me off guard, but my sense of loss and my sense of incompetency seemed to be compounded by my own experience of grief and trauma aroused by the event. I was not prepared to be an effective helper under these conditions.

---

1 Excerpt from: George S. Everly, Jr., Randal D. Beaton, Betty Pfefferbaum, and Cindy L. Parker, "Training for Disaster Response Personnel: The Development of Proposed Core Competencies in Disaster Mental Health," *Public Health Reports*, vol. 123, no. 4, pp. 539–542. Copyright © 2008 by SAGE Publications. Reprinted with permission.

2. Identify areas of specialized knowledge and skill required for those providing crisis and trauma counseling;

3. Describe the core dispositions, values, and attitudes necessary for effective crisis/trauma counselors; and

4. Explain the need for cultural consideration when providing crisis, trauma, or disaster mental health services.

While the current chapter serves as an introduction to the knowledge, skills, and dispositions required of those engaged in crisis and trauma work, it is suggested that all who may be interested in serving at times of crisis and disaster seek additional training as provided by agencies such as the American Red Cross (http://www.redcross.org/take-a-class/disaster-training), the Federal Emergency Management Agency (http://www.fema.gov), and the National Center for Post-Traumatic Stress Disorder (http://www.ncptsd.org).

The Need for Special Knowledge and Skills

As noted in our opening vignette, the timing, circumstances, and pressing needs presented at the time of crisis and disaster do not allow for the successful engagement of traditional counseling and therapeutic models. While it is true that the fundamentals of the helping relationship and dynamic continue to apply and the basic skills necessary for attending and focusing clients or victims remain essential, additional knowledge of approaches and skills to employ these approaches are required.

Crisis Intervention

The very nature of a crisis demands a response, an intervention that might be best described as Psychological First Aid. The intervention during times of crisis, as contrasted to the more traditional forms and models of mental health intervention, is short-termed, time-limited, goal-focused, and highly directive. Given these characteristics, the knowledge and skills employed by the crisis worker often differ from those typically found within a counseling or therapy setting.

Connecting

Because of the unique demands encountered by the client, who, by definition, has overwhelmed his/her resources and has thrown him/herself into a state of disequilibrium, it is important to: (a) quickly establish rapport and a working relationship; (b) address immediate threats and concerns including resolving the client's basic and pressing needs; and (c) provide the client with information about what to expect and the steps to be taken.

Assessment

Another demand is for the crisis worker to quickly assess the current crisis and relevant pre-disaster stressors. It is important to identify the degree to which impairment to the client's functioning is affective, behavioral, and cognitive and identify a client's problem-solving and coping capabilities, as well as the extent of his or her support system.

During the assessment, it is important to identify the existence of warning signs of maladaptive coping behaviors and responses, including suicidal ideation, and explore the client's adaptive coping behaviors that may be substituted for exhibited behaviors. As one attempts to assess the client, it is important to be aware of risk factors, such as a depressed state, social isolation, level of losses as a result of the disaster, and significant pre-disaster losses (e.g., recent divorce, unemployment, death of significant other, etc.) that may indicate a need for a more enduring form of intervention. The PsychSTART Mental Health Triage system (Schreiber, 2005) provides a process for identifying evidenced-based risk markers and serves as a tool for identifying those who will need additional assessment and intervention. Figure 11.1 provides the items to consider in PsychSTART, with any identified red factors marking the higher likelihood of a client's elevated clinical distress, and purple triage risk factors highlighting those with compelling and immediate emergencies. Clearly, the greater the number of risk factors, or the presence of emergency factors, the greater the need for alternative interventions, including possible hospitalization.

Goals and Interventions

As with all forms of therapeutic support and intervention, it is important to present as a caring, calming force. It is vital to engage in active listening and nonjudgmental and empathic responding, reflecting crisis-related feelings and clarifying crisis facts, while instilling a sense of realistic hope. It is also important to facilitate the client's expression of feelings about the current crisis, including any sense of guilt or responsibility. While being nonjudgmental, it is important to use challenging skills to help reframe and interpret any misunderstandings or maladaptive beliefs displayed by the client.

In helping the client reduce current anxiety and begin to gain a sense of control, it is important to help him or her articulate the nature of the problem(s) being confronted. It is critical to not only inquire about what happened, but also help the client identify specific, immediate, and concrete issues and needs. Once these have been identified, the crisis worker needs to assess the client's emotional readiness to begin to problem solve and explore past coping strategies. While attempting to identify strategies that may have worked in the past, it is also important to help the client explore new coping strategies, including some alternatives suggested by the crisis worker. Throughout this entire process, it is central to provide encouragement and convey confidence in the client's ability to manage the current situation, highlighting his or her strengths.

Figure 11.1 PsychSTART

PsychSTART™ Mental Health Triage System		
DANGER TO SELF OR OTHERS?	⬡ STOP	Y ☐
FELT/EXPRESSED EXTREME PANIC or FEAR?	⚠	Y ☐
FELT DIRECT THREAT TO LIFE OF SELF and/or FAMILY MEMBER?	⚠	Y ☐
SAW/HEARD DEATH or SERIOUS INJURY OF OTHER?	⚠	Y ☐
DEATH OF PARENT, CHILD or FAMILY MEMBER?	⚠	Y ☐
DEATH OF PET?	⚠	Y ☐
SIGNIFICANT DISASTER-RELATED ILLNESS or PHYSICAL INJURY TO SELF or FAMILY MEMBER?	⚠	Y ☐
TRAPPED or DELAYED EVACUATION?	⚠	Y ☐
FAMILY MEMBER CURRENTLY MISSING or UNACCOUNTED FOR?	⚠	Y ☐
UNACCOMPANIED CHILD?	⚠	Y ☐
HOME NOT LIVABLE?		Y ☐
SEPARATED FROM IMMEDIATE FAMILY DURING EVENT?		Y ☐
PRIOR HISTORY OF MENTAL HEALTH CARE?		Y ☐
PRIOR HISTORY OF DISASTER EXPERIENCE?		Y ☐
NO TRIAGE FACTORS IDENTIFIED		Y ☐

⬡ STOP If yes, immediately contact site supervisor and DMH or call 911.

⚠ If yes, contact DMH as soon as possible.

Contact DMH at the end of your shift for all other risk factors.

© 2001–2012 Marritt D. Schreiber, Ph.D.

Action Plan

Once the issues have been concretely identified, it is important to move the client into finding and engaging with solutions. Given the nature of crisis as a destabilizing experience, clients are typically receptive to suggested action plans. Stress resulting in the experience of crisis and trauma causes disorganized thinking, concentration problems, and difficulty planning and making decisions.

Even with this major destabilization and disruption to their problem solving ability, it is important to engage and empower clients as much as possible. This may require the crisis worker to be more active in guiding the client through problem-solving steps and strategies. As suggested by the U.S. Department of Health and Human Services (2005), crisis support involves guiding, listening, reassuring, and providing practical assistance. As such, it is important to start with current needs and pressing concerns. Asking clients to identify problems or challenges that they are currently facing and helping to identify tasks that are easily completed can help restore a sense of control and capability. It is also important when selecting a strategy to have the client identify coping strengths and tactics that worked previously, as well as current resources and social supports that may be available.

With a direction and plan in place, the crisis worker needs to break down goals and subgoals into manageable chunks and provide specific tasks to be completed. For example, rather than identifying the need to find alternative housing, it is more helpful to direct the client to investigate available apartments, or determine the amount of money one can spend on a new living space. In outlining the specific steps to be taken by the client, it is also important to provide a sense of confidence in the ability to take the steps and to be successful. Even though the crisis worker will be actively engaged and somewhat directive throughout process, it remains important to engage the client in a collaborative relationship to ensure not only that the client owns the action plan and is capable of implementing it, but that she or he also feels empowered.

Referral

For some clients and workers, these immediate interventions are not enough to alleviate their distress or mitigate long-term consequences. In those cases, additional interventions targeted to specific client needs may be necessary.

Disaster Responders

While the same set of competencies and approaches listed for crisis counselors applies to those responding at times of disaster, a set of core competencies were developed for mental health professionals engaged in disaster work. The Disaster Mental Health Collaborative Group (DMHCG) identified five core competencies for disaster mental health providers (Everly et al., 2008). While the list is viewed as foundational, the group recognized that a set of more advanced competencies, built upon this core, will be needed to address the needs and concerns of specialized subgroups and uniquely challenging situations (Everly et al., 2008). Exercise 11.1 invites you to reflect upon these core competencies. You are asked to assess your level of knowledge and skill and to develop a professional plan for those areas needing development.

EXERCISE 11.1

CORE COMPETENCIES FOR DISASTER MENTAL HEALTH PROVIDERS

Directions: Review the five core areas of competency along with the specific competencies identified as foundational by Disaster Mental Health Collaborative Group. For those who desire additional training, check the resources listed at the end of the chapter for training materials and opportunities.

Core area	Specific competency	Self-evaluation: 1 = need training 2 = some knowledge and skill 3 = mastery	Plan for professional development
I. Disaster response personnel will demonstrate the ability to define and/or describe the following key terms and concepts related to disaster mental/psychosocial/behavioral health preparedness and response:	1. The biopsychosocial and cultural manifestations of human stress. 2. Phases of psychosocial disaster and recovery reactions at the community level. 3. The effects of psychological trauma and disaster-related losses and hardships. 4. Incident management structure and the role of disaster mental health in a multidisciplinary disaster response. 5. Disaster mental health intervention principles. 6. Crisis intervention(s) with disaster-affected individuals. 7. Population-based responses before, during, and after a disaster (e.g., evacuation, shelter in place).		
II. Disaster response personnel will demonstrate the following skills needed to communicate effectively:	1. Establish rapport. 2. Employ active/reflective listening skills. 3. Display effective nonverbal communications. 4. Establish realistic boundaries and expectations for the interaction. 5. Use a culturally competent and developmentally appropriate manner of communication.		
III. Disaster response personnel will demonstrate skill in assessing the need for, and type of, intervention (if any) including, but not limited to, the ability to:	1. Gather information by employing methods such as observation, self-reporting, other reports, and other assessments. 2. Identify immediate medical needs, if any. 3. Identify basic human needs (e.g., food, clothing, shelter). 4. Identify social and emotional needs.		

	5. Determine level of functionality (e.g., the ability to care for self and others, follow medical advice and safety orders). 6. Recognize mild psychological and behavioral distress reactions and distinguish them from potentially incapacitating reactions. 7. Synthesize assessment information.		
IV. Disaster response personnel will demonstrate skill in developing and implementing an action plan (based upon one's knowledge, skill, authority, and functional role) to meet those needs identified through assessment including, but not limited to, the following behaviors:	1. Disaster response personnel will demonstrate skill in developing an action plan including the ability to: (*1*) identify available resources (e.g., food, shelter, medical, transportation, crisis intervention services, local counseling services, financial resources), (*2*) identify appropriate stress management interventions, and (*3*) formulate an action plan consisting of sequential steps. 2. Disaster response personnel will demonstrate skill in initiating an action plan including the ability to: (*1*) provide appropriate stress management, if indicated, (*2*) connect to available resources (e.g., food, shelter, medical, transportation, crisis intervention services, local counseling services, financial resources), (*3*) connect to natural support systems (e.g., family, friends, coworkers, spiritual support), and (*4*) implement other interventions as appropriate. 3. Disaster response personnel will demonstrate the ability to evaluate the effectiveness of an action plan considering changes in situation or disaster phase through methods such as observation, self-report, other reports, and other assessments. 4. Disaster response personnel will demonstrate the ability to revise an action plan as needed (e.g., track progress and outcomes).		
V. Disaster response personnel will demonstrate skill in caring for responder peers and self, including, but not limited to, the ability to:	1. Describe peer-care techniques (e.g., buddy system, informal town meetings).		

	2. Describe self-care techniques (e.g., stress management, journaling, communication with significant others, proper exercise, proper nutrition, programmed downtime, sufficient quality sleep). 3. Describe organizational interventions that reduce job stress (e.g., organizational briefings, adjustment of shift work, job rotations, location rotations, effective and empathic leadership, work/rest/nourishment cycles, and support services, as indicated).		

Dispositions and Attitudes

When considering the types of attitudes, dispositions, or values required of one working in crisis intervention, it is important to reflect upon the core qualities necessary of all mental health providers. Research (e.g., Tepper & Hass, 2001) has highlighted the need for mental health providers, including those engaged in crisis intervention, to embody each of the following.

Acceptance

At the time of crisis or in the wake of a disaster, those needing services are often stripped of those symbols of status, role, and position. They are confused, and their view of self and the world may be somewhat muddled. It is at these times that they need to experience acceptance for where they are and who they are.

To accept another demands that one be able to put aside status or informal social roles that might interfere with a mutual, open relationship. This is not the time to be the "helper" and the other to be in a position of needing "help." Rather, in approaching our service, we need to ignore labels, stereotypes, and role assignments and engage as two individuals attempting to navigate the circumstances of the moment.

In accepting the other, we do not demand that the other behave or think in any certain way or try to impose a role on him or her, but instead, allow people to be who they are and where they are at any one moment. This acceptance of others does not mean we give wholesale approval of all that they did or are choosing to do, but rather accept the fact that given their experience of reality and sense of self at this moment, those decisions made sense.

Unconditional Positive Regard and Valuing

In addition to conveying an acceptance of the client's current sense of self and worldview, it is important to convey an attitude of deep valuing and respect for this other. It is important, especially for one whom in the moment of crisis may feel defeated, to experience the prizing, the valuing, and the non-possessive warmth and respect of the client or disaster survivor. This valuing of the other allows the helper to look beyond the conditions of that person's life or current situation, conditions that can serve as filters coloring our valuing of another, and instead simply embrace and value them as a fellow human being.

The ability to convey unconditional value and regard is especially important to those individuals whose status, power, and social standing or prestige have been shattered. Research points to the fact that the presence of such unconditional positive regard appears to be significantly associated with therapeutic success (Farber & Lane, 2012).

Genuineness

Being real and genuine positions us to interact with another to from a truly authentic position, one in which we are without a game face or a scripted role, and present as real, as opposed to phony. Genuineness allows us to be congruent in a way that our words, actions, tone, thoughts, and feelings are all conveying the same message (Parsons, 2011). It is this genuineness that positions us for true, meaningful contact with another (Moursund & Kenny, 2002).

Self-Awareness as a Foundation for Empathy

The conditions of one in crisis certainly can, and likely will, elicit sympathy from those engaged in caring and intervening. Our sympathy emerges from our viewing the conditions of another from our point of reference, our perspective, as if this was happening to me. While our sympathy may move us, it moves us from the perspective of our world and self-views.

CASE ILLUSTRATION 11.2

CHAOS, SMOKE, AND TEARS

It looked like a war zone. Clothes were scattered all over, rooftops came to rest on top of cars, smoke and fire billowed from down power lines, and through it all, the tears of young and old permeated the sounds of the evening. This was the setting to which we are called to serve. This was the impact of the tornado that devastated my community on March 11th.

While, thankfully, there were no fatalities and only a handful of individuals with minor injuries, it felt like hundreds of people were in a state of absolute panic, all seeking assistance. Immediately upon exiting my car, I was confronted by a number of individuals, all clearly upset, clearly disoriented, and seeking answers and direction. Between the tears, the anger, the confusion, and the absolute disbelief about the loss they just encountered, they asked questions regarding the location of loved ones and demanded direction as to what they were to do or where were they were to go. It was hard to have them focus. It was difficult to attend to one when so many were in need. To say it was an experience of unbridled chaos is understatement. Yet, it was an experience, a situation, which demanded a calming presence, and I thank God for the training I had received.

EXERCISE 11.2

UNIQUE DISPOSITIONS, ATTITUDES, AND PROFESSIONAL STYLE

Directions: In the first column, you will note characteristics of crisis and disaster work that make it unique from the more traditional counseling practice. The second column addresses some of the dispositions and attitudes required to function within this unique form of service. Your task is to personally assess your current level of comfort in working with those client/setting demands and the disposition required.

In contrast to "traditional" counseling	Dispositions, attitude, and style required	Personal comfort level (0 = could not function, 3 = somewhat distracting, 5 = no negative impact on effective functioning)
Worksite: In the field, at a shelter, or with an unexpected walk-in, rather than designated office, space, desk, appointment schedule, etc.	A comfort with responding on your feet, creatively making use of resources available and dealing with the unexpected	
Collaboration: Work typically involves multiple professionals in coordination, rather than the one-on-one typically encountered.	A valuing of teamwork and a comfort surrendering absolute authority that comes with working alone.	
Engagement: Rather than client self-or-other referred, may be required to make initial contact with clients who are unable or initially unwilling to engage.	Secure when working in difficult circumstances with resistant, distracted, or otherwise pre-occupied clients	
Boundaries: While there remain clear professional boundaries in both crisis work and traditional practice, the parameters may be less clear and formal. Defining the relationship and its parameters may be more fluid than typically experienced.	Comfort with engaging in more social service activity, vis-à-vis traditional counseling and, thus, stepping out of the role of counselor to support in a variety of non-counseling ways.	
Approach: As opposed to the opportunity to employ client-centered or other classical therapeutic approaches, this work is time-limited, requiring increased direction by the counselor and reliance, when needed, on referral for longer-term issues.	Valuing short-term, directive, problem-solving strategies	
Focus: While certainly addressing client emotional states, the focus is on the here and now task issues, which may often be "non-psychological" and practical in nature (e.g., finding shelter, reconnecting with loved ones, etc.).	Flexibility and appreciation for shifting from interest in intrapsychic dynamics and family history to practical concerns as primary focus on your interventions	
Contact and Schedule: While most traditional practices are scheduled and anticipated, crisis and disaster work is most often spontaneous and unplanned.	Flexibility with the unanticipated and comfort addressing multiple stressors and needs.	

For one to truly understand and to assist a client in need, one needs to step outside of their own frame of reference in order to step into the client's. To be able to step from one's own frame of reference and become attuned to that of another, to have direct and visceral understanding of that person's current state, is essential to truly understanding the issues confronting that person (Aragno, 2008).

Many times, a client in crisis or one surviving trauma or disaster may stir up painful memories from your own past. To be effective in these circumstances, helpers need to be aware of their own triggers and have spent time in counseling or other self-awareness programs to process these personal experiences. It is essential to work through our own points of sensitivity if we are going to be able to empathize with clients without becoming personally involved or emotional when subjects arise that have personal meaning.

High Tolerance for Chaos

The very nature of crisis and trauma work positions helpers in a context where chaos, stress, and overstimulation are maximized (see Case Illustration 11.2).

As noted in our case illustration, individuals in crisis present in a highly emotional state. They may be disoriented and feel panic and, as a result, exhibit outbursts or even threats. To help the client through the chaos, it is essential that the helper remain calm, non-reactive, and supportive. Presenting as a stable, balancing force is essential if one is to assist the client to trust in the help being offered and be hopeful about the direction that is being taken. This demands that crisis and trauma workers have a high tolerance for chaos and dramatic situations and a special resiliency under these conditions.

The unique nature of the work experienced by those engaged in crisis and trauma counseling places demands on the helper not typically encountered in a more traditional counseling setting. Exercise 11.2 provides a listing of unique characteristics found in crisis and disaster. You are invited to review these characteristics, as well as the implied types of attitudes and dispositions that would be required of one serving as a helper in those situations. You are asked to then assess the degree to which you feel able and ready to serve within a crisis or disaster context.

Cultural Consideration (revisited)

In Chapter 1, we noted that trauma and crisis are socially constructed within the context of the culture in which they occur (Silvoe, 2000). It is also true that the impact of crisis, as well as the approach to crisis resolution, are filtered through the lens of one's culture. Culture is a lens through which people view their experience, express their traumatic reactions, and view healing. As such, it is important for crisis workers to increase their personal awareness of culturally biased assumptions (see Pederson, 1987, in Chapter 1).

But beyond identifying one's biased assumptions, it is also of value for helpers to under-stand the need and value for community-based, culturally responsive services. This is especially true when attempting to intervene at times of catastrophe and disaster.

Looking at communities from an ecological perspective, that is viewing the physical and social environments of individuals and collectives as of equal importance in shaping human welfare, can be critical in times of crisis. This ecological perspective helps to promote understanding of how community resources, including people, information, services, and capital, can be mobilized in times of catastrophe, as well as a recognition of the need for external support (Kelly, 2002). This perspective directs crisis workers to attend to cultural norms and traditions of those impacted by the crisis (Dubrow & Nader, 1999). For example, in reviewing the response to Hurricane Katrina (see Chapter 10), it was discovered that the interventions perceived as helpful to survivors were grounded in the context of their culture, race, ethnicity, and sociopolitical history (Boyd, Quevillon, & Engdahl, 2010).

Planning an intervention without any knowledge of the affected group or the care they may need is grossly inappropriate (Boyd, Quevillon, & Engdahl, 2010). In addition, responders need to understand that their presence in the community may be a political act and, thus, must continually ask themselves, "Whose interests am I serving? Whose interests may be overlooked through this work?" (Wessells, 1996).

When considering specific forms of service and intervention, it is important to un-derstand culture as it sets the tone and direction for appropriate psychosocial inter-ventions. The importance of culture has been highlighted in the Inter-Agency Standing Committee's (IASC; 2007) *Guidelines on Mental Health and Psychosocial Support in Emergency Settings*. This document not only sets a framework for mobilizing community resources following a disaster but also provides action sheets with suggested activities and process indicators of success.

Central to these guidelines is the need for relief workers to understand power struc-tures and communication networks and methods, as well as identify those who stand as community opinion leaders. Further, the guidelines direct those intervening to be aware of locally available cultural resources, including traditional and spiritual healers, leaders, elders, and practices (e.g., sharing of a meal, presenting gifts of welcome, etc.).

On a practical note, it is clear that crisis situations are even more challenging when English is not the primary language. It is important to convey cultural sensitivity by pro-viding information, notifications, and support services in the primary spoken language. Further, for many cultures, the experience of violence, terrorism, and displacement as a result of disaster are filtered through the experience of prior traumatization and, thus, have impacts that are compounded and reactions that can be defensive and reactionary. According to the U.S. Department of Health and Human Services (2005) *Mental Health Mass Violence and Terrorism Handbook*, crisis workers should learn about the affected group's cultural norms, practices, and traditions and communicate cultural sensitivity by not only employing culturally accepted courteous behaviors (e.g., greetings, personal space, etc.) but also developing and adapting services to fit special group needs and reflect cultural practices and resources.

Summary

- The timing, circumstances, and pressing needs presented at the time of crisis and disaster do not allow for the successful engagement of traditional counseling and therapeutic models.

- Interventions employed during times of crisis are, by necessity, short-termed, time-limited, goal-focused, and highly directive.

- At time of crisis and disaster, it is important to: (a) quickly establish rapport and a working relationship; (b) address immediate threats and concerns including resolving basic and pressing client needs, and (c) provide the client with information about what to expect and the steps to be taken.

- In assessing clients at times of crisis and disaster, it is important to identify the existence of warning signs of maladaptive coping behaviors and responses, including suicidal ideation, and explore the clients' adaptive coping behaviors that may be substituted for behaviors being exhibited.

- One process for identifying evidenced-based risk markers is PsychSTART Mental Health Triage system.

- Given the nature of crisis as a destabilizing experience, clients are typically receptive to suggested action plans.

- Those engaged in providing crisis, trauma, and disaster mental health services need to demonstrate: acceptance, valuing, genuineness, non-judgment, empathy, a high tolerance for chaos, and cultural sensitivity.

Important Terms

Acceptance

Cultural considerations

Destabilizing experience

Empathy

Genuineness

High-chaos tolerance

Inter-Agency Standing Committee's

Psychological First Aid

PsychSTART Mental Health Triage system

Self-awareness

State of disequilibrium

Unconditional positive regard

Warning signs

Additional Resources

In Print

American Red Cross. (2012). Disaster Mental Health Handbook. Retrieved October 23, 2016, from http://www.cdms.uci.edu/pdf/disaster-mental-health-handbook-oct-2012.pdf

Nader, K., Dubrow, N., Stamm, B. & Hudnall, N. (2014). *Honoring Differences: Cultural Issues in the Treatment of Trauma and Loss (Series in Trauma and Loss)*. Philadelphia, PA: Brunner/Mazel.

U.S. Department of Health and Human Services. (2005). *Mental Health Response to Mass Violence and Terrorism: A Field Guide*. DHHS Pub. No. SMA 4025. Rockville, MD: Center for Mental Health Services, Substance Abuse and Mental Health Services. Administration.

On the Web

Red Cross Training Opportunities: http://www.redcross.org/take-a-class/disaster-training Federal Emergency Management Agency: http://www.fema.gov International Society for Traumatic Stress Studies: http://www.istss.org

National Center for Post-Traumatic Stress Disorder/ U.S. Department of Veteran Affairs: http://www.ncptsd.org

National Child Traumatic Stress Network: http://www.nctsnet.org

References

Aragno, A. (2008). The language of empathy: An analysis of its constitution, development and role in psychoanalytic listening. *Journal of the American Psychoanalytic Association, 56*, 709–740.

Boyd, B., Quevillon, R. P., & Engdahl, R. M. (2010). Working with rural and diverse communities after disaster. In P. Dass-Brailsford (Ed.), *Crisis and Disaster Counseling* (pp. 149–163). Thousand Oaks, CA: Sage.

Dubrow, N., & Nader, K. (1999). Consultations amidst trauma and loss: Recognizing and honoring differences among cultures. In K. Nader, N.Dubrow, & B. Hudnall Stamm (Eds.), *Honoring differences: Cultural issues in the treatment of trauma and loss* (pp. 267–280). Philadelphia, PA: Brunner/Mazel.

Everly, G. S., Beaton, R. D., Pfefferbaum, B., & Parker, C. L. (2008). Training for disaster response personnel: The development of proposed core competencies in disaster mental health. *Public Health Reports,123*(4), 539–542.

Farber, A. A., & Lane, J. S. (2002). Positive regard. In J.C. Norcross (Ed.*), Psychotherapy relationships that work: Therapist contributions and responsiveness to patients (*pp. 175–194). New York, NY: Oxford University Press.

Guo, Y. J., Wang, S. C., Lok, H. K., Phillips, A., & Statz, S. (2016). Crisis counseling courses in counselor preparation. *VISTAS*, retrieved October 23, 2016, from http://www.counseling.org/docs/default-source/vistas/article_458bfd25f16116603abcacff0000bee5e7.pdf?sfvrsn=4

Kelly, J. G. (2002). The spirit of community psychology. *American Journal of Community Psychology, 30*, 43–63.

IASC (Inter-Agency Standing Committee). (2007). IASC guidelines on mental health and psychosocial support in emergency settings. Geneva, Switzerland: IASC. Retrieved October 25, 2016, from http://www.unicef.org/protection/guidelines_iasc_mental_health_psychosocial_june_2007.pdf

Minton, C. A. B., & Pease-Carter, C. (2011). The status of crisis preparation in counselor education: A national study and content analysis. *Journal of Professional Counseling: Practice, Theory, and Research, 38*, 5–17.

Morris, C. A. W., & Minton, C. A. B. (2012). Crisis in the curriculum? New counselors' crisis preparation, experiences, and self-efficacy. *Counselor Education & Supervision, 51*, 256–269.

Moursund, J., & Kenny, M.C. (2002). *The Process of Counseling and Therapy* (4th ed.). Upper Saddle River, NJ: Prentice Hall.

Parsons, R.D. (2011). *Fundamentals of the Helping Process* (2nd ed). Long Grove, IL: Waveland Press, Inc.

Schreiber, M. (2005). Learning from 9/11: Toward a national model for children and families in mass casualty terrorism. In Y. Daneli & R. Dingman (Eds.), *On the ground after September 11: Mental health responses and practical knowledge gained* (pp. 605–609). New York, NY: Haworth Press.

Smith, H. (2005). The American Red Cross: How to be part of the solution, rather than part of the problem. In J. Webber, D. D. Bass, & R. Yep (Eds.), *Terrorism, trauma, and tragedies: A counselor's guide for preparing and responding* (pp. 37–38). Alexandria, VA: American Counseling Association Foundation.

U.S. Department of Health and Human Services (2005). *Mental Health Response to Mass Violence and Terrorism: A Field Guide*. DHHS Pub. No. SMA 4025. Rockville, MD: Center for Mental Health Services, Substance Abuse and Mental Health Services. Administration.

Webber, J., & Mascari, J. B. (2009). Critical Issues in implementing the new CACREP standards for disaster, trauma and crisis counseling. In G.R. Waltz, J. C. Bleur, & R. K. Yep (Eds.), *Compelling counseling interventions: VISTAS, 2009* (pp. 125–138). Alexandria, VA: American Counseling Association.

Webber, J., & Mascari, J. B. (2005). September eleventh: Lessons learned. In J. Webber, D. D. Bass, & R. Yep (Eds.), *Terrorism, trauma, and tragedies: A counselor's guide for preparing and responding*. Alexandria, VA: American Counseling Association Foundation.

Wessells, M. (1996). Culture, power and community: Intercultural approaches to psychosocial assistance and healing. In K. Nader, N. Dubrow, & B. Hudnall Stamm (Eds.), *Honoring differences: Cultural issues in the treatment of trauma and loss* (pp. 267–282). Philadelphia, PA: Brunner/Mazel.

CHAPTER 12

Developing an Identity as a Crisis Counselor

I remember when I was in school, I had a professor tell me, "You know what the difference is between an expert and everyone else in the counseling field? About 5% more training or experience." I used to think that was true until I started doing crisis work. This is hard, and it takes a lot of understanding. I feel like I've started to commit my life to it, yet I still feel like I have so much to learn.

T his was a statement made by an experienced therapist who has been doing crisis work for some time. It captures the essence of the challenges of the work; becoming a crisis counselor is sometimes far harder than we are ready for. A crisis happens, and we are often thrown out of the frying pan and into the fire. Yet, to be a qualified, skilled crisis counselor, we need more than just "5% more training or experience" than the next person.

The following chapter describes the historical development of crisis intervention as a subset of professional counseling, as well as the integration of crisis intervention into our professional identity. As part of the understanding of that identity, this chapter also examines the concept of Post-Traumatic Growth. After reading this chapter, you should be able to:

1. Identify the historical underpinnings of the field of crisis counseling;
2. Know how crisis intervention has developed as a subset of counseling, including the various certifications and professional organizations associated with crisis intervention; and
3. Understand the concept of Post-Traumatic Growth and its relationship to identity as a professional counselor.

Historical Underpinnings of Crisis Intervention

As James and Gilliland (2001) argue, crisis intervention has developed as a major specialty within counseling and other human service fields. Crisis intervention work was initially a volunteer-based, grassroots undertaking that was almost exclusively reactive in nature (James & Gilliland, 2013). Historically, crisis intervention volunteers responded to a specific need, and it was not until there was a critical mass of public pressure that crisis counseling developed as a subset of the larger human service fields.

Most people who volunteer as crisis interventionists are concerned with a specific type of crisis (e.g., natural disasters, suicidality, terrorism, etc.) (James & Gilliland, 2013). Their interest in volunteering tends to arise from their personal investment in the type of crisis for which they want to help. For example, some people volunteer for suicide hotlines, because someone in their family has attempted suicide or they have considered taking their own lives. However, as the need for volunteers in a particular area grows, so does the impetus for more formalized organization, training, and implementation of services.

As these groups of volunteers have begun to develop into more organized groups with policies, organizational structures, and financial needs, they have also require trained consultants to educate and prepare volunteers for the type of work they will be asked to do in the field (James & Gilliland, 2013). As consultation develops into formalized training, these groups of volunteers gain legitimacy in their communities and are able to garner a sense of professionalism, as well as the resources and attention that are necessary for growth and success.

As crisis intervention has grown from small groups of volunteers to a subset of the human service profession, it is difficult to identify exactly how or why this work has experienced such extraordinary growth. The most logical answer to this question would be that our society, and our world, continues to experience crises that are increasing in severity and frequency. As discussed in previous chapters, situational and environmental crises continue to challenge our available physical, financial, and psychological resources. Mass shootings, terrorism, hurricanes, tsunamis, nuclear accidents, earthquakes, transit accidents, and other crises happen daily. As these crises continue to occur, the need for fully trained, well-prepared crisis counselors continues to grow.

As we look to the future, there is very little indication that this need will wane any time soon. Global environmental crises are predicted throughout the 21st century as climate change continues unabated and human beings continue to act in ways that challenge the planet's limited resources. Population growth continues to expand without the resources to support it. Wars, terrorism, and smaller scale violence continues to occur every day.

Issues related to disease (e.g., Ebola, Zika, etc.), proliferation of drug abuse, and economic challenges will continue to place stresses on society, at both micro and global levels. With these stresses comes the continued need for highly skilled crisis interventionists.

Exercise 12.1 invites you to delve more deeply into the many different trends in the field of crisis intervention.

Integration of Crisis Intervention into Professional Counseling and Other Human Service Fields

As the field of crisis intervention has continued to grow under the weight of the needs described previously, there has been a need for the mental health

---

EXERCISE 12.1

THE MANY FACETS OF CRISIS INTERVENTION

Directions: In this book, we have discussed a number of factors that challenge our communities, our societies, and our world. Some examples include: wars, terrorism, natural disasters, man-made catastrophes, interpersonal violence (murder, sexual assault, etc.), disease, terrorism, and many more. In this exercise, we invite you to choose one of these issues and conduct your own research on the topic. Specific questions you may want to examine include:

1. What is the prevalence of this issue in your local community? In your country? Worldwide?

2. Is this issue trending higher or lower? That is, will this concern grow in prevalence or wane?

3. Are there any professional organizations, peer-reviewed journals, or specific trainings or certifications related to this issue? How are these crises typically addressed?

professions to respond accordingly in order to prepare professionals to work in crisis situations. While there is no specific state license to work as a crisis counselor, many academic training programs are integrating crisis intervention into their preparation of mental health professionals. For example, the Council for the Accreditation of Counseling and Related Educational Programs (CACREP) implemented a number of educational requirements related to crisis intervention and trauma counseling in its 2016 standards. In the Professional Identity Standards, located in Section 2, CACREP (2016) identifies the following standards that have been, or will be, addressed in this text.

- 2.F.1.c. counselors' roles and responsibilities as members of interdisciplinary community outreach and emergency management response teams
- 2.F.3.g. effects of crisis, disasters, and trauma on diverse individuals across the lifespan
- 2.F.5.l. suicide prevention models and strategies
- 2.F.5.m. crisis intervention, trauma-informed, and community-based strategies, such as Psychological First Aid
- 2.F.7.c. procedures for assessing risk of aggression or danger to others, self-inflicted harm, or suicide
- 2.F.7.d. procedures for identifying trauma and abuse and for reporting abuse

Additionally, CACREP identifies a number of crisis-related standards for specific program tracks (e.g., Clinical Mental Health Counseling, School Counseling, Higher Education Counseling, etc.). The following are the 2016 CACREP standards related to the specialty areas accredited by CACREP:

- 5.C.2.f. impact of crisis and trauma on individuals with mental health diagnoses (Clinical Mental Health Counseling)
- 5.D.2.h. impact of crisis and trauma on individuals with disabilities (Clinical Rehabilitation Counseling)
- 5.E.2.b. roles of college counselors and student affairs professionals in relation to the operation of the institution's emergency management plan, and crises, disasters, and trauma (College Counseling/Student Affairs)
- 5.E.2.e. models of violence prevention in higher education settings (College Counseling/Student Affairs)
- 5.F.2.g. impact of crisis and trauma on marriages, couples, and families (Marriage, Couples, and Family Counseling)

- 5.G.2.e. school counselor roles and responsibilities in relation to the school emergency management plans, and crises, disasters, and trauma (School Counseling)

In addition to formal educational standards in the preparation of counselor trainees, certifications and training are available for counselors who want to develop additional knowledge and skill in the area of crisis intervention and treating survivors of trauma. Some of these opportunities are included in Table 12.1.

Table 12.1 Crisis Intervention and Trauma Counseling Training and Certification

Crisis Intervention Training	<ul><li>QPR Suicide Prevention: www.qprinstitute.org</li><li>American Red Cross Disaster Mental Health Services: http://www.redcross.org/take-a-class/disaster-training</li><li>American Institute of Health Care Professionals: http://aihcp.net/crisis-intervention-counseling-certification/</li><li>Crisis Prevention Institute (CPI): https://www.crisisprevention.com</li><li>Nonviolent Crisis Intervention: https://www.crisisprevention.com/Specialties/Nonviolent-Crisis-Intervention</li><li>National Association for Victim Assistance: www.trynova.org</li><li>National Action Alliance for Suicide Prevention: http://zerosuicide.actionallianceforsuicideprevention.org</li><li>Crisis and Trauma Resource Institute (CTRI): http://www.ctrinstitute.com/</li></ul>
Trauma Counseling Resources	<ul><li>EMDR Institute: www.emdr.com</li><li>Trauma-Focused Cognitive Behavioral Therapy: https://tfcbt.musc.edu/</li></ul>

In addition to the many options for training and certifications, there are also a host of professional journals and organizations that hold professional meetings. These organizations have done a great deal to advance the fields of crisis intervention and traumatology. A few examples of peer-reviewed journals are listed in Exercise 12.2.

Exercise 12.2 invites the reader to learn more about these specific peer-reviewed journals and the types of articles they publish.

Finally, as the counseling profession has increased its efforts to better clarify and communicate its professional identity, there has been a movement among many professional counselors to draw the subfields of crisis intervention and trauma counseling in to the identity of professional counseling. One of the core tenets of professional counseling is a focus on wellness, holism, and a strength-based approach to therapeutic work. While this may seem incongruent with the pathogenic nature of crisis work, the emerging field of Post-Traumatic Growth is showing promise as a way of integrating wellness and strength-based counseling into crisis intervention.

Post-Traumatic Growth

While the literature is rich with descriptions of pathogenic responses to trauma, there has been little attention paid to the potential for personal growth from the experience of trauma. However, there recently has been a paradigm shift among some researchers from pathogenic to salutogenic approaches to trauma responses (Morris, Shakespeare-Finch, Rieck, & Newberry, 2005). Salutogenesis is a term coined by Aaron Antonovsky (1979) with its origins in Greek (Salut = Health and Genesisi = Origin). Briefly defined, salutogenesis examines the sources of health, or why some respond positively to life events while other respond negatively. The reason we have chosen to include a discussion on salutogenic approaches to crisis and trauma counseling is because we believe these approaches are congruent with our historical roots in the counseling profession; specifically, that our profession is entrenched in a wellness and developmental approach to human behavior, rather than a pathogenic one.

The assumption that all trauma causes negative consequences has been replaced with the notion that there exists the potential for positive, personal development that can result from exposure to trauma. This phenomenon has been defined in the literature as Post-Traumatic Growth (PTG) (Calhoun & Tedeschi, 1998). Despite its relatively recent addition to the literature, the notion of PTG has received significant attention (Helgeson, Reynolds, & Tomich, 2006).

Calhoun and Tedeschi (1998) provided one of the earliest descriptions of PTG found in the literature. According to Tedeschi and Calhoun (2004) PTG is the "experience of positive change that occurs as a result of the struggle with highly challenging life crises" (p. 1). PTG can manifest itself in a variety of ways: increased self-esteem, improved personal relationships, increased appreciation for life in general, and an increased sense of self-efficacy or personal strength. PTG can result from a variety of experiences, including: chronic or severe illness, sexual assault, combat, natural disasters, shootings, injury, and recovery from substance abuse (Linley & Joseph, 2004).

CASE ILLUSTRATION 12.1

THE CASE OF MAX

Max is a 33-year-old survivor of childhood sexual assault. Specifically, when Max was seven, he was sexually abused by his uncle over the course of four years. His abuser had told him that the abuse was a "secret" and that if Max ever told anyone, the police would come and take Max's parents to jail, and Max would have to live in a foster home. Max kept the secret for many years, only telling his mother about the abuse after his father's death when Max was 22. Max's uncle had died several years earlier.

For many years after the abuse had ended, Max struggled with a host of concerns. Max was diagnosed with severe depression at the age of 14. He attempted suicide at 15 and was hospitalized for almost two months. Throughout his teens and early 20s, Max struggled with depression and severe anxiety. In hindsight, Max was experiencing Post-Traumatic Stress Disorder (PTSD), but it had gone undiagnosed, because the abuse had never been disclosed. After telling his mother about the abuse, Max entered therapy again, this time telling his counselor about his uncle and the abuse. Max was diagnosed with PTSD and was treated with a combination of medication and Cognitive Behavioral Therapy. In the weeks and months that followed, Max experienced significant reduction of symptoms, eventually terminating therapy and going on to live a content, happy life. Max eventually married and had two children.

But Max's story doesn't end there. As Max got older, he began to get involved with survivor's groups, volunteering his time and energy to help others who had experienced similar abuse. He was praised by others for his ability to help those who have experienced such violence and harm.

Max has been through quite a bit as an adult, with his father passing away at a young age and his youngest child needing a (successful) liver transplant when she was seven years old. But, people are always impressed with Max's resilience and openness to emotion. He was the "rock" in his family when his father died and was a significant source of support for his wife, son, and daughter during his daughter's illness. When people ask him how

Growth does not occur as a result of trauma but rather new cognitive schemas that develop following the traumatic incident (Calhoun & Tedeschi, 2014). PTG suggests that the traumatic incident can cause the individual to re-evaluate their worldview (Calhoun & Tedeschi, 2014). In contrast to the negative reactions that typically occur in trauma, Calhoun and Tedeschi (2014) suggest a traumatic experience can certainly cause a negative reaction initially, but that, with time, that negative reaction may manifest itself in to a more positive, hopeful perception of the world and one's place in that world. People who experience PTG may experience an increased sense of resilience, hardiness, and optimism (Calhoun & Tedeschi, 2014).

Calhoun and Tedeschi (2014) suggest that PTG begins with a major life crisis that shatters the individual's sense of self and place in the world. Previously held beliefs, attitudes, and coping systems are challenged, and in some cases, dismantled. The individual may initially respond negatively, but through cognitive processing and the development of new coping strategies, the person may begin to experience positive development. Cognitive processing and social support are considered central to the PTG process. Over time, new cognitive schemas develop to replace those that were initially lost or damaged.

The concept of PTG is explained further in Case Illustration 12.1, where we explore a case of PTG in the context of crisis.

Others' discussions of PTG have been identified in the literature. Stuhlmiller and Dunning (2000a, 2000b) have examined the move from pathogenic to salutogenic models of secondary trauma response in working with first responders and others who help survivors of trauma. They suggest that the pathogenic response is incorporated in the medicalization of American culture. That is, Americans tend to focus on diagnoses, symptoms, treatment, and even medications when addressing physical and psychological distress. Stuhlmiller and Dunning (2000a, 2000b) also discuss the growth of debriefing models for addressing trauma and those who respond to traumatic incidents. These authors suggest that debriefing may not only fail to help, but may instead serve to re-traumatize people or hinder the potential for Post-Traumatic Growth by interrupting the development of positive schemas.

he can handle so much adversity with such a positive attitude, Max usually answers, "I've been through a lot in my life. It's really given me perspective and taught me how to handle adversity. I figure with all that I've been through, there's really nothing life can throw at me that I can't handle."

In making these points, Stuhlmiller and Dunning (2000a) provide a quote from a firefighter following a debriefing intervention:

> "You know, I didn't like being put on the spot like that ... it was like, show and tell, show me your trauma and I'll get the chief to lay off ... Either they accuse you of not being tough enough or of being a cry baby. Am I supposed to get these symptoms or what? If I do, is that good or bad?" (p. 311)

Janoff-Bullman (2004) discussed three other models of PTG found in the literature. The first model involves uncovering strengths the individual may possess that were not obvious to the survivor prior to experiencing the traumatic event. This model also involves the development of new coping strategies for life's challenges. The second model describes the creation of a new sense of psychological preparedness. Here, the individual overcomes the irrational belief that traumatic life events cannot happen and accepts that traumatic experiences can occur to anyone, but these experiences need not be detrimental. Rather, one can find strength in surviving a trauma. The third model is one based in existential philosophy. This model stresses that tragedy can lead to a new appreciation for life, as well as the positive characteristics of our existence.

Tedeschi and Calhoun (1996) developed the Post-Traumatic Growth Inventory, designed to measure the positive outcomes reported by people who have experienced traumatic events. The instrument contains 21 items and consists of five areas of evaluation: Spiritual Change, Appreciation of Life, New Possibilities, Relating to Others, and Personal Strength. According to the authors, "the scale appears to have utility in determining how successful individuals, coping with the aftermath of trauma, are in reconstructing or strengthening their perceptions of self, others, and the meaning of events" (Tedeschi & Calhoun, 1996, p. 455).

Summary

- Crisis intervention has developed as a major specialty within counseling and other human service fields. Crisis intervention work was initially a volunteer-based, grassroots undertaking that was almost exclusively reactive in nature.

- Situational and environmental crises continue to challenge our available physical, financial, and psychological resources. Mass shootings, terrorism, hurricanes, tsunamis, nuclear accidents, earthquakes, transit accidents, and other crises happen daily. As these crises continue to occur, the need for fully trained, well-prepared crisis counselors continues to grow.

- The Professional Identity Standards in Section 2 of the 2016 CACREP standards identify seven of the following standards that have been, or will be, addressed in this text. Additionally, CACREP identifies six crisis-related standards for specific program tracks.

- There are a host of professional organizations and peer-reviewed journals that are specific to the fields of trauma counseling and crisis intervention.

- There recently has been a paradigm shift among some researchers from pathogenic to salutogenic approaches to trauma responses, which focuses on why some respond positively to traumatic events while other respond negatively.

- The assumption that all trauma causes negative consequences has been replaced with the notion that there exists the potential for positive, personal development that can result from exposure to trauma. This phenomenon has been defined in the literature as PTG.

- Growth does not occur as a result of trauma but rather new cognitive schemas that develop following the traumatic incident.

- Calhoun and Tedeschi (2014) suggest that PTG begins with a major life crisis that shatters the individual's sense of self and place in the world. Previously held beliefs, attitudes, and coping systems are challenged and, in some cases, dismantled.

Important Terms

Council for the Accreditation of Counseling and Related Educational Programs (CACREP) standards

Debriefing

Existential philosophy

Global environmental crises

Medicalization of American culture

Post-Traumatic Growth (PTG)

Salutogenesis

Additional Resources

In print

Antonovsky, A. (1979). *Health, stress, and coping.* San Francisco, CA: Jossey-Bass.

Calhoun, L. G., & Tedeschi, R. G. (2014). *Handbook of Posttraumtic Growth: Research and practice.* New York, NY: Psychology Press.

Janoff-Bullman, R. (2004). Posttraumatic growth: Three explanatory models. *Psychological Inquiry, 15,* 30–34.

Violanti, J. M., Paton, D. & Dunning, C. (2000), *Posttraumatic stress intervention: Challenges, issues, and perspectives.* Springfield, IL: Charles C. Thomas.

On the Web

American Institute of Health Care Professionals: http://aihcp.net/crisis-intervention-counseling-certification/

Crisis Prevention Institute (CPI): https://www.crisisprevention.com

Crisis and Trauma Resource Institute (CTRI): http://www.ctrinstitute.com/

References

Antonovsky, A. (1979). *Health, stress, and coping.* San Francisco, CA: Jossey-Bass.

CACREP (2015). *2016 standards.* Alexandria, VA: Author.

Calhoun, L. G., & Tedeschi, R. G. (1998). Posttraumatic growth: Future directions. In R. G. Tedeschi, C. L. Park, & L. G. Calhoun (Eds.), *Posttraumatic growth: Positive changes in the aftermath of crisis* (pp. 215–238). Mahwah, NJ: Lawrence Erlbaum.

Calhoun, L. G., & Tedeschi, R. G. (2014). *Handbook of Posttraumtic Growth: Research and practice.* New York, NY: Psychology Press.

Helgeson, V. S., Reynolds, K. A., &. Tomich, P. L. (2006). A meta-analytic review of benefit finding and growth. *Journal of Consulting and Clinical Psychology, 74,* 797–816.

James, R. K., & Gilliland, B. E. (2001). *Theories and strategies in counseling and psychotherapy* (5th ed.). Boston, MA: Allyn & Bacon.

James, R. K., & Gilliland, B. E. (2013). *Crisis intervention strategies* (7th ed.). Belmont, CA: Brooks-Cole.

Janoff-Bullman, R. (2004). Posttraumatic growth: Three explanatory models. *Psychological Inquiry, 15,* 30–34.

Linley, P. A., & Joseph, S. (2004). Positive change following trauma and adversity: A review. *Journal of Traumatic Stress, 17,* 11–21.

Morris, B.A., Shakespeare-Finch, J., Rieck, M., & Newbery, J. (2005). Multidimensional nature of posttraumatic growth in an Australian population. *Journal of Traumatic Stress, 18*, 575–585.

Stuhlmiller, C., & Dunning, C. (2000a). Concerns about debriefing: Challenging the mainstream. In B. Raphael, & J. P. Wilson (Eds.), *Psychological debriefing* (pp. 305–320). Cambridge, UK: Cambridge University Press.

Stuhlmiller, C., & Dunning, C. (2000b). Challenging the mainstream: From pathogenic to salutogenic models of posttrauma intervention. In J. M. Violanti, D. Paton, & C. Dunning (Eds.), *Posttraumatic stress intervention: Challenges, issues, and perspectives* (pp. 10–42). Springfield, IL: Charles C. Thomas.

Tedeschi, R. G., & Calhoun, L. G. (1996). Posttraumatic growth: Conceptual foundations and empirical evidence. *Psychological Inquiry, 15,* 1–18.

Tedeschi, R. G., & Calhoun, L. G. (2004). The Posttraumtic Growth Inventory: Measuring the positive legacy of trauma. *Journal of Traumatic Stress, 9,* 455–471.

CHAPTER 13

Challenge and Care of the Crisis Worker

I've been doing this a long time. I've heard all kinds of stories, and some of them really get to you; but you learn to let things go and move on after a while. I mean, you can't let things get to you, or you'll burn out in a hurry. But after I spent that week deployed with the families of the shooting victims, it was all really different. I didn't sleep well; I kept having nightmares. I stopped trusting people, and I was angry all of the time. It was like I had turned into a different person, and I didn't know what to do.

This statement, made by a disaster worker who had responded to a mass shooting, similar to the ones described in Chapter 7, is indicative of the long-term impact crisis work can have on counselors, even those with years of

210

experience. As a crisis interventionist, helpers need to be aware of the impact and effect that clients' stories can have. It is unrealistic to believe that we can listen to stories of trauma, time and again, without being influenced and impacted.

The following chapter describes the most common impact of crisis on those who provide counseling and care. After reading this chapter, you should be able to:

1. Identify the various types of responses helpers have to stories of crisis and trauma;

2. Recognize specific forms of assessment for the various negative effects of crisis on the helper;

3. Appreciate the importance of mitigating these potential negative outcomes on individual and systemic levels; and

4. Understand the concept of Vicarious Post-Traumatic Growth.

Impact of Crisis on the Helper

As described in the opening vignette, working with survivors of crisis can have detrimental and lasting effects on the crisis worker. Hearing personal stories of tragedy and loss is seldom easy; it is often made worse when the client's pain is palpable, and as a helper, you know there is very little you can do in the immediate aftermath of a crisis. Clients are looking for help, for answers, and we often do not have them. Sitting with someone who is injured, frightened, and has experienced a major loss will effect anyone, and when we are attuned to the thoughts and emotions of those in crisis, it can be especially difficult.

What follows are descriptions of a number of responses counselors may have to working with individuals in crisis. If you consider them on a continuum, from least to most severe, they include: countertransference, burnout, secondary traumatic stress, and finally, vicarious traumatization.

Countertransference

The concept of countertransference was introduced by Freud (1910) to define the reciprocal relationship between counselor and client that occurs during the counseling process. According to Freud, it was a common occurrence for clients to project their cognitions and affect onto the clinician. Freud defined this process as transference. Countertransference is the yang to the yin of transference; it is the process of the therapist projecting his or her beliefs, attitudes, and feelings, onto the client. Freud never fully developed the notion of countertransference but believed countertransference resulted from unresolved conflicts in the counselor's own life, and resolution of these conflicts was necessary for effective helping (Gorkin, 1987).

Corey (2005) argues that countertransference occurs when counselors become too familiar with clients and begin to identify with them or when they see themselves in relation to the client. It may also occur when helpers try to meet their own needs through the therapeutic relationship. However, an opposing perspective on countertransference suggests that it is to be expected in the therapeutic process and is a natural consequence of empathy development and a working alliance between counselor and client (Wilson & Lindy, 1994). Rather than viewing countertransference negatively, some research suggests that countertransference can be useful in the counseling relationship in that it can help counselors better understand their clients and, at worst, should be evaluated and used carefully (McCann & Colletti, 1994).

Transference and countertransference should be viewed through a different lens when working with survivors of trauma. Neumann and Gamble (1995) discussed the nature of transference and countertransference when counseling clients who have survived crises. They argue that helpers may find themselves fantasizing about rescuing their clients and that these rescue fantasies may lead to preoccupation. They also suggest that counselors who work with traumatized clients are at risk of questioning their beliefs and the propensity people have toward evil. As a result, helpers may attempt to distance themselves from clients by intellectualizing their clients' stories or making unfounded generalizations about the nature of trauma (Neumann & Gamble, 1995).

Burnout

Freudenberger (1974, 1975) is credited with introducing the term *burnout* to describe a consequence of human service work and discussed burnout as it related to career counseling. Freudenberger and Richelson (1980) identified burnout as the process of continually attempting to meet self-imposed but unrealistic goals; this self-defeating process leads to the exhaustion of emotional, mental, and physical resources. Others have also examined the relationships between work environment and employee burnout (Elloy, Terpening, & Kohls, 2001; Maslach & Jackson, 1986; Zunker, 1998).

Maslach (1982) examined the experience of burnout as a relationship between the individual and their environment. She defined burnout as a "syndrome of emotional exhaustion, depersonalization, and reduced personal accomplishment that can occur among individuals who do 'people work' of some kind" (p. 3). Burnout is a response to the powerful strain of working closely with other people, especially people who have experienced traumas and crises (Maslach, 1982). Burnout is characterized by chronic stress that results from the frequent and intense personal relationships found in the helping professions. Unlike other types of stress, burnout is unique in that it results from the social interaction between counselor and client (Maslach, 1982).

Maslach's (1982) definition of burnout has three distinct elements: (1) depersonalization, (2) emotional exhaustion, and (3) reduced personal accomplishment. Maslach, Jackson, and Leiter (1996) described *depersonalization* as the development of cyclical negative beliefs about clients; Maslach (1982) defined depersonalization as "viewing other people through rust-colored glasses—developing a poor opinion of them, expecting the worst from them, and even actively disliking them" (p. 4). *Emotional exhaustion* is characterized by the belief that the helper's emotional resources are spent, and there is nothing left to give (Maslach, Jackson, & Leiter, 1996). Finally, *reduced personal accomplishment* is the "tendency to evaluate oneself negatively, particularly with regard to one's work with clients" (Maslach, Jackson, & Leiter 1996, p. 4). In short, burnout is a response to working with people who are in need of help and results from the emotional strain of consistently being needed by others.

Case Illustration 13.1 provides an example of a clinician who is struggling with burnout. After reading Maslach's (1982) definition of burnout, consider the symptoms of burnout you see in this case.

Burnout is cumulative, that is, it typically manifests initially with mild symptoms but progressively increases in severity if left unchecked (Gentry, Baranowsky, & Dunning, 2002; Maslach, 1982). Burnout typically results from feelings of powerlessness, frustration, and inadequacy in meeting goals and can manifest itself through physical and emotional symptoms, such as: sleeplessness, nightmares, headaches, back and neck pain, physical exhaustion, repeated illnesses, irritability, emotional exhaustion, and aggressive behavior (Maslach, 1982; McMullen & Krantz, 1988). It can result from intense work stressors or from pressures from supervisors or subordinates (Valent, 2002). Additionally, misunderstanding among coworkers may also lead to increased degrees of burnout.

CASE ILLUSTRATION 13.1

BURNING OUT? THE CASE OF ALLISON

Allison is a new graduate of a clinical mental health counseling program and has been working as an in-home mobile therapist for a year since she graduated. It was the same position she had held through her clinical practicum and internship courses, and when she was offered a full-time position, she was thrilled, because she loved the work and the impact she had on her clients.

For the first six or seven months in her job, she continued to find great satisfaction in her work. She enjoyed meeting new clients, traveling to their homes and truly getting to put her newly acquired clinical skills to work. She realized that she wasn't getting much supervision from her agency, but she got enough to process the most serious cases, and she was successful, so she continued on. She did wish she had more time and opportunity to process things though, not only so she could further develop her clinical skills, but also to vent some of her frustrations.

In the last two months, Allison has noticed her attitude towards work has changed. Clients with whom she once enjoyed working, she now dreaded seeing. She hated going from home to home throughout the day, and all she could think about as she traveled to her clients' homes was how needy they were, how annoying they were, and how they didn't really want to be helped. She stopped thinking about them as people, and all she could think about was the problems they brought, and the challenges they presented to her.

Allison started to realize that she really hadn't been very effective at all; in fact, she was pretty sure she hadn't made any real progress with her clients in weeks. That would have bothered her before, but now she didn't even seem to care. Sure, she could see some minor improvement, but it had taken so long to get that little result; it all seemed hopeless. Allison also found herself tired all of the time. She had trouble concentrating and had taken a few days off recently, her first sick leave since she had started as a practicum student. She was just too tired to care most of the time, and even if she did, it wouldn't make much of a difference. She seriously considered quitting several times but wasn't sure what she would do if she did.

EXERCISE 13.1

HAVE YOU EXPERIENCED BURNOUT?

Directions: We encourage you to assess your own level of burnout (as well as compassion fatigue or compassion satisfaction, especially if you are currently working in a human services field). To do so, go to www.proqol.org and review the self-score PROQol instrument. The instrument is designed in a way that you can assess your own levels of burnout, even if you aren't currently working as a counselor but if you are helping people in some capacity. After completing the instrument, consider the questions below.

Reflection:

1. What were your scores on the three scales of the PROQol?

2. Were you surprised (in a positive or negative way) by any of the scores?

3. If you were surprised in a positive way, what do you think you're doing to generate those positive scores?

4. If you were surprised in a negative way, what do you think you could do differently moving forward to improve the situation?

Compassion Fatigue and Secondary Traumatic Stress

In order to understand the concepts of compassion fatigue and secondary traumatic stress, it is important to first examine the notion of trauma. A definition of trauma is provided in Chapter 5, but for the purposes of this discussion, the critical element of this definition is that one does not have to experience the traumatic event firsthand to experience a traumatic response (APA, 2013). Learning about traumatic events can also illicit a trauma response, and people can be traumatized without directly experiencing the event. The *Diagnostic and Statistical Manual of Mental Disorders, 5th Edition*, (DSM-5) also identifies a wide variety of specific events that can be considered traumatic and may result in Post-Traumatic Stress Disorder (PTSD) (APA, 2013).

Figley (1995) originally developed the term *compassion fatigue* to describe the PTSD-type symptoms that may emerge among individuals who learn about trauma secondhand. Figley (1995) later redefined compassion fatigue as *Secondary Traumatic Stress* (STS) and defined STS as "the natural, consequent behaviors and emotions resulting from *knowing about* a traumatizing event experience by a significant other. It is the stress resulting from *helping or wanting to help* a traumatized or suffering person" (p. 10). Figley (1999) suggests that STS symptoms can be nearly identical to those of PTSD, except that some symptoms may be experienced vicariously. For example, symptoms of PTSD include re-experiencing the traumatic event. In the case of STS, the symptom may be the recall of the experience of the traumatic event as described by the traumatized person (Figley, 1999).

Figley (1998) suggests that any number of people can suffer from STS. Family and friends of a traumatized person may experience STS, as can helping professionals. For Figley (1998), one must be empathetically involved with the traumatized person in order to be susceptible to STS. Research into STS has suggested that individuals who work with survivors of trauma often experience similar symptoms to those whom they help (Beaton & Murphy, 1995; Figley, 1995, 1999; Hyatt-Burkhart, 2014; Owens, 2011; Wilson & Lindy, 1994). These symptoms can include sleep disturbances, flashbacks, nightmares, anxiety, avoidance, and hyperarousal (Figley, 1999).

Vicarious Traumatization and Constructivist Self-Development Theory

In an effort to better describe the consequences of trauma on the helper, McCann and Pearlman (1990a) introduced the term *vicarious traumatization*. Vicarious traumatization has been defined in a number of ways. For example, McCann and Pearlman (1990b) stated that "persons who work with victims may experience profound psychological effects, effects that can be disruptive and painful for the helper and can persist for months or years after work with traumatized persons" (p. 133). Pearlman and Saakvitne (1995) defined vicarious traumatization as "a transformation in the therapist's (or other trauma worker's) inner experience resulting from empathic engagement with the victim's trauma material" (p. 151). Regardless of the language, the issue remains: exposure to graphic accounts of traumatic experiences and the reality that human beings can behave in inhumane ways can cause a traumatic reaction for the helper.

Vicarious traumatization is cumulative and permanent and will manifest itself in both the helper's personal and professional lives. Additionally, it involves a profound change in the helper's core sense of self (Pearlman & Saakvitne, 1995). These changes can cause a disruption in one's identity and worldview, the ability to manage emotions, to maintain positive self-esteem, and to connect to others. Vicarious traumatization can also have an impact on the helper's basic needs and mental schemas about issues such as "safety, esteem, trust and dependency, control, and intimacy" (Pearlman & Saakvitne, 1995, p. 152). Individuals suffering from vicarious traumatization are also vulnerable to intense images and other PTSD symptomology. There are two factors than can impact a helper's susceptibility to vicarious traumatization: the nature of the therapy, as well as the characteristics and vulnerabilities of the helper (Pearlman & Saakvitne, 1995).

CASE ILLUSTRATION 13.2

DR. PAPELBON: A CASE OF VICARIOUS TRAUMATIZATION

Dr. Papelbon is a Licensed Professional Counselor and a faculty member at a local university. She has been a clinician for over 30 years and a professor for over 10. She has a long history of working with trauma survivors, especially children and adolescents who have experienced violence. She has spent years researching trauma and crisis intervention and has a strong reputation as a therapist, as well as a teacher and a scholar.

Several years ago, Dr. Papelbon decided to become a Disaster Mental Health responder for the American Red Cross and has responded to a number of crisis situations in her community. She has responded mainly to personal tragedies, such as house fires, victims of violent crime, and recently worked with survivors of a commuter train accident. She has received accolades, not only for the countless hours she has spent volunteering, but for the quality of the service she has provided and the number of people she has helped through crises.

Recently, there was a plane crash in a city a few hundred miles away. In the accident, 161 passengers and crew members were killed; there were no survivors. The American Red Cross asked for volunteers to deploy to the area for 14 days to work with the families and first responders to provide Psychological First Aid, as well as more intensive psychological services. Dr. Papelbon was on sabbatical for the semester, so she volunteered to deploy. During her deployment, she worked closely with firefighters and other first responders who were the first at the crash site. During her work, she heard countless tales that were deep with sadness, fear, and specific sensory details (e.g., the sights, sounds, and smells at the scene). Dr. Papelbon was even permitted to go to the crash site several days in to her deployment, so she could see first-hand what these women and men had seen.

When she returned home, Dr. Papelbon was a different person. She was having trouble sleeping and was very short-tempered. She would have nightmares that included the accounts she heard from the firefighters and found herself constantly "on edge." Every time a plane or helicopter flew by, she would find herself duck or cringe, and she cancelled a flight to Europe where she was supposed to work with colleagues on a year-long research project, the focus of her sabbatical and the culmination of a many years of work.

More importantly, Dr. Papelbon felt like the world was different. She found that she was having trouble feeling connected to friends and felt like the intimacy was gone with her partner. She had trouble trusting people, even people she had known and cared about for many years. She felt like there was nothing in the world that she could believe in and assumed the worst of people, when she had always been an eternal optimist. She felt like she was disconnecting from reality and often wondered if she would ever be herself again. She started to realize she was falling into depression, and her anxiety was preventing her from leaving the house some days.

Case Illustration 13.2 describes what vicarious traumatization might look like in a seasoned clinician, especially one who works primarily with trauma and crisis intervention.

Vicarious traumatization is best understood in the context of what McCann and Pearlman (1990a) defined as Constructivist Self-Development Theory (CSDT). CSDT suggests that individuals possess the ability to construct their own realities as they interact with their environments. CSDT focuses on three psychological systems: (1) the self, (2) an individual's psychological needs, and (3) cognitive schemas (McCann & Pearlman, 1990a). The premise of CSDT is that individuals balance these three systems in order to make sense of the world and interpret new experiences. Since new data is always being evaluated in terms of these systems, a person's constructed reality is constantly changing in reaction to the new information (McCann & Pearlman, 1990b). These cognitive schemas are based on the individual's beliefs, assumptions, and expectations about the self and environment. When disturbing, frightening, and traumatic experiences are introduced into this constructivist system, it can impact the individual's entire worldview.

Assessing Negative Impact

Armed with an understanding of the various ways that crisis can impact the interventionist, it can be beneficial to understand the tools that are available for measuring these effects on the helper. What follows are a few examples of methods of assessing these negative counselor outcomes.

Burnout: The Maslach Burnout Inventory

The Maslach Burnout Inventory (MBI) was developed by Maslach, Jackson, & Leiter (1996) in order to measure the three elements related to burnout: depersonalization, emotional exhaustion, and reduced personal accomplishment. The MBI consists of 22 items, which are divided into three subscales specific to these elements of burnout. Each of the items is scaled from zero to six, where respondents identify the frequency of feelings or attitudes. For example, one item on the instrument, *I don't really care what happens to [clients]*, is scaled from zero (never) to six (every day).

The Emotional Exhaustion scale consists of nine items that measure "feelings of being emotionally overextended and exhausted by one's work" (Maslach, Jackson, & Leiter, 1996, p. 194). The Depersonalization scale consists of five items that measure a response toward clients that is unfeeling and impersonal. The Personal Accomplishment scale consists of eight items and measures self-efficacy and feelings of achievement. The instrument is scored in such a way that higher scores on the Emotional Exhaustion and Depersonalization scales indicate higher levels of burnout, while the opposite is true of the Personal Accomplishment scale.

While the MBI was designed to measure burnout in human service occupations, alternate versions of the instrument have been developed for specific professions. For example, the Maslach Burnout Inventory-Educators Survey (MBI-ES) is designed to measure burnout among teachers. Another version of the instrument, the MBI General Survey (MBI-GS) is designed for those not in human service work. The most recent version of the instrument, the MBI Third Edition, has been norm referenced and has been found reliable and valid.

Secondary Traumatic Stress

Bride, Robinson, Yegidis, and Figley (2004) developed the Secondary Traumatic Stress Scale (STSS) to measure STS. The STSS is a 17-item self-report instrument that is designed to measure the frequency of symptoms related to STS. Specifically, the instrument measures experiences of intrusion, avoidance, and arousal that are symptoms of STS. Respondents are asked to indicate the frequency of these experiences on a five-point Likert scale (from never to very often).

The STSS consists of three subscales: Intrusion, Avoidance, and Arousal. The Intrusion scale consists of five items that measure the frequency of negative, intrusive thoughts. The Avoidance scale consists of seven items that gauge how often the respondent avoids negative thoughts and experiences related to the source of the STS. Finally, the Arousal subscale consists of five items that measure emotional arousal to STS experiences. Eight of the items are specific to therapeutic work stressors, while nine of the items are non-specific.

Vicarious Traumatization

One measure of vicarious traumatization found in the literature is the Traumatic Stress Institute (TSI) Belief Scale. The TSI Belief Scale was constructed using CSDT and was designed to measure the disruption of beliefs and attitudes that are consistent with vicarious trauma (Adams, Matto, & Harrington, 2001). Rather than measuring specific symptomology, the TSI Belief Scale measures one's attitudes, beliefs, and internal experiences. Adams, Matto, and Harrington (2001) established reliability and validity for the TSI Belief Scale as a measure of vicarious traumatization.

The TSI Belief Scale, Revision L, consists of 49 items, incorporating the use of six subscales, which include measures of safety and trust. Respondents are asked to respond to statements on a six-point Likert Scale ranging from "Disagree Strongly" to "Agree Strongly." Higher scores on the TSI Belief Scale indicate higher levels of vicarious traumatization. Some examples of items on the TSI Belief Scale include (some of which are reverse scored):

- "I usually feel safe when I'm alone."
- "I worry a lot about the safety of loved ones."
- "Trusting other people is generally not smart."
- "I often think the worst of others."

Multiple Measures: The Professional Quality of Life Inventory

The Professional Quality of Life Inventory (ProQOL), Fifth Edition, is a free instrument that has been norm referenced and has demonstrated reliability and validity (Stamm, 2010). The ProQOL is a 30-item instrument that contains three subscales measuring: Compassion Satisfaction, Compassion Fatigue, and Burnout. Respondents are asked to answer each item on a five-point Likert Scale, ranging from one (Never) to five (Very Often). Each of the three scales consists of 10 items, some of which are reverse scored. Results of each subscale indicate a level from Low to High for compassion satisfaction, burnout, and compassion fatigue. The instrument can be self-scored or scored by an administrator and is available at www.proqol.org.

Table 13.1 Overview of Negative Impacts of Crisis on the Helper

Type of Impact	Key Symptoms	Method of Assessment
Countertransference	Therapist projecting own beliefs, attitudes, and feelings, onto the client	Countertransference is best assessed through clinical supervision.
Burnout	Emotional Exhaustion Depersonalization Reduced Personal Accomplishment	Maslach Burnout Inventory ProQOL
Secondary Traumatic Stress	• Post-Traumatic Stress Disorder Symptomology • Flashbacks • Intrusive Thoughts • Avoidance • Sleep disturbances • Arousal symptoms (e.g., hypervigilance, emotional dysregulation)	Secondary Traumatic Stress Scale ProQOL

Vicarious Trauma	Change in Core Sense of Self • Changes in sense of safety • Changes in sense of good in the world • Loss of trust in others • Assuming the worst in others and the world • Feelings of loss of control • Difficulty creating and maintaining intimacy • Post-Traumatic Stress Disorder Symptomology	Traumatic Stress Institute Belief Scale

Mitigating Negative Outcomes

While this chapter has focused on many of the negative outcomes that can occur for crisis workers, these negative outcomes are not necessary. There are a number of practices that can be implemented to prevent burnout, STS, and vicarious traumatization. The first, and likely most important, element of any strategy to avoid negative outcomes begins with the realization and acceptance that these negative effects are possible. Too many helpers ignore themselves and their needs in an altruistic, yet dangerous, effort to help others at their own expense. However, burnout, STS, and vicarious traumatization result in impaired practice, which helps no one.

Interventions for mitigating negative outcomes can occur on the individual or systemic level. On an individual level, successful intervention is most often found in appropriate self-care. Wicks (2007) writes on self-care in his book, *The Resilient Clinician.* In this text, he provides a number of questions to consider in the development of a self-care protocol. Specifically, Wicks (2007) looks at self-care planning as a balance of being realistic and creative. If the plan is unrealistic, it won't be successful; if it does not incorporate risks, it could be better. The challenge, he argues, is to answer the question, "How do we formulate a protocol that we are likely to use beneficially and regularly rather than in spurts." (Wicks, 2007, p. 50).

Trippany, White Kress, and Wilcoxon (2004), identify a number of needs counselors should attempt to meet in an effort to help mitigate the potential negative effects of working with those who have experienced traumatic events:

- Safety needs: working with those who have experienced crises and trauma can cause the helper to question their basic sense of safety.

- Trust needs: This includes trust of self and trust of others. Traumatic stories can cause one to question whether it is wise to trust others.

- Esteem needs: Esteem for self can be questioned when the helper feels they cannot really help. Esteem for others can be called into question when the helper begins to wonder if people are inherently bad or evil.

- Intimacy needs: Feeling connected to others is a basic need for all people. When working with those in crisis, the helper may feel empty and disconnected from others.

- Control needs: Most crises represent a loss of control. When we work consistently with clients who have experienced this loss of control over self and situations, we may begin to question our own sense of control: of ourselves, of others, and of influences around us.

Trippany et al. (2004) also recommended the following to prevent negative outcomes. These practices are sometimes referred to as self-care:

- Peer supervision: supervision provides feedback and normalization of the experiences of the helper.

- Education and training: feeling one has the requisite skills and knowledge to handle crisis situations can mitigate burnout, STS, and vicarious trauma.

- Personal coping mechanisms: balancing work, play, and rest is critical for remaining a healthy practitioner. Not only do we enjoy rest and leisure, but restorative activities (e.g., vacations) have been found to mitigate the impact of vicarious trauma. Also, a strong support network of friends and family can counteract the negative impact on trust that is sometimes found in this type of work.

- Spirituality: Research suggests that counselors with a sense of connection and meaning with the world are less likely to develop vicarious traumatization. Spirituality can provide the means of making sense of a sometimes dangerous and troublesome world.

- Agency responsibility: Agencies that employ counselors who work in crisis situations have a responsibility to provide a healthy workplace. How this can be done is described in the next section of this chapter.

On a systemic level, East, James, and Keim (2001) identify a number of important elements to preventing burnout and other negative outcomes. In examining the work of a child abuse treatment center, they found the following practices to be critical in preventing burnout and other negative outcomes:

- Limit the number of hours worked: No one should work more than 40 hours in a week.

- Continuing education: In-services help staff stay refreshed and energized.

- Quality supervision: The supervisor to clinician ratio at the center they examined was never more than 1:6.

- Environmental settings: Offices are well lit and well purposed. Therapy rooms should be colorful and bright, and clinicians should have access to necessary media and other supplies. Support is available to reduce the burden of paperwork and other administrative duties.

- Team approach: Supervisors and staff work collaboratively on cases. Mission and goals of the organization are clear and understood by everyone, and no one is "above" performing any given task, regardless of title or position.

- Work/home balance: Home and family is prioritized over work.

- Spirituality: Spiritual renewal and growth is encouraged. This approach is non-denominational, but staff are encouraged to explore their spiritual selves for growth and strength.

- Debriefing: This process is incorporated continuously.

- Variety: Staff are encouraged and challenged to explore and include a variety of different tasks in their daily work.

- Technology: Clinicians are equipped with up-to-date technology (e.g., computers, video, mobile devices, etc.).

- Safety: Clear policies and procedures are designed, communicated, and implemented to ensure the safety of staff and clients.

- Manageable workload: As additional clients are brought into the center, additional staff are hired. Clinicians' caseloads are kept manageable through advocacy for additional resources.

- Networking: The center has developed strong relationships with partner organizations in the community to increase visibility, cooperation, and credibility.

- Hiring: Candidates are carefully selected to ensure they fit in the mission and culture of the organization.

- Positive reinforcement: Intrinsically and extrinsically, staff are rewarded for their good work.

EXERCISE 13.2

HOW DO YOU PRACTICE SELF-CARE?

Directions: Below are a number of questions related to developing a self-care plan (as adapted from Wicks, 2007). Consider each, and perhaps write a few notes about each one. Then, with a partner, evaluate the self-care protocol of the other person and provide feedback, suggestions, and considerations.

Reflection:

1. What forms of exercise would be realistic to participate in regularly?

2. In your circle of friends, who are the people who encourage you and give you life? (e.g., challenge you, support you, laugh with, and inspire you?) How do you stay in touch with those people?

3. What is the perfect balance for you between personal and professional time? How well do you maintain this balance? What will you do to maintain this balance?

4. Self-care means staying emotionally disconnected from the strong emotions that are often prevalent in our work. What do you do to support a healthy sense of detachment?

5. How do you maintain a balance between rushing in too quickly and procrastination?

6. How do you feel about change? How do you prepare for, and react to, change?

7. How can you balance between silent time and time that is full of sensory stimulation?

8. How do you process unfinished business?

9. What are the forces in your life that bring you stability and provide your "anchor?"

10. How do you set high but realistic goals?

11. How do gender, race, ethnicity, sexual orientation, or other elements of diversity factor in to your self-care? Do you need to take any specific steps for self-care that others who are from different groups do not?

12. How have your established habits made self-care difficult?

13. What elements of self-care are more important to you at this stage of life that maybe weren't as important in the past?

14. What are your "red flags?" (e.g., warnings that you're burning out, making poor choices, becoming impaired, blurring boundaries, etc.). What do you do when the red flags are raised?

15. What do you already do for self-care?

16. What are your next steps for self-care?

17. Do you balance your holidays and vacations? How is this time best spent for your self-care? Is this how you traditionally spend it?

18. What types of "daily holidays" do you take (e.g., walking outside, short breaks for coffee, tea, or water, visiting friends, etc.)? Are they sufficient?

Vicarious Post-Traumatic Growth

While the literature is rich with descriptions of pathogenic responses to trauma, there has been little attention paid to the potential for personal growth from the experience of trauma. However, there has been a paradigm shift among some researchers from pathogenic to positivist approaches to trauma responses (Morris, Shakespeare-Finch, Rieck, & Newberry, 2005). The assumption that all trauma causes negative consequences has been replaced with the notion that there exists the potential for positive personal development that can result from exposure to trauma. This phenomenon has been defined in the literature as Post-Traumatic Growth (PTG) and is described at a greater detail in Chapter 12.

As discussed in Chapter 12, PTG is positive change that occurs as a result of the struggle with negative events, such as crises and traumas. Growth does not occur because a person experienced a crisis but rather because the traumatic event challenges the individual to examine the world in a new way and create new, positive, cognitive schemas (Tedeschi & Calhoun, 2004). Similar to CSDT, PTG suggests that a crisis can influence the person in crisis to reexamine their perception of the world. In contrast to the negative reactions of CSDT, Tedeschi and Calhoun (2004) suggest a traumatic experience may cause a positive reevaluation of that worldview.

While the literature on PTG has focused mainly on the experiences of trauma survivors or first responders, Arnold, Calhoun, Tedeschi, & Cann (2005) conducted a study on the possibility that psychotherapists may experience vicarious Post-Traumatic Growth. In their study, they used convenience and snowball sampling to select 21 licensed psychotherapists from one United States city for the research. All of the participants indicated they regularly worked with survivors of trauma, and 17 of the 21 participants indicated some personal trauma history. Through qualitative inquiry, the authors examined if these helpers had experienced symptoms of either vicarious traumatization or PTG. The reports of secondary PTG were quite similar to those described by people who experienced primary PTG. These results suggest that there may be potential for growth on the part of the helper who works with survivors of trauma and point to the possibility of vicarious PTG (Arnold et al., 2005). While the methodology limits the generalizability of the study (e.g., sampling methods, small sample size, and the qualitative nature of the inquiry), the results certainly imply that vicarious PTG may be possible.

Summary

- Working with survivors of crisis can have detrimental and lasting effects on the crisis worker.

- The concept of countertransference was introduced by Freud (1910) to define the reciprocal relationship between counselor and client that occurs during the counseling process. It is the process of the therapist projecting his or her beliefs, attitudes, and feelings, onto the client.

- Maslach (1982) explained the experience of burnout as a "syndrome of emotional exhaustion, depersonalization, and reduced personal accomplishment that can occur among individuals who do 'people work' of some kind" (p. 3). Burnout has three distinct elements: (1) depersonalization, (2) emotional exhaustion, and (3) reduced personal accomplishment.

- Figley (1995) originally developed the term *compassion fatigue* to describe the PTSD-type symptoms that may emerge among individuals who learn about trauma secondhand. Figley (1995) later redefined compassion fatigue as STS. STS symptoms can mirror those of PTSD.

- One must be empathetically involved with the traumatized person in order to be susceptible to STS.

- Pearlman and Saakvitne (1995) defined vicarious traumatization as "a transformation in the therapist's (or other trauma worker's) inner experience resulting from empathic engagement with the victim's trauma material."

- Vicarious traumatization is cumulative and permanent and will manifest itself in both the helper's personal and professional lives; vicarious traumatization involves a profound change in the helper's core sense of self.

- Vicarious traumatization is best understood in the context of what McCann and Pearlman (1990a) defined as CSDT.

- The MBI can be used to measure burnout, the STSS can be used for STS, and the TSI Belief Scale can be used for vicarious trauma. The ProQOL is a multifaceted instrument that can be used to measure Compassion Satisfaction, Compassion Fatigue, and Burnout.

- Interventions for mitigating negative outcomes can occur on the individual or systemic level.

- While the literature on PTG has focused mainly on the experiences of trauma survivors or first responders, Arnold et al. (2005) conducted a study on the possibility that psychotherapists may experience vicarious PTG.

Important Terms

Burnout

Compassion fatigue

Constructivist Self-Development Theory (CSDT)

Countertransference

Depersonalization

Emotional exhaustion

Maslach Burnout Inventory (MBI)

Reduced personal accomplishment

Secondary Traumatic Stress (STS)

Secondary Traumatic Stress Scale (STSS)

Self-care

Traumatic Stress Institute (TSI) Belief Scale

Vicarious Post-Traumatic Growth

Vicarious traumatization

Additional Resources

In Print

Figley, C. R. (1999). *Secondary traumatic stress: Self-care issues for clinicians, researchers, & educators*. Lutherville, MD: Sidran Press.

Maslach, C. (1982). *Burnout: The cost of caring*. Englewood Cliffs, NJ: Prentice-Hall.

McCann, I. L., & Pearlman, L. A. (1990a). *Psychological trauma and the adult survivor: Theory, therapy, and transformation*. New York, NY: Brunner/Mazel

Wicks, R. J. (2007). *The resilient clinician*. New York, NY: Oxford.

On the Web

Professional Quality of Life Inventory (ProQOL), Fifth Edition: www.proqol.org

Vicarious Trauma Institute: www.vicarioustrauma.com

References

Adams, K. B., Matto, H. C., & Harrington, D. (2001). The Traumatic Stress Institute Belief Scale as a measure of vicarious trauma in a national sample of clinical social workers. *Families in Society, 82,* 363–371.

American Psychological Association. (2013). *Diagnostic and Statistical Manual of Mental Disorders* (5th ed.). Arlington, VA: Author.

Arnold, D., Calhoun, L. G., Tedeschi, R., & Cann, A. (2005). Vicarious posttraumatic growth in psychotherapy. *Journal of Humanistic Psychology, 45,* 239–263.

Beaton, R., & Murphy, S. A. (1995). Working people in crisis: Research implications. In C. R. Figley (Ed.), *Compassion Fatigue: Coping with secondary PTSD among those who treat the traumatized.* New York, NY: Brunner Mazel.

Bride, B. E., Robinson, M. M., Yegidis, B., & Figley, C. R. (2004). Development and validation of the Secondary Traumatic Stress Scale. *Research on Social Work Practice, 14,* 27–35. doi: 10.1177/1049731503254106

Corey, G. (2005). *Theory and practice of counseling & psychotherapy* (7th ed.). Belmont, CA: Brooks/Cole.

East, T. W., James, R. K., & Keim, J. (2001). *The best little vicarious trauma prevention program in Tennessee.* Paper presented at the 25th Annual Convening of Crisis Intervention Personnel, Chicago.

Elloy, D. F., Terpening, W., & Kohls, J. (2001). A causal model of burnout among self-managed work team members. *The Journal of Psychology: Interdisciplinary and Applied, 135*(3), 321–334.

Figley, C. R. (1995). Compassion fatigue as secondary traumatic stress disorder: An overview. In C. R. Figley (Ed.), *Compassion fatigue: Coping with secondary traumatic stress disorder in those who treat the traumatized* (pp. 1–20). Bristol, PA: Brunner/Mazel.

Figley, C. R. (1998). Burnout in families. In C. R. Figley (Ed.), *Burnout in families: The systematic costs of caring* (pp. 15–28). Boca Raton, FL: CRC Press.

Figley, C. R. (1999). Compassion fatigue: Toward a new understanding of the costs of caring. In B. H. Stamm (Ed.), *Secondary traumatic stress: Self-care issues for clinicians, researchers, & educators* (2nd ed., pp. 3–28). Lutherville, MD: Sidran Press.

Freud, S. (1910). The future prospects of psycho-analytic theory. *Standard Edition, 11,* 141–151.

Freudenberger, H. J. (1974). Staff burnout. *Journal of Social Issues, 30,* 159–165.

Freudenberger, H. J. (1975). The staff burn-out syndrome in alternative institutions. *Psychotherapy, Theory, Research and Practice, 12,* 73–82.

Freudenberger, H. J., & Richelson, G. (1980). *Burnout: The high cost of high achievement.* Garden City, NY: Anchor Press.

Gentry, J. E., Baranowsky, A., & Dunning K. (2002). ARP: The accelerated recovery program (ARP) for Compassion Fatigue. In C. R. Figley (Ed.), *Treating compassion fatigue* (pp. 123–138). New York, NY: Brunner-Routledge.

Gorkin, M. (1987). *The uses of countertransference.* Northvale, NJ: Jason Aronson.

Hyatt-Burkhart, D. (2014). The experience of vicarious posttraumatic growth in mental health workers. *Journal of Loss and Trauma, 19,* 452–461. doi: 10.1080/15325024.2013.797268

Maslach, C. (1982). *Burnout: The cost of caring.* Englewood Cliffs, NJ: Prentice-Hall.

Maslach, C., & Jackson S. E. (1986). *Maslach Burnout Inventory.* Palo Alto, CA: Consulting Psychologists Press.

Maslach, C., Jackson S., & Leiter, M. P. (1996). *Maslach Burnout Inventory* (3rd ed.). Palo Alto, CA: Consulting Psychologists Press.

McCann, I. L., & Colletti, J. (1994). The dance of empathy: A hermeneutic formulation of counter-transference, empathy, and understanding in the treatment of individuals who have experienced early childhood trauma. In J. P. Wilson & J. D. Lindy (Eds.), *Countertransference in the treatment of PTSD* (pp. 87–121). New York, NY: The Guilford Press.

McCann, I. L., & Pearlman, L. A. (1990a). *Psychological trauma and the adult survivor: Theory, therapy, and transformation.* New York, NY: Brunner/Mazel.

McCann, I. L., & Pearlman, L. A. (1990b). Vicarious traumatization: A framework for understanding the psychological effects of working with victims. *Journal of Traumatic Stress, 3*(1), 131–149.

McMullen, M. B., & Krantz, M. (1988). Burnout in day care workers: The effects of learned helplessness and self-esteem. *Child and Youth Care Quarterly, 17*, 275–280.

Morris, B.A., Shakespeare-Finch, J., Rieck, M., & Newbery, J. (2005). Multidimensional nature of posttraumatic growth in an Australian population. *Journal of Traumatic Stress, 18*, 575–585.

Neumann, D. A., & Gamble, S. J. (1995). Issues in the professional development of psycho-therapists: Countertransference and vicarious traumatization in the new trauma therapist. *Psychotherapy, 32*, 341–347.

Owens, E. W. (2011). *The resident assistant as paraprofessional counselor and crisis interventionist: A study of lived experience* (Doctoral Dissertation). Retrieved from ProQuest.

Pearlman, L. A., & Saakvitne, K. W. (1995). Treating therapists with vicarious traumatization and secondary traumatic stress disorders. In C. R. Figley (Ed.), *Compassion fatigue: Coping with secondary traumatic stress disorder in those who treat the traumatized* (pp. 150–177). New York, NY: Brunner Mazel.

Stamm, B. H. (2010). *The concise ProQOL manual* (2nd Edition). Retrieved from www.proqol.org

Tedeschi, R. G., & Calhoun, L. G. (2004). Posttraumatic growth: Conceptual foundations and empirical evidence. *Psychological Inquiry, 15*, 1–18.

Trippany, R. L., White Kress, V. E., & Wilcoxon, S. A. (2004). Preventing vicarious trauma: What counselors should know when working with trauma survivors. *Journal of Counseling and Development, 82*, 31–37.

Valent, P. (2002). Diagnosis and treatment of helper stresses, traumas, and illnesses. In C. R. Figley (Ed.), *Treating compassion fatigue.* (pp. 17–37). New York, NY: Brunner-Routledge.

Wicks, R. J. (2007). *The resilient clinician.* New York, NY: Oxford.

Wilson, J. P., & Lindy, J. D. (1994). Empathic strain and countertransference. In J. P. Wilson & J. D. Lindy (Eds.), *Countertransference in the treatment of PTSD* (pp. 5–30). New York, NY: The Guilford Press.

Zunker, V. G. (1998). *Career counseling: Applied concepts of life planning.* New York, NY: Brooks/Cole Publishing Company.

CHAPTER 14

Legal and Ethical Issues in Crisis Intervention

When he told me he was thinking about killing himself, I knew there were all of these assessments I'd need to do. But when it was all over and I decided he really wasn't going to do it, I was left wondering if I'd made the right decision … you know, not sending him to the hospital and not telling his wife. If that was my spouse, I'd want to know.

Counselors who work with people in crisis will certainly face a situation like the one described above. As we discussed in Chapter 4, knowing how to assess a client's suicidal or homicidal intent is a challenging process. But, perhaps even more challenging is knowing how those assessments intertwine with our ethical codes as professional counselors.

The following chapter describes a number of specific ethical and legal challenges for the crisis counselor. As we explain the various ethical issues facing crisis workers, we will refer to the American Counseling Association's (2014) *2014 ACA Code of Ethics* with the caveat that different professional organizations (e.g., American Psychological Association, National Association of Social Workers, etc.) have their own ethical codes and expectations for practice. It's critical to understand the ethical guidelines of your own profession in the context of the issues that will be presented here.

After reading this chapter, you should be able to:

1. Identify the various ethical issues facing crisis counselors;

2. Understand how laws impact crisis intervention, as well as the legal pitfalls inherent in this type of work;

3. Identify issues specific to counseling contexts and areas of practice (e.g., K–12 schools, colleges and universities, etc.); and

4. Develop strategies for addressing these various ethical and legal challenges in crisis intervention.

Ethics and Laws

The purpose of this chapter is not to provide a thorough explanation of the *2014 ACA Code of Ethics* (ACA, 2014), nor is it intended to explain the process of resolving ethical or legal decisions. There are a number of excellent resources for understanding professional ethics, ethical decision-making, and legal issues in the field of professional counseling (see the resources section at the end of this chapter for examples). The goal of this chapter is to explore the most significant ethical and legal issues in crisis intervention. But first, it is important to understand the *difference* between ethics and laws.

Professional ethics are codes written by professional organizations (e.g., American Counseling Association, American Psychological Association, National Association of Social Workers, etc.) that guide professional practice. These ethical codes have been developed with consideration given to legal concerns, as well as the mission, goals, and values of the professions that write the ethical guidelines. Ethics tend to be subjective, and it is sometimes difficult to apply ethical codes to real life situations, because they are, by their nature, open to a degree of interpretation. For this reason, it is crucial that practitioners use an ethical decision-making model (e.g., Welfel, 2015) when applying ethical codes to their practice. Violations of ethical codes do not, in and of themselves, result in legal issues; violating an ethical code may result in the loss of one's credentials (e.g., license, certificate, etc.) and other sanctions from state-level credentialing bodies.

Laws are written by local, state, and federal governments to regulate the behavior of citizens. While violating an ethical code may result in serious penalties, violations of the law may result in criminal or civil action. Criminal violations may result in fines, probation, or incarcerations, while violations of civil laws may result in lawsuits. Laws are also interpreted by courts through legal proceedings, where precedents are set that can establish expected behavior in the future.

As we explore these issues, we'll first examine professional ethics, followed by a cursory review of specific legal concerns. Throughout, we will attempt to provide guidance on how crisis counselors can avoid these pitfalls. It is also important to consider that ethical codes and legal obligations may conflict, especially when services are offered during a crisis. The *2014 Code of Ethics* explains how counselors should best address this issue.

I.1.c. Conflicts Between Ethics and Laws

> If ethical responsibilities conflict with the law, regulations, and/ or other governing legal authority, counselors make known their commitment to the ACA Code of Ethics and take steps to resolve the conflict. If the conflict cannot be resolved using this approach, counselors, acting in the best interest of the client, may adhere to the requirements of the law, regulations, and/or other governing legal authority. (ACA, 2014, p.19)

Ethical Concerns in Crisis Intervention

As we begin to unpack the ethics of effective crisis intervention work, we will explore several specific areas of the *2014 Code of Ethics* (ACA, 2014), including: Record Keeping, Informed Consent, Confidentiality, Competence, and Issues of Impairment.

Record Keeping

It is an ethical responsibility of professional counselors to maintain records of their work with clients in order to provide the highest-quality services. The *2014 Code of Ethics* (ACA, 2014) outlines several areas related to record keeping that are important in a discussion of crisis intervention. They include sections A.1.b, B.6.a and B.6.b of the *Code* (ACA, 2014):

A.1.b. Records and Documentation

Counselors create, safeguard, and maintain documentation necessary for rendering professional services. Regardless of the medium, counselors include sufficient and timely documentation to facilitate the delivery and continuity of services. Counselors take reasonable steps to ensure that documentation accurately reflects client progress and services provided. If amendments are made to records and documentation, counselors take steps to properly note the amendments according to agency or institutional policies (p.4).

B.6.a. Creating and Maintaining Records and Documentation

"Counselors create and maintain records and documentation necessary for rendering professional services" (p.7).

B.6.b. Confidentiality of Records and Documentation

"Counselors ensure that records and documentation kept in any medium are secure and that only authorized persons have access to them" (p. 8).

While these are certainly important ethical guidelines to maintain in the course of traditional counseling practice, they can be especially difficult to adhere to when working in a disaster situation. For example, what will a crisis counselor use to maintain the records of discussions with clients in the hours and days following a hurricane? The area may not have power to maintain secure electronic records, and it may be unrealistic to keep progress notes on interactions with clients that occur in temporary shelters or while standing in lines waiting for clean water or food.

The PsychSTART process described in Chapter 11 offers a good way of maintaining brief records on client interactions during a disaster or situational crisis. However, this is only one element of an effective record-keeping process during a disaster. Unfortunately, there are no specific suggestions in the literature on best practices for developing and maintaining records during crisis situations in the field. The most important piece for crisis interventionists to consider is what is required by one's professional code of ethics and how they can best meet the expectations of the *Code* while deployed after a major disaster.

For example, crisis counselors may want to consider using more traditional forms of record keeping while working in crisis situations, since technology may not be readily available. SOAP (i.e., Subjective data, Objective data, Assessment, and Plan) or DAP (i.e.,

Data, Assessment (and response), and Plan) notes can be kept on paper and secured in a locked briefcase or messenger bag while working in the field, and that bag can then be locked again in a hotel room or car, providing two layers of security. There are no specific means of maintaining client records during a disaster, and it may be the last thing the crisis worker is considering. However, the ethical codes suggest that it should be more than merely considered, and the crisis worker should be proactive in planning how to meet these ethical requirements, prior to a crisis occurring or going on a crisis deployment.

Informed Consent

The *2014 Code of Ethics* clearly describes the issue of informed consent. It states:

A.2.a. Informed Consent in the Counseling Relationship

> Clients have the freedom to choose whether to enter into or remain in a counseling relationship and need adequate information about the counseling process and the counselor. Counselors have an obligation to review, in writing and verbally with clients the rights and responsibilities of both counselors and clients. Informed consent is an ongoing part of the counseling process, and counselors appropriately document discussions of informed consent throughout the counseling relationship.

A.2.b. Types of Information Needed

> Counselors explicitly explain to clients the nature of all services provided. They inform clients about issues such as, but not limited to, the following: the purposes, goals, techniques, procedures, limitations, potential risks, and benefits of services; the counselor's qualifications, credentials, relevant experience, and approach to counseling; continuation of services upon the incapacitation or death of the counselor; the role of technology; and other pertinent information. Counselors take steps to ensure that clients understand the implications of diagnosis and the intended use of tests and reports. Additionally, counselors inform clients about fees and billing arrangements, including procedures for nonpayment of fees. Clients have the right to confidentiality and to be provided with an explanation of its limits (including how supervisors and/or treatment or interdisciplinary team professionals are involved), to obtain clear information about their records, to participate in the

ongoing counseling plans, and to refuse any services or modality changes and to be advised of the consequences of such refusal. (ACA, 2014, p. 4)

As discussed throughout this text, crisis intervention is often very different from traditional therapeutic models, requires different skills and interventions, and is often extremely time-limited. As you read the sections on informed consent, you probably envision a counselor and client sitting in an office reviewing an informed consent document that clearly outlines issues such as autonomy, limits to confidentiality, laws covering practice and privacy, and so forth.

Instead, consider how informed consent might be delivered when sitting with a family in a tent surrounded by damaged and destroyed homes after a community is ravaged by floods. It is still absolutely necessary to inform clients of the issues related to informed consent; it is also important to be realistic and consider how that might best be done. Exercise 14.1 invites you to consider how you might meet the ethical guidelines for record keeping and informed consent while providing crisis intervention services following a disaster.

Confidentiality

Issues related to confidentiality are discussed throughout the *2014 Code of Ethics*, so it is important for crisis counselors to be familiar with the entire document and all of the elements related to confidentiality. Those that are most important to consider when working with crises include:

EXERCISE 14.1

RECORD KEEPING AND INFORMED CONSENT DURING A DISASTER

Directions: As previously discussed, record keeping and informed consent can be difficult to maintain when responding to a disaster situation. Mental health services are less formalized and often delivered in unfamiliar settings and in brief interactions. Consider the following scenario, and then respond to the questions below.

Scenario:

You've been deployed as a disaster mental health responder following an earthquake that has damaged several sections of a large United States city. Thousands of residents have been displaced and without essential resources, such as food, water, shelter, clothing, and connections to loved ones. You're working in a temporary shelter that is housing approximately 100 families in a high school gymnasium. You're distributing food, water, and clothing while also talking with families and serving as a referral resource for other responders who do not have mental health training.

Reflection:

1. How will you provide informed consent as you're working with people who present with mental health needs?

2. Will you provide informed consent to everyone with whom you work? If so, how will you do this? If not, how will you decide when to engage the informed consent process and when not to?

3. How will you keep records of your mental health work? Consider issues like: what medium/media will you use (paper/pencil, technology, etc.)? How will you secure these records? What will you do with the records after your deployment? What information will you record (names, presenting concerns, treatment interventions, etc.)?

B.1.c. Respect for Confidentiality

Counselors protect the confidential information of prospective and current clients. Counselors disclose information only with appropriate consent or with sound legal or ethical justification.

B.2.a. Serious and Foreseeable Harm and Legal Requirements

The general requirement that counselors keep information confidential does not apply when disclosure is required to protect clients or identified others from serious and foreseeable harm or when legal requirements demand that confidential information must be revealed. Counselors consult with other professionals when in doubt as to the validity of an exception. Additional considerations apply when addressing end-of-life issues.

B.3.c. Confidential Settings

Counselors discuss confidential information only in settings in which they can reasonably ensure client privacy. (ACA, 2014, p. 7)

Limits to confidentiality are discussed widely in counseling texts and throughout the literature. It is important to appreciate that counselors have both an ethical and legal obligation to breech confidentiality in situations where the counselor assesses serious and foreseeable harm to a client or others, such as when a client is actively suicidal or homicidal. Additional information on the legal issues related to breeching confidentiality will be provided later in this chapter.

However, another important element of confidentiality related to crisis intervention is found in section B.3.c, related to conducting counseling in confidential settings. Again, when one reads this section, it's easy to imagine a comfortable office with a closed door, white noise machine outside, and where it is free from distractions or other people. However, crisis intervention is often not this easy. Sometimes, crisis counselors are passing out bottled water and working with people who are displaced and sleeping on cots in a high school gymnasium. As with the other elements of the *2014 Code of Ethics*, counselors need to use sound judgment and determine when a conversation has moved beyond just talk and toward counseling. At these times, it might be necessary to secure a private space where the client can talk confidentially without concern for others hearing.

Competence

The ACA (2014) *Code of Ethics* speaks specifically to practicing within one's area of competence:

C.2.a. Boundaries of Competence

> Counselors practice only within the boundaries of their compe-
> tence, based on their education, training, supervised experience,
> state and national professional credentials, and appropriate
> professional experience. Whereas multicultural counseling compe-
> tency is required across all counseling specialties, counselors gain
> knowledge, personal awareness, sensitivity, dispositions, and skills
> pertinent to being a culturally competent counselor in working with
> a diverse client population. (p. 8)

Trained and credentialed counselors should be competent to handle some crises by the nature of their education, training, and supervised practice. For example, it is unfortunate, but clients at risk of harm to self or others are commonplace in counseling practice. Individuals who have experienced trauma and are exhibiting symptoms of the diagnoses described in Chapter 5 are a regular part of a helping practice. However, some clients may require a level of care that cannot be provided by the clinician, because he or she lacks the specialized training to help. In these cases, referral may be necessary and warranted.

It should be noted that training and preparation in crisis intervention and trauma counseling has not always been a requirement of counselor education programs. As described in Chapter 12, the Council for Accreditation of Counseling and Related Educational Programs (CACREP) recently began requiring preparation in these areas in their educational standards, including 12 standards related to crisis and trauma counseling in the *2016 Standards* (CACREP, 2015). Also, research has indicated the importance of teaching these standards to counselors-in-training in order to prepare them for the realities of working in the field. Webber and Mascari (2009) discuss the positive implications for both individual practice and the counseling profession, as we require more training and preparation in areas related to trauma and crisis counseling.

However, during a large-scale crisis, competence becomes more complicated. During or after a crisis, people often want to help. It is especially common for coun-selors to want to volunteer, since most counselors enter the field because they want to help others. When a crisis happens, people line up to donate blood; send monetary donations; collect clothing, food, water, and other essentials; and sometimes volunteer their time and services to those in need. For those in the helping professions, it may be instinctive to want to donate time and services to those who are hurting after a crisis.

CASE ILLUSTRATION 14.1

WE JUST WANTED TO HELP

Dr. Hooks is a counselor educator at a state university in the Northwest United States. Dr. Hooks is teaching a course on crisis intervention at his university during a semester when wildfires are ravaging Northern California, killing several dozen people and displacing hundreds of residents. While discussing the wildfire crisis in class, one of Dr. Hooks' students suggests the small class of eight people could go to the scene of the fires to provide support and mental health services to those affected. Thinking this could be a great way to not only help, but to provide practical experience, Dr. Hooks agrees, secures a university van, and drives the students south to the scene of the fires.

As they arrive in California, they realize the situation is far more dangerous than they expected when they left. Roads are closed, in part, because the flames are crossing highways and spreading across the area. Dr. Hooks and his students become trapped on a state highway and have to abandon their vehicle on the side of the road. Without food, water, or adequate supplies, they begin to walk, looking for help themselves. Their mobile devices are not able to acquire signals, as cell towers are damaged by the flames, and the system is overloaded by residents attempting to contact help, loved ones, or get vital information about the crisis. One of the students has chronic asthma, and while walking for over an hour in the smoke-filled valley, has an asthma attack and is having trouble breathing. A crew of firefighters stops to help the stranded SUVs and drives them to a local Red Cross shelter.

Dr. Hooks finds a Disaster Mental Health volunteer and explains that he and his class have come to help. The volunteer looks concerned and takes Dr. Hooks to her supervisor. The supervisor explains to Dr. Hooks that he and his students cannot assist with the disaster response. The supervisor can't verify Dr. Hooks' credentials, and the students are not licensed to practice independently in their own state or in California. The supervisor cannot perform criminal or child abuse background checks and is already working

There are organized ways to do this that require specific training, preparation, and credentialing. As described previously in this text, the American Red Cross trains and deploys Disaster Mental Health volunteers locally, regionally, and nationally after crises. However, being part of this process requires a level of competence and understanding of how crises unfold, the specific needs of people and communities in crisis, and how to best provide services while avoiding harm.

After a crisis, Spontaneous Uninvited Volunteers (SUVs) may come to the scene to offer help. However, their presence can create a host of problems for those attempting to resolve the crisis. For instance, there may not be a need for these helpers, or the people who come on scene may not be trained or prepared to help. Those organizing the delivery of services are not planning for SUVs and may not be able to accommodate them. Credentials cannot be verified during an emergency situation, so those lacking competence to provide services may try to provide those services anyway. Background checks cannot be performed to ensure the safety of those in the community, and burnout, secondary traumatic stress (STS), or vicarious trauma may occur for those not trained to recognize it in themselves. In fact, their arrival may cause another crisis in and of itself.

Case Illustration 14.1 describes what can happen when SUVs attempt to intervene in a crisis.

Impairment

As we discussed in Chapter 13, there are costs to helping, especially during times of crises. Burnout, STS, and vicarious traumatization are all dangers for the crisis worker, especially when unmonitored or left unchecked. A number of researchers have examined the impact of these conditions on crisis interventionists and the impact on counselor impairment. While some counselors may leave the field as a result of the personal costs related to the work (Figley, 1995; Harris, 1995), others may continue to practice, despite being impaired and being unable to practice competently (Catherall, 1999; Munroe, 1999; Sommer, 2008). The *2014 Code of Ethics* defines impairment:

C.2.g. Impairment

Counselors monitor themselves for signs of impairment from their own physical, mental, or emotional problems and refrain from offering or providing professional services when impaired. They seek assistance for problems that reach the level of professional impairment, and, if necessary, they limit, suspend, or terminate their professional responsibilities until it is determined that they may safely resume their work. Counselors assist colleagues or supervisors in recognizing their own professional impairment and provide consultation and assistance when warranted with colleagues or supervisors showing signs of impairment and intervene as appropriate to prevent imminent harm to clients. (ACA, 2014, p. 9)

While the *Code* outlines the necessity for self-monitoring, that can be especially difficult when coping with STS or vicarious traumatization. One element of the *Code* that is especially important in crisis work is the requirement that colleagues assist one another in recognizing impairment and providing feedback supervision, and referral, when necessary. These interventions are especially important in crisis work, as outlined in Case Illustration 14.2

diligently to deploy the resources she has at her disposal. "I wish you'd gone through the proper processes," the supervisor says to Dr. Hooks. "We could use the help, but right now, it looks like the nine of you will just be taking up food, water, and cots in our shelter that we could have used for the people who live here. If I get you a phone, do you think you could arrange for you and your students to go home?"

Dr. Hooks wonders what the university will think about the abandoned van that has certainly been engulfed in flames by now.

CASE ILLUSTRATION 14.2

DEPLOYED AFTER A MASS SHOOTING

Kelsey is a seasoned counselor who has been working in crisis and disaster work for about 18 months when she is called upon to provide mental health crisis intervention after a school shooting in a local community. Wanting to use her skills and training, Kelsey agrees to respond and drives across town where two middle school students entered their school with handguns and pipe bombs. The two shooters killed seven of their classmates and two teachers, while wounding another 23. They then shot themselves as police entered the school.

Kelsey has been asked to sit with families of the children in the school while they are reunited with their children, who were evacuated to a nearby high school and debriefed. Kelsey is friends with several of the parents and has two children in an elementary school in the district. She listens and provides comfort and watches as tearful parents are connected with their frightened but unharmed children. However, after the families are reunited, Kelsey is left with those whose children have been killed or wounded. Kelsey cries along with the families of those lost in the violence.

Wanting to continue to help, Kelsey stays connected with many of these families as funerals are planned, vigils are held, and people begin to process their emotions. As a member of the community and a parent herself, Kelsey knows she is shaken. She has trouble sleeping, has become irritable and unfocused, and finds she is scared much more than she used to be. However, she also knows that this is probably temporary and she will likely be fine after things go back to normal.

After Kelsey returns to work at a local counseling agency, she finds she is having difficulty staying focused on her clients. During sessions, her mind keeps going back to that day at the high school gym, hearing parents crying and screaming as police came in to tell them their children were gone. Kelsey refuses to silence her phone during sessions, because she wants to be sure to be available if anything should happen to her own children or if those families need her again. She has been late to work, and when she is there, she's rarely paying attention to her clients. Her supervisor approaches her and asks if she's okay. She's always been a great counselor, but she seems to be doing more harm than good lately. The supervisor is especially concerned since Kelsey snapped at a client the day before, telling the mother of three, "You have NO IDEA what real problems are. You need to grow up and figure this out!"

Legal Issues

As discussed previously, ethical codes and legal obligations address different areas of concern. Now, we will explore some common legal issues facing crisis interventionists, and it is important to remember that, similar to our discussion on ethics, this list is not exhaustive. Professionals in the helping field must be aware of their legal obligations to clients and their communities. With that being said, some of the most common legal issues facing those who work with individuals in crisis include: Duty to Protect, Issues of Involuntary Hospitalization, Record Keeping Requirements, and Mandated Reporting.

Duty to Protect

The concept of Duty to Protect stipulates that counselors have a legal obligation to breech confidentiality when a client is an imminent threat to self or others. The legal obligation to breech confidentiality in these cases was established in the landmark court case *Tarasoff v Regents of the University of California* (1976). In 1968, Prosenjit Poddar confided to his psychologist at the University of California, Berkley, that he intended to kill his love interest, Tatiana Tarasoff. The psychologist did not immediately warn Tarasoff of the threat, but after consulting with a supervisor, did notify campus police, who interviewed Poddar and determined he was not a threat. Several months later, Poddar stabbed and killed Tarasoff.

Tarasoff's family filed a lawsuit against several employees of the university and eventually won the case. In their ruling, the California Supreme Court determined that breeching confidentiality is a legal necessity when there is foreseeable harm:

> When a therapist determines, or pursuant to the standards of his profession should determine, that a patient presents a serious danger of violence to another, he incurs an obligation to use reasonable care to protect the intended victim against such danger … it may call for him to warn the intended victim of that danger, to notify police or to take whatever other steps are reasonably necessary under the circumstances. (Tarasoff v Regents of the University of California, 1976, p. 340)

Subsequent rulings in other cases have confirmed this duty to protect others in the event of foreseeable harm (e.g., *Jablonski v. United States*, 1983; *Hamman v. County of Maricopa*, 1989; *Currie v. United States*, 1986; *Schuster v. Altenberg*, 1988).

Involuntary Hospitalization

In cases where a client is a threat to others, law enforcement may make a determination that the client is psychologically disturbed to a point that hospitalization is necessary. In other cases, clients may be unable to keep themselves safe and may be an imminent threat to take their own life. In these cases, hospitalization may be necessary, as well.

In cases where hospitalization is warranted, some clients may voluntarily choose to admit themselves to a psychiatric facility. However, in cases where a client is unwilling or unable to admit oneself, involuntary hospitalization may be warranted. It is important to remember that involuntary hospitalization should be seen as a last resort, when all other efforts to maintain the safety of the client or others have failed. When clients are hospitalized against their will, several things must be considered. First, while such action is necessary to ensure safety, the therapeutic relationship may be damaged if the client feels as if the counselor has betrayed them in some way. More importantly, involuntary hospitalization removes the client's most important choices, choices over control of one's surroundings, decisions, movements, clothing, meals, recreation, and so forth. In short, while it is sometimes necessary, it is a decision that should be made only after careful deliberation and assessment of the client's capacities.

Each state has its own laws and regulations regarding involuntary hospitalization. For example, in Pennsylvania, such a decision can only be made by a medical doctor or law enforcement official. The initial hospitalization may only last up to 72 hours, at which time the client is either released or a hearing is conducted to determine if the client should remain in the hospital or be released. Other states will certainly have different regulations, and each state has nuances to these laws that are important to understand.

We strongly encourage you to study the laws of the state(s) in which you intend to practice. A good place to start is the website http://www.treatmentadvocacycenter.org/browse-by-state, which provides an overview of the involuntary hospitalization laws in each state. Again, it is advisable to delve more deeply in to your own state's laws, but this website provides an overview.

HIPAA & FERPA: Record Keeping Requirements

As described in the section on ethics, counselors have an ethical obligation to maintain notes on their work with clients. How those notes are treated, and the legal obligations counselors have to protect those notes, are covered under two federal laws. The Health Insurance Privacy and Accountability Act of 1996 (HIPAA) was enacted to improve the efficiency and effectiveness of the healthcare system and create national standards for the security and privacy of healthcare records. Sometimes referred to as the HIPAA Privacy Rule, one part of the law requires healthcare providers to protect individuals' healthcare records and personal information, as well as limiting when, how, and with whom these records may be shared, and under what circumstances. While a thorough overview of HIPAA regulations is not warranted here, it is important to note that HIPAA does allow for disclosure of personal health information when there is an imminent threat to oneself or the public (U.S. Department of Education, 2008).

The Family Educational Rights and Privacy Act of 1974 (FERPA) is a federal law that protects the privacy of students' educational records. FERPA covers most K–12 and higher education institutions in the United States, excluding only those that do not accept federal funding of any kind. FERPA creates a number of safeguards for students' educational records, including limiting who has access to those records, when records can be disclosed or shared, what information is contained within an educational record, how records must be stored, and so forth. FERPA rights typically reside with the parents until a student turns 18 years of age or graduates from high school (U.S. Department of Education, 2008). Similar to HIPAA, the law is too complex for a complete review here; however, it should be noted that FERPA also has provisions for disclosure of educational records during crises and emergencies (more information on the specifics of this exception will be discussed later in this chapter).

Mandated Reporting

As a professional counselor, you will be a *mandated reporter*. Mandated reporting is the legal requirement for counselors and others who work with children, the elderly, or other vulnerable populations to report suspected cases of abuse. Similar to the issue of involuntary hospitalization, each state has established its own laws and regulations regarding mandated reporting. For example, in Pennsylvania, school counselors and Licensed Professional Counselors (LPCs) are both considered mandated reporters, as are licensed social workers and psychologists. As a requirement for licensure, professionals are required to complete a mandated reporter training and must completed additional training every two years as a condition of maintaining their licenses.

The purpose of mandated reporting is to protect children and others from abuse: physical, emotional, sexual, and neglect. Counselors and others in the helping professions must be aware of the laws, processes, and policies in their jurisdictions in order to not only protect children from abuse, but also to ensure that perpetrators of abuse are reported to the authorities. Also critical are the criminal penalties when mandated reporters fail to fulfill their legal obligations. For example, in Pennsylvania, failure to report child abuse may result in felony charges that, if convicted, can carry large fines and significant prison terms.

Another element of mandated reporting that is of significance for crisis interventionists is that crisis workers are sometimes deployed out of state when a need arises. For example, the American Red Cross will often call for volunteers from across the country to assist with mental health services in times of crisis. During crises, we also see predators emerge who may attempt to take advantage of vulnerable populations that are made more vulnerable by the impact of the crisis. It is important that prior to or during a deployment out of state, crisis interventionists make themselves familiar with the laws and regulations of that state relating to mandated reporting.

Exercise 14.2 invites you to examine the mandated reporting laws in your state and consider situations in your practice when you might need to report abuse.

Context-Specific Legal and Ethical Considerations

This chapter has focused largely on the ethical and legal considerations related to work in crisis intervention. While the discussion thus far has focused on general concerns, we believe it is important to focus on two specific areas of practice where crisis intervention often occurs: K–12 school settings and college campuses.

Ethics and Legal Issues in K–12 Schools

The most significant issue related to crisis counseling in K–12 schools relates to the fact that most students in school are minors, and schools hold a responsibility of *in loco parentis*, or in place of parents. The concept of *in loco parentis* is that the school, and by extension, employees of the school, hold a responsibility for the safety and welfare of children while in the supervision of the school. Students' minor status and the notion of *in loco parentis* complicate issues for professional school counselors.

Glosoff and Pate (2002) identify a number of challenges facing school counselors related to the issues of confidentiality described previously in this chapter. Because school students are often minors, the legal right to confidentiality is complicated and often lies

---

EXERCISE 14.2

MANDATED REPORTING

Directions: We've discussed how mandated reporting laws differ across states. This exercise asks you to research the laws in your state. Several questions to consider when researching these laws are provided below.

Reflection:

1. Who is a mandated reporter in your state?

2. In what cases are you mandated to make a report? (e.g., child abuse, elder abuse, etc.)

3. What is the reporting procedure? To whom do you report? What information will you need to report?

4. How long do you have to make a report?

5. What are the legal definitions of abuse in your state? (e.g., definitions of physical, emotional, and sexual abuse, as well as neglect)

6. Do you have criminal and/or civil immunity if you make a report in good faith? How is good faith defined in your state?

7. What are the criminal and/or civil penalties for failing to make a report when mandated to do so?

8. Is specific training on mandated reporting required for licensure and/or certification in your jurisdiction? If so, what are the regulations about this?

with the parent. In fact, the rights under FERPA specifically belong to the parent(s) until a student reaches the age of 18 or graduates from high school (U.S. Department of Education, 2008). There are also developmentally appropriate limits to confidentiality; for example, a school counselor could not realistically promise confidentiality to a kindergarten student at the age of five.

As Glasoff and Pate (2002) describe, issues related to informed consent and confidentiality become murky when working with students in school settings. For example, parents must consent to counseling for their minor children; the child provides assent rather than consent. The authors encourage school counselors to engage both parents and students in the informed consent process, as to educate both on the limits to confidentiality, with whom information can be shared, and when. In many cases, school policies may also regulate the disclosure of information (Glasoff & Pate, 2002). An example of this may include non-lethal self-injurious behavior. While self-injury might not be disclosed in a clinical setting, it might be disclosed in a K–12 setting.

Another important element for school counselors to consider is the issue of suicidality among K–12 students. Rates of suicide have increased 300% since the 1950s among adolescents while remaining mostly static among adult populations. Capuzzi (2002) identifies a number of important considerations for school counselors when working with students experiencing suicidal ideation. These include:

- Remembering what crisis intervention is: The school counselor's role is to manage the unusual situation and ensure the student's safety.

- Be calm and supportive: It's critical to respect the pain of the student while providing safety and a sense of balance through a calm demeanor.

- Be nonjudgmental: Respecting the student's reality without judgment or comparison is key.

- Encourage self-disclosure: The school counselor may be the first person to whom the student has disclosed the intention. Long-term healing can begin through disclosure at this stage.

- Acknowledge the reality of suicide as a choice without normalizing it: While the student is not alone in their thoughts of suicide, there are better options with better outcomes.

- Listen actively and provide positive reinforcement: Indicate emphatic understanding through active listening.

- Do not attempt to provide in-depth, therapeutic intervention: At this stage, triage and assessment is critical. In-depth therapy is not appropriate in a school setting, especially with a suicidal student.

- Do not conduct an assessment alone: When possible, conduct the suicide assessment with another professional. This provides for consultation, more thorough assessment, and risk management.

- Assess lethality: Ask specific questions to assess the imminent risk of lethality. See Chapter 4 for specific suicide assessment methods.

- Notify parents: Legal and ethical guidelines require notification of parents. The *ACA Code of Ethics*, the *American School Counselors Association Ethical Standards for School Counselors*, and legal precedent all require a breach of confidentiality when a student is suicidal. School policy likely will, as well.

- Consider hospitalization: See the previous section on involuntary hospitalization for more information on how to engage this process in your state.

- Require formal assessment before the student can return to school: Suicidal students are disruptive to the educational environment and can be dangerous for the student at risk. Requiring a third party assessment provides a layer of safety for the student as well as for the school system and its employees.

It is important to note that confidentiality is not required when a student in a K–12 school expresses suicidal ideation (Remley & Herlihy, 2001). In fact, the case of *Eisel v. Board of Education of Montgomery County* (1991) describes this notion of confidentiality. In this case, a middle school student made threats of suicide to friends, who informed a school counselor. After consulting with colleagues, the counseling staff assessed the student who had made the threats and determined the student was not suicidal and did not contact her parents. She eventually did take her own life, and the student's parents sued the school district and won. This seminal case has laid the groundwork for school counselors to disclose self-injurious threats, even if they might not meet the threshold for hospitalization or a breach of confidentiality in clinical practice.

Finally, FERPA makes clear exceptions for the disclosure of educational records in the event of crisis or other emergency. Specifically, the law states, "An educational agency or institution may disclose personally identifiable information from an education record to appropriate parties, including parents of an eligible student, in connection with an emergency if knowledge of the information is necessary to protect the health or safety of the student or other individuals" (FERPA, 1974, §99.36). The law requires educational institutions to consider the "totality of the circumstances pertaining to a threat to the health or safety of a student or other individuals" (FERPA, 1974, §99.36). The law continues by stating that the judgment of the educational institution will not be challenged by the Department of Education after the fact.

Ethics and Legal Issues in Colleges and Universities

One of the most significant legal questions in crisis intervention on college campuses concerns the relationship between HIPAA and FERPA and how these laws regulate the work of counselors and other crisis interventionists on campus. This has become a complicated and convoluted issue, one which is often referred to legal counsel on many campuses. The U.S. Department of Education has issued guidance on this issue in their document, *Joint Guidance on the Application of the Family Educational Rights and Privacy Act (FERPA) And the Health Insurance Portability and Accountability Act of 1996 (HIPAA) To Student Health Record* (U.S. Dept. of Education, 2008). This document attempts to clarify the applicability of these federal regulations in K–12 and college settings.

While the document outlines cases where both HIPAA and FERPA would apply to mental health records maintained by college counselors, the guidance in the document refers mostly to the application of FERPA. While FERPA would apply to the college setting, FERPA makes a distinction for mental health treatment records and indicates that these records are excluded from the provisions of FERPA. However, under the exceptions described previously in this chapter, these records could be disclosed in the event of a health or safety emergency.

Another important element for college counselors to consider is the legal implications when working with students who are suicidal or otherwise at risk for self-injurious behavior. As Lake and Tribbensee (2002) discuss, colleges place themselves in legal jeopardy when maintaining the confidentiality of students who may be at risk of suicide or self-injury. Specifically, they argue that courts are increasingly finding colleges at fault in cases where family members sue, arguing that campus staff could have prevented the suicide of a student. While legal protections are still in place to protect the confidentiality of clients on campus, the legal threshold for responsibility has lowered in recent years.

Summary

- Professional ethics are codes written by professional organizations that guide professional practice. Violations of ethical codes do not, in and of themselves, result in legal issues; violating an ethical code may result in the loss of one's credentials (e.g., license, certificate, etc.) and other sanctions from state-level credentialing bodies.

- Laws are written by local, state, and federal governments to regulate the behavior of citizens. While violating an ethical code may result in serious penalties, violations of the law may result in criminal or civil action. Criminal violations may result in fines, probation, or incarcerations, while violations of civil laws may result in lawsuits.

- It is an ethical responsibility of professional counselors to maintain records of their work with clients in order to provide the highest-quality services for those who receive professional services. The crisis worker should be proactive in planning how to meet these ethical requirements, prior to a crisis occurring or going on a crisis deployment.

- While informed consent is also an ethical responsibility, it can be challenging in crisis situations, especially during disasters or situational crises.

- Counselors have both an ethical and legal obligation to breech confidentiality in situations where the counselor assesses serious and foreseeable harm to a client or others, such as when a client is actively suicidal or homicidal.

- Sometimes after a crisis, SUVs will come to the scene to offer help, but this can create a host of problems for those attempting to resolve the crisis.

- Burnout, STS, and vicarious traumatization are all dangers for the crisis worker, especially when unmonitored or left unchecked. These can lead to impairment, a breach of professional ethics.

- The concept of Duty to Protect stipulates that counselors have a legal obligation to breech confidentiality when a client is an imminent threat to self or others.

- In cases where a client is unwilling or unable to admit themself, involuntary hospitalization may be warranted. It is important to remember that involuntary hospitalization should be seen as a last resort, when all other efforts to maintain the safety of the client or others have failed. Each state has its own laws and regulations regarding involuntary hospitalization.

- HIPAA was enacted by to improve the efficiency and effectiveness of the health-care system, as well as create national standards for the security and privacy of healthcare records. FERPA is a federal law that protects the privacy of students' educational records. Both provide exclusions to protect the client or the community.

- As a professional counselor, you will likely be what is often called a *mandated reporter*. Mandated reporting is the legal requirement for counselors and others who work with children, the elderly, or other vulnerable populations to report suspected cases of abuse. Similar to the issue of involuntary hospitalization, each state established its own laws and regulations regarding mandated reporting.

- Confidentiality and suicide intervention are crucial issues for counselors working in K–12 school settings. In higher education settings, legal issues around HIPAA, FERPA, and culpability for student self-harm and suicide have been concerns in recent years.

Important Terms

2014 ACA Code of Ethics

Competence

Confidentiality

Duty to Protect

Eisel v. Board of Education of Montgomery County

Family Educational Rights and Privacy Act of 1974 (FERPA)

Health Insurance Portability and Accountability Act of 1996 (HIPAA)

Impairment

Informed consent

In loco parentis

Involuntary hospitalization

Mandated reporting

Laws

Professional ethics and ethical codes

Record keeping

Serious and foreseeable harm

Spontaneous Uninvited Volunteers (SUVs)

Tarasoff v. Regents of the University of California

Additional Resources

In print

U.S. Department of Education & U.S. Department of Health and Human Services. (2008). Joint Guidance on the Application of the Family Educational Rights and Privacy Act (FERPA) and the Health Insurance Portability and Accountability Act of 1996 (HIPAA) To Student Health Record. Washington, D.C.: Authors.

Webber, J. M., & Mascari, J. B. (2009). Critical issues in implementing the new CACREP standards for disaster, trauma, and crisis counseling. In G. R. Walz, J. C. Bleuer, & R. K. Yep (Eds.), *Compelling counseling interventions: Celebrating VISTAS 2009* (pp. 126–138). Alexandria, VA: American Counseling Association.

Welfel, E. R. (2015). *Ethics in counseling & psychotherapy: Standards, research, & emerging issues* (6th ed.). Belmont, CA: Cengage.

On the Web

American Counseling Association Code of Ethics: https://www.counseling.org/resources/aca-code-of-ethics.pdf

Legal information on involuntary hospitalizations by state: http://www.treatmentadvocacycenter.org/browse-by-state

References

American Counseling Association. (2014). *2014 ACA Code of Ethics.* Alexandria, VA: Author.

CACREP (Council for Accreditation of Counseling and Related Educational Programs). (2015). *2016 standards.* Alexandria, VA: Author.

Capuzzi, D. (2002) Legal and ethical challenges in counseling suicidal students. *Professional School Counseling, 6,* 36–45.

Catherall, D. (1999). Coping with secondary traumatic stress: The importance of the therapist's professional peer group. In B. H. Stamm (Ed.), *Secondary traumatic stress: Self-care issues for clinicians, researchers, and educators* (2nd ed., pp. 80–92). Lutherville, MD: Sidran Press.

Eisel v. Board of Education of Montgomery County. 597 A.2d 447. (1991).

FERPA (Family Educational Rights and Privacy Act). (1974). 22 United States Code § 1232g.

Figley, C. R. (1995). Compassion fatigue as secondary traumatic stress disorder: An overview. In C. R. Figley (Ed.), *Compassion fatigue: Coping with secondary traumatic stress disorder in those who treat the traumatized* (pp. 1–21). New York, NY: Brunner/Mazel.

Glasoff, H. L. & Pate Jr., R. H. (2002). Privacy and confidentiality in school counseling. *Professional School Counseling, 6,* 20–28.

Harris, C. (1995). Sensory-based therapy for crisis counselors. In C. R. Figley (Ed.), *Compassion fatigue: Coping with secondary traumatic stress disorder in those who treat the traumatized* (pp. 101–114). New York, NY: Brunner/Mazel.

HIPAA (Health Insurance Portability and Accountability Act of 1996). (1996). Pub. L. No. 104–191.

Lake, P., & Tribbensee, N. (2002). The emerging crisis of college student suicide: Law and policy responses to serious forms of self-inflicted injury. *Stetson Law Review, 32,* 125–157.

Munroe, J. (1999). Ethical issues associated with secondary trauma in therapists. In B. H. Stamm (Ed.), *Secondary traumatic stress: Self-care issues for clinicians, researchers, and educators* (2nd ed., pp. 211–229). Lutherville, MD: Sidran Press.Remley, T. E, Jr., & Herlihy, B. (2001). *Ethical, legal, and professional issues in counseling. Upper Saddle River, NJ: Merrill/Prentice Hall.*

Sommer, C. A. (2008). Vicarious traumatization, trauma-sensitive supervision, and counselor preparation. *Counselor Education & Supervision, 48,* 61–71.

Tarasoff v. Regents of the University of California. 551 P.2d 334. (1976). Vacating and modifying 529 P.2d 553 (Cal 1974).

U.S. Department of Education & U.S. Department of Health and Human Services (2008). *Joint Guidance on the Application of the Family Educational Rights and Privacy Act (FERPA) and the Health Insurance Portability and Accountability Act of 1996 (HIPAA) to Student Health Record.* Washington, D.C.: Authors.

Welfel, E.R. (2015). *Ethics in counseling & psychotherapy: Standards, research, & emerging issues.* (6th ed.). Belmont, CA: Cengage.

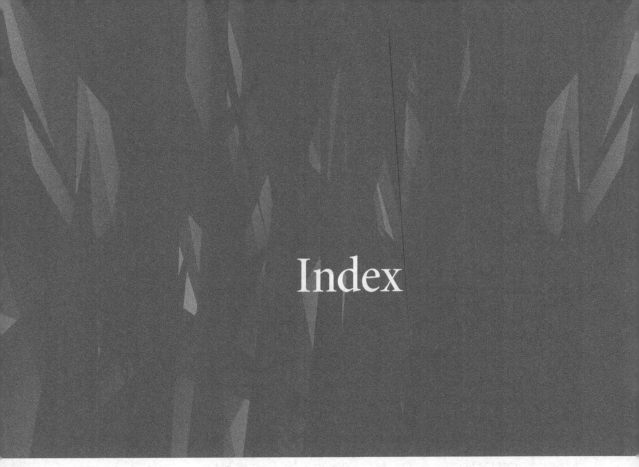

Index

C

CPSIA information can be obtained
at www.ICGtesting.com
Printed in the USA
BVHW071925020721
610878BV00003B/87

9 781516 528035